Invisible Victims

Invisible Victims

WHITE MALES AND THE CRISIS OF AFFIRMATIVE ACTION

Frederick R. Lynch

PRAEGER

New York
Westport, Connecticut
London

Library of Congress Cataloging-in-Publication Data

Lynch, Frederick R.
    Invisible victims : White males and the crisis of affirmative action /
Frederick R. Lynch.—Paperback ed.
        p.   cm.
    Includes index.
    ISBN 0-275-94102-7 (pbk. : alk. paper)
    1. Discrimination in employment—United States.   2. Reverse
discrimination in employment—United States.   3. Affirmative action
programs—United States.   I. Title.
HD4903.5.U58L96   1991
331.6'9034073—dc20   91-15268

British Library Cataloguing in Publication Data is available.

A hardcover edition of *Invisible Victims* is available from the
Greenwood Press imprint of Greenwood Publishing Group, Inc.
(Contributions in Sociology, no. 80; ISBN 0-313-26496-1).

Library of Congress Catalog Card Number: 91-15268
ISBN: 0-275-94102-7

First published in 1989
Paperback edition 1991

Praeger Publishers, One Madison Avenue, New York, NY 10010
An imprint of Greenwood Publishing Group, Inc.

Printed in the United States of America

The paper used in this book complies with the
Permanent Paper Standard issued by the National
Information Standards Organization (Z39.48—1984).

10 9 8 7 6 5 4 3

For the memory of Mother and Dad

Over the last twenty years, the new liberal vision, implemented by means of the policy of preferential treatment and quotas, has led to a number of perfectly disastrous and perfectly predictable results—predictable, that is, to anyone willing to think about what it means to apportion the goods of society according to the color of one's skin.

Hardly a policy maker or academic anywhere wants to examine these results, and fewer still want to speak of them.

Charles Murray, "The Coming of Custodial Democracy"
Commentary, September 1988

CONTENTS

TABLES

PREFACE

For the past twenty years, a system of taboos has structured the analysis of race relations in this country. Fostered by intellectual, political, and media elites, these taboos suppressed stereotypical thinking about women and minority groups. The taboos also discouraged criticism of social programs designed to aid the occupational and social mobility of these same oppressed populations.

The taboos may have been well intentioned. Looking away from awkward matters was supposedly for a good cause. Initially, it was easy to do: accentuate the positive and suppress the negative. As the 1970s wore on, however, outright distortion was required to maintain the taboos. Large numbers of journalists and social scientists felt compelled to avoid close scrutiny of race-related topics, such as violent crime, forced busing, and affirmative action quotas. Important issues were perceived to be off-limits. Sociologists and political scientists who once craved the respectability and objectivity of the physical sciences caved in to political fashion.

The taboos became increasingly intense and violators were threatened with being labeled "racist." This New McCarthyism, as I term it, prevented recognition and discussion of race-related problems. For example, the deterioration of family structures in urban, black communities and the rise of violence and drug-dealing among urban, minority, youth gangs were ignored until these problems reached crisis proportions and burst into the national consciousness.

The New McCarthyism also masked the transformation of affirmative action programs from equality of opportunity for individuals to group-based quotas. The original, individualistic ideals were replaced by the collectivist philosophy of proportional representation. Groups, not individuals, were to be accorded jobs or promotions based on their proportion in the labor force or general population. A drive to restructure society by race and gender produced a series of government-sponsored group preferences.

The moral fervor with which affirmative action policies were steamrollered into place suppressed recognition or discussion of a number of complexities, contradictions, and new injustices. For example, few scholars or policy makers noted that the various subpopulations included in affirmative action programs differed enormously in cultural values, aspirations, age structures, and other important variables. There was little mention that affirmative action quotas included many newly arrived immigrants who thus obtained preference over citizens who had resided in this nation for many generations.

Few analysts observed that older members of corporate and government elites imposed affirmative action quotas upon younger, working, and middle-class white males. There was little mention of the additional stress placed upon the huge Baby Boom generation, already locked in fierce competition for educational slots, jobs, and promotions. Only a handful of scholars and policy makers seemed willing to counter arguments that meritocratic criteria, such as grades and test scores, were inherently biased against minorities and women. Finally, few scholars pointed out that race and gender are but two of a large variety of important factors that structure human destinies. The drive for ethnic and gender equity and diversity suppressed recognition of enormous individual variations in motivation, drive, and intelligence. The use of race-and-gender categories also overlooked the independent influence of social class.

The use of race-and-gender preferences to restructure American society has produced a good deal of conflict, resentment, and other problems. These problems, in turn, have generated a growing sense of crisis and doubt about affirmative action. Yet among intellectuals and policymakers pressures also exist to remain "politically correct" and redouble allegiance to policies of preferential treatment—especially in the wake of conservative political trends. On the other hand, evidence continues to mount that a once lofty sounding theory has degenerated into a real-world racial spoils system. The ideals of equal treatment and selection-by-merit have been replaced by a bureaucratic drive for ethnic/gender "diversity." Group-based quotas have been mandated and filled, regardless of individual qualifications.

Cognitive dissonance—the psychological state caused by two contradictory conceptions—is provoking doubt and unease about affirmative action quotas. The gap between American legal principles and the actual practice of social policy has grown too wide to ignore. For academics, affirmative action policies and problems have been "coming home" as university hiring has begun to accelerate after a fifteen-year lull. All of a sudden, the complaints voiced by academic outsiders concerning the dilemmas and complexities involved in implementing affirmative action policy could no longer be labeled as mere vestiges of racism.

Since the mid-1980s, social scientists and journalists have been breaking away from rapid-fire labeling and the ideological orthodoxy of the New McCarthyism (Coleman, 1988; Lieberson, 1988). One well-known breakaway event was the January 1985, Bill Moyers' television documentary on the crisis in urban, ghetto, black families. The program revived widespread debate on a topic suppressed since the mid-1960s. Another recent media event that punctured the New McCarthyist taboos was the 1988 film *Colors,* which catapulted more inner city realities into public consciousness. Though there had been sporadic media recognition of increasing violence and drug-dealing among urban, minority, youth gangs, *Colors* literally made the issue a box-office topic. The nightly newscasts began to cover urban gangs in depth.

Taboo-breaking also proved bankable in the book world. By 1987, heretical volumes were atop the best-seller list. Allan Bloom's *The Closing of the American Mind* ripped the academic establishment for lowering or abandoning academic standards in favor of egalitarian value relativism. Tom Wolfe's thinly fictional *Bonfire of the Vanities* probed racial cynicism, hypocrisy, and tensions in New York City. And Randy Shilts' *And the Band Played On* described how a combination of conservative apathy and liberal ideological taboos obscured social realities and delayed response to the *AIDS* (Acquired Immune Deficiency Syndrome) epidemic.

Like these books, *Invisible Victims: White Males and the Crisis of Affirmative Action* is concerned with the costs of public ignorance as well as the manipulation of law and social reality by ideological elites. The book explores how an official system of race-and-gender preferences was imposed upon American life in spite of laws and massive public opinion against such policies. The focus of the book is on how affirmative action has actually operated in everyday settings, as opposed to its early, airy "ideals." A particular aim of the book is to discover how white males, their co-workers, and families reacted to reverse discrimination situations. The role of the mass media and social sciences in portraying—or ignoring—affirmative action is also examined. Finally, I examine the latent, or hidden and unintended, consequences of affirmative action policies.

This is an issue-raising, not an issue-solving, enterprise. I am trying to get at the reality behind the few statistical studies that purportedly measure the mobility of women and minorities in education and the occupational structure. To use Erving Goffman's terminology, I am looking at the "backstage" realities of affirmative action processes (1955).

Because of its behind-the-scenes realities, the topic of affirmative action has been resistant to the large-scale, quantitative methods preferred by many sociologists. Data can and has been gathered on changes in the race-

and-gender compositions of work forces and student enrollments. But one cannot necessarily state why those changes occur. Thus, the major quantitative studies differ on the effects of affirmative action policies (Leonard, 1984a, 1984b; Smith and Welch, 1986; and U.S. Commission on Civil Rights, 1986.)

Therefore, the approach in this book is decidedly investigatory and qualitative. A case-study method has been used to assess reactions of white males to affirmative action barriers. The thirty-two individuals interviewed for that phase of the study were gathered by networking, chain-sampling methods (Biernacki, 1988: 200–221). Count-and-prove techniques were employed in the chapter on the mass media and affirmative action. Again, such data tell only a small part of the story. Materials from secondary sources are both quantitative and qualitative.

I have discovered that people are remarkably resistant to "inconvenient facts" on this topic (Weber, 1946). Even Ph.D.s see only what they want to see when it comes to affirmative action. With this in mind, I have used many direct, detailed quotations in this book.

Affirmative action has been a radioactive topic among both professionals and laypersons. The issue has been heavily self-censored by social scientists, journalists, personnel managers, and even those who lost jobs and promotions due to affirmative action barriers.

Affirmative action should no longer be regarded as an article of political faith; rather, it should be seen as a major social revolution to be studied sociologically. It is high time we examined the use and the effects of race-and-gender preferences in the restructuring of American society.

ACKNOWLEDGMENTS

I am grateful to the Institute for Educational Affairs for providing seed money for the interviewing phase of this study in 1984–85. In 1986, the Earhart Foundation provided me with a research fellowship, which enabled me to put the book together.

Three wonderful colleagues and friends listened for more than a decade to my ramblings on this radioactive topic: Monica Morris, Frances Coles, and Jan Allard. They provided argument and feedback on sensitive matters when most other social scientists had their heads in the sand.

Research assistants Tom Byrne and Ron O'Dell did a fine job of locating and interviewing subjects.

William Beer provided encouragement and a fine critique of the original draft of the book, and Monica Morris provided detailed editorial help on that same draft.

Ralph Rossum provided support for this project in many ways.

Chapter 1

INTRODUCTION: SOCIAL POLICY BY STEAMROLLER

Some Baby Boomers born in the late 1940s and 1950s may recall Margaret Wise Brown's whimsical children's story of a little girl who received an adult-sized steamroller as a Christmas gift (Brown, 1948: 54–58). The excited child climbed aboard the colossal machine, started it up, blew the whistle, and put the machine into gear. But, once in motion, the little girl did not know how to stop her giant toy. She smashed through the wall of her parents' home, flattened a fence, and, despite her cries of warning to all concerned, "squished" assorted animals and persons in her neighborhood. Finally, of course, the machine was brought to a halt and—this being a wholesome, happy story—all the flattened people and animals were scooped up and popped back to life. All was forgiven, and there were no hard feelings or lawsuits.

The evolving systems of race-and-gender quotas known as "affirmative action" can be likened to the steamroller story. As in the 1940s tale, the mating of machine and operator began with the best intentions. Then, however, things got out of control and much damage was done.

But there are some important differences between the happy, magical ending of a 1940s children's story and the real-world effects of a contemporary social policy. I shall try to demonstrate in this book that the injuries wrought by the affirmative action steamroller have been both deep and possibly extensive. While some of those squashed in the steamroller story did pop back up and go on their way, real-life people who lost jobs or promotions because of affirmative action may have been permanently crippled in careers and livelihoods. Occupational markets during the 1970s and the 1980s were highly competitive, and many fields were stagnant; policies of race and sex preference meant that, when one person was quotaed in, another was ipso facto quotaed out.

Another crucial difference between the 1940s story and the realities of the ever-more-aggressive polices of affirmative action is that the havoc wrought by the steamroller in the story was seen and acknowledged. The little girl and her parents clearly saw that the machine was out of control, yelled warnings, and tried to avoid subsequent injuries. But operators and supporters of today's affirmative action steamroller indicate few regrets about running over anyone; indeed, a number still refuse to admit any damage whatsoever. Here is California Congressman Democrat Don Edwards writing for the Op Ed page of *The New York Times*:

In fact, it has been pretty hard to find any quota users at all. In recent hearings on Capital Hill, groups advocating the elimination of affirmative action requirements such as the United States Chamber of Commerce and the Associated Builders and Contractors, were asked to name companies using quotas. They couldn't.

The same story applies to tales that goals and timetables result in reverse discrimination against white males, and that they act as a ceiling to exclude qualified minority members and women from opportunities. Despite claims that both of these problems have reached epidemic proportions, no one has been able to back up these claims with actual cases. (February 13, 1986)

The congressman's statements are quite extraordinary, insofar as the U.S. Supreme Court had just heard three important cases involving use of affirmative action quotas and, within weeks of Edwards' words, would hand down decisions in those same cases (in *Wygant v. Jackson Board of Education* [1986], *Local 93 of the International Association of Firefighters vs. City of Cleveland* [1986], and *Local 28 of the Sheet Metal Workers v. Equal Employment Opportunity Commission* [1986]). The Justice Department would shortly release documents that showed that government contractors had been ordered to use rigid quotas in at least fifty-six cases (*Los Angeles Times*, April 3, 1986).

In fairness to Congressmen Edwards, it is worth pointing out that many in the Democratic Party hierarchy had lost touch with the controversial realities of affirmative action. Most officials and candidates had given quiet, routine assent to the use of affirmative action quotas in society at large and in the selection of delegates to conventions. Yet some in the Democratic/liberal intelligentsia knew that there was widespread disapproval of quotas in public-opinion polls (see Chapter 2). Thus, quotas were rarely called quotas or even affirmative action. Instead, Democrats/liberals tried to camouflage use of quotas with buzz words such a "justice," "fairness," and especially "equity."

But the voters saw through such codes. Democrats lost more than 70 percent of the white male vote in the 1984 elections; in some regions the figure approached 90 percent. The party and its union affiliates then commissioned political scientist Stanley Greenberg to investigate the attitude of white, male, blue-collar voters in the industrial heartland. The study of "Reagan Democrats" had begun.

Greenberg and his associates read the group a statement by Robert Kennedy that "Americans ought to honor a special obligation to black citizens who lived through the slave experience and racial discrimination." The responses:

That's bullshit.

No wonder they killed him.

I can't go along with that.

This happened years ago. And they talk to you about it as if it was happening right now.

I'm fed up with it, man.

I really feel that they have had so much just handed to them. . . . Most of them are abusing it. It's where now, it's almost like a turnaround. They're getting, getting, getting, and the whites are becoming the minority. (1985: 15)

Much to the surprise and dismay of both Greenberg and his sponsors, white fury over affirmative action emerged as a top voter concern in Greenberg's 1985 report and in a second report in 1987. Quotas and minority preferences were a primary source of anti-government, anti-Democrat anger among white blue-collar voters. Democratic campaign themes such as "fairness," "equity," and "justice" had been perceived—not without justification—as code words for quotas. Therefore, white voters had become, in Greenberg's terms, "de-aligned" from the Democratic Party.

The inability of Congressman Edwards, the Democratic Party, and millions of other Americans to see the affirmative action steamroller and heed its victims is a fascinating phenomenon. Such blindness begs many questions: How did a major social revolution evolve without being seen? How did a major drive to restructure society with race-and-gender preferences get as far as it did?

FROM EQUAL OPPORTUNITY TO RACIAL SPOILS SYSTEM

Affirmative action originally began as a series of presidential directives designed to encourage recruitment of qualified minorities and women through advertising and training programs. Under the old version of affirmative action, women and minorities attracted to an applicant pool would then compete on a non-discriminatory, colorblind, gender-neutral basis for jobs, promotions, or educational positions.

The former goal of equal opportunity has been progressively abandoned in favor of a "new," more radical vision of affirmative action emphasizing equality-of-results. Women and minorities are to be hired in proportion to their numbers in labor pools or the general population. For example, an employer might be asked to demonstrate considerable effort or "good faith" to increase the proportion of minorities in his workplace to 20 percent black and 15 percent Hispanic by a specific date. These "goals and timetables" are to be set based upon the proportion of blacks and

Hispanics already in his labor force compared with the proportion of blacks and Hispanics available in the appropriate labor pools. If the employer does not agree to set goals and timetables, or if he does not try to meet them once they were established, he might be considered guilty of discrimination. He would then be subject to fines or other penalties levied by government agencies or courts. Colleges and universities are accorded similar treatment.

Proponents of the new, proportionally based affirmative action have tried to avoid the term "quota." The word implies exclusion and the use of lower standards of selection for groups favored by quotas. Quotas clearly identified as such have not been regarded favorably by the courts. Therefore, nearly every affirmative action plan refers to "goals and timetables." However, in organizational practice, goals and timetables have often become quotas used to rapidly boost the percentage of minorities or women and to exlude better-qualified whites, especially white males (Glazer, 1975; Jencks, 1985b).

In *Invisible Victims*, I am much more concerned with how affirmative action actually operated in organizational contexts, rather than with its abstract, idealistic formulation. Throughout this book, therefore, I use the term "affirmative action" to refer to a system of racial-and-ethnic preferences or "quotas" that have been the real-world results of "goals and timetables." I use interchangeably the terms affirmative action quotas, preferential affirmative action (Auerbach, 1988), affirmative action preferences, race-and-gender preferences, or, simply, preferences. I am somewhat less concerned with affirmative action in the form of gender preferences; for the cutting edge in rhetoric and effort appears to have been with regard to racial/ethnic matters.

For twenty years, the shift in affirmative action policy has gone unnoticed by all but a handful of social scientists, jurists, and journalists. As Supreme Court Justice Antonin Scalia bitterly remarked, affirmative action has been formulated "without the slightest justification or analysis" (*Johnson v. Transportation Agency of Santa Clara*, 1987). Few scholars or commentators have asked why this has happened or what the consequences have been, especially for white males. The social psychological impact of affirmative action policies on white males and the lack of response to these policies by the mass media and social scientists are two key topics addressed in this book.

Any set of policies has both manifest and latent functions (Merton, 1968). What attention the press and the media have paid affirmative action has focused heavily on the policies' manifest, or obvious and intended, functions: increasing female or minority representation in higher education and the professions. But what have been the latent, or hidden and unintended, consequences of affirmative action? What unforeseen and unnoticed results occurred? That is another concern of this book.

By way of both preview and overview, it will be useful to briefly outline five factors which made possible a silent social policy revolution.

Factor One: Bureaucrats and Judges Implemented Affirmative Action

Affirmative action policies have been unilaterally formulated and imposed in a behind-the-scenes fashion through administrative or court decrees (Glazer, 1975; Capaldi, 1985). The mere threat of such decrees has led to "voluntary" or home-grown quota programs in many public and private organizations. Such policies have served as pre-emptive defense measures against charges of discrimination. Thus, insofar as it is a "social revolution," affirmative action has been forced upon society "from above." Public opinion polls have usually found that 80 percent of the public is opposed to affirmative action in the form of quotas. (On the depth and stability of public opposition to quotas or preferential treatment see Lipset and Schneider, 1978; Ladd and Lipset, 1980; Bunzel 1986; Kluegel and Smith, 1986.)

Factor Two: "Word Comes Down But Does Not Go Out"—Affirmative Action Has Been Largely an Informal, Oral Policy

The affirmative action revolution has proceeded quietly in a behind-the-scenes process, "back stage," rather than "front stage," to use Erving Goffman's terms (1955). It has not been a publicly viewed or noticed phenomenon. Specific orders to hire by race or gender have usually been issued orally behind the cover of more general and vaguely phrased "equal opportunity" guidelines.

The day-to-day reality of affirmative action as a back-stage process has been accurately captured in a letter to the editor in the *Los Angeles Times* by Darlene Murphy, a personnel secretary in a defense contractor's office:

The problems with well-intentioned theories are the real victims they leave in their wake.

From 1974 to 1976 I was employed by a major manufacturer at its sales office and plant in the Los Angeles area. This was one of those facilities that have a billboard outside announcing what jobs are available. One of my duties included working part time in the reception area where people would come in to fill out job applications.

When receiving an application, I was instructed to thank the person, wait until they left, then pencil in their race in the upper right hand corner. You see, we had "enough" whites and Hispanics at the facility; we needed more blacks. If the applicant was not black, no matter what his qualifications, the applications went into an inactive file to be considered no further.

I've always wondered about those Hispanics and whites who came back in to submit applications when we were only considering black applicants. What must they have thought when they drove by and saw the "Jobs Available" sign still out? How many weeks did it take before they began to realize that they had been dealt with unfairly? That, in bad faith, we had led them to believe they were in the running for jobs when in fact they never had been allowed in the race?

Let's face it; if we had been honest, the sign outside would have read "Jobs Available—only blacks need apply." But, then, that would have been discrimation. (October 2, 1983: II, 6)

Murphys's description echoes that of Harvard political scientist Harvey Mansfield, who aptly remarked of affirmative action programs: "Word comes down, but it does not go out" (1984, 28).

Factor Three: Constitutional and Legal Foundations Have Been Unclear

A major reason for the back-stage, oral nature of affirmative action processes is that employers have faced legal uncertainties whether they did or did not implement affirmative action programs. Without affirmative action programs, government contractors could lose their contracts or be more vulnerable to lawsuits by minorities or women charging discrimination. On the other hand, if they implemented affirmative action, they could be sued for reverse discrimination by white males.

Though Title VII of the 1964 Civil Rights Act expressly discouraged state-sponsored group preferences, the precise legal status of the various forms of affirmative action has never been quite clear. In *Defunis v. Odegaard* (1974), the U. S. Supreme Court dodged the issue of affirmative action preferences in law school admissions. In the famous 1978 *Regents of the University of California v. Bakke* case, the court ruled that race could be one factor in admissions to universities and professional schools.

While waiting for district, appellate, and Supreme Court decisions, a tacit social contract was arranged among corporate, government, and civil-rights elites. The bargain was basically understood as follows: workers who had already obtained jobs and promotions would not be affected by race-and-gender quotas. Race-and-gender preferences would mainly affect job applicants and persons seeking lower-level promotions (Jencks, 1985b: 754). The Baby Boomer white males would shoulder the burden of affirmative-action quotas.

During the 1980s, the Supreme Court gradually ratified the tacit corporate/government contract through a series of decisions that held that hiring and promotion using race-and-gender criteria was permissible but that such criteria may not be used to abrogate seniority criteria in lay-off situations. In early 1989, in *Richmond v. Croson*, the Supreme Court declared unconstitutional the use of state and local set-aside programs for minority contractors. The decision also implied that any racial classifications are "constitutionally suspect" and that white males are protected by the Equal Protection clause of the Fourteenth Amendment. Whether the *Richmond* decision will significantly alter affirmative action procedures remains to be seen.

Factor Four: The Complicity of the Victims and the Futility of Legal Recourse

The questionable legal status of affirmative action preferences, coupled with the informal, behind-the-scenes enforcement of such policies, has kept whites from realizing fully when and how often they have been shut out of jobs or promotions. Indeed such semi-secret operations make it difficult for anyone to determine just how often reverse discrimination has occurred.

In a poll conducted by Gordon Black Associates in September 1984, one out of ten white males in a telephone survey indicated that they had lost a job or promotion due to affirmative action quotas. As for officially reported complaints: "In the four years ending in 1983, for example, more than 1,500 complaints were filed with the U.S. Equal Employment Opportunity Commission by white males charging racial discrimination by public employers" (*Los Angeles Times*, April 16, 1985). In 1984, the State of California's Department of Fair Employment and Housing received 418 job-related discrimination complaints from whites out of a total number of 7,161 filings. Yet the data in this study indicate that white males were reluctant to complain openly of reverse discrimination, much less take official action. Therefore, any "official complaint" records are likely an understatement of the actual incidence of this phenomenon.

A naive assumption among many political scientists, jurists, and rank-and-file citizens is that victims of race-and-gender discrimination can easily obtain justice by filing a complaint with the Equal Employment Opportunity Commission or by going to court. However, victims of race-and-gender discrimination often sense—or quickly learn—that discriminatory behavior by employers or universities has been difficult to prove in legal forums. Justice in discrimination cases usually has been expensive, time-consuming, and may demand a great deal of effort and research. Thus, the legal machinery appears daunting, unapproachable, and an uncertain dispenser of justice. In behavioristic terms, the rewards aren't worth the costs (Homans, 1958; 1974).

It is of crucial importance to keep in mind throughout this book that employers and educational institutions have also been aware of the long odds against a disgrunted white male winning a reverse discrimination lawsuit, much less even filing one. The "you-can't-fight-city-hall" attitude among white-male victims of reverse discrimination has been a major factor in the institutionalization of affirmative action preferences.

Only three men interviewed for this study took legal action—thus far, without any success. The rest found it easier merely to get on with their lives in spite of reverse discrimination losses. Like other victims of discrimination, "they choose to rely on strategies for economic and personal survival that perpetuate their victimization but are seen as more desirable than submitting to the terms of legal discourse" (Bumiller, 1988: 109). Others who even tentatively considered filing complaints or taking legal action were quickly discouraged.

But if legal action against reverse discrimination was rare, what other forms of responses were there? If these men did not take legal action or even complain openly, why? How did co-workers, friends, and family respond to such situations? How did institutions, such as government, mass media, and corporations, react? Why was there never any large-scale, organized response by white males to programs of race-and-gender preference? These are the questions addressed in Chapters, 4, 5, and 6.

Factor Five: A New McCarthyism and the Spiral of Silence Suppressed Discussion and Dissent

One possible source of the lack of response by white males has been the misperception that the majority of Americans favor affirmative action. Such misperceptions can lead to what Elisabeth Noelle-Neumann (1974; 1975; 1984) has termed a "spiral of silence," whereby people keep silent rather than voice what they perceive to be dissident viewpoints.

As mentioned in the preface, a set of taboos suppressing discussion of race-related problems and policies arose during the past twenty years. This New McCarthyism, as we shall see, affected not only white males and the general public but also journalists, social scientists, policy makers, and members of corporate and government elites. (On the effects of the taboos in journalism and social science see: Adelson, 1978; Glazer, 1975; Douglas, 1977; Podhoretz, 1979; Lynch, 1984; 1985; Capaldi, 1985; Bloom, 1987; Sobran, 1987). The New McCarthyism stifled critical discussion of affirmative action and prevented recognition of the change in policy from equality of opportunity to equality of results via quotas.

PLAN OF THE BOOK

The thesis of this book is that the transformation of affirmative action from equal opportunity to racial quotas and proportional representation was a product of:

1. The implementation and interpretation of these policies by relatively independent government administrators and judges
2. The back-stage manner in which affirmative action was implemented

3. The complicity of white male victims
4. The failure of social scientists and the mass media to focus upon the issue
5. The influence of the New McCarthyism and the spiral of silence.

All of these factors contributed to widespread confusion and ignorance concerning affirmative action policies and realities on the part of the public. The topics of chapters in this book reflect the importance of these factors.

The next chapter provides a brief overview of the legal history of affirmative action and the shape of public opinion on the issue. Chapter 3 provides a sampler of press accounts of affirmative action as ordered and implemented in actual organizational settings. The chapter provides a context for the rest of the book.

Chapter 4 looks at the individual response to affirmative action setbacks by thirty-two white males interviewed for this study. Chapter 5 focuses upon the responses of friends, relatives, and co-workers. Chapter 6 examines how sex role behavior and larger organizational reactions to affirmative action affected white males' encounters with affirmative action.

Chapter 7 is concerned with the mass media's coverage of affirmative action both as news and as entertainment. The effects of the New McCarthyism and the spiral of silence are the subjects of Chapter 8. The impact of affirmative action and the New McCarthyism upon universities and the field of sociology is the focus of Chapter 9.

The behavior of elites and three logical/sociological flaws in affirmative action provide a dual focus in Chapter 10. Chapter 11 contains an assessment of the manifest or intended functions of affirmative action while the final chapter is concerned with the latent or unintended consequences of these policies.

Chapter 2

AFFIRMATIVE ACTION: LEGAL HISTORY AND PUBLIC OPINION

In this chapter, I shall briefly outline the key developments in affirmative action law and the shape of public opinion on affirmative action. The chapter is not a treatise on either topic. These pages provide a simple overview for the primary question of the book: what has actually happened with affirmative action?

A BRIEF LEGAL OUTLINE OF AFFIRMATIVE ACTION

In 1941, Executive Order 8802 was issued by Franklin Roosevelt to prohibit racial discrimination in defense industries. President Truman and Eisenhower issued additional executive orders extending the ban on discrimination to all government contractors.

Brown v. Board of Education (1954) struck down the concept of "separate but equal" racial segregation. But enforcement of this and similar cases was difficult. Therefore, in 1964 Congress passed the Civil Rights Act and in 1965 the Voting Rights Act. With regard to the future of affirmative action, Charles Murray has noted that

the core legislation was Title VII of the 1964 Civil Rights Act which forbade discrimination in hiring, promotion, firing, transfer, training, and pay, among all employers, employment agencies, and labor unions engaged in industry affecting commerce. In 1972, an amendment to the act extended its provisions to include any business employing more than fifteen workers and to employees of state and local governments and educational institutions. (1984: 93)

The words "affirmative action" were first used (vaguely) in Executive Order 11246 issued in September 1965. The directive required government contractors to take "affirmative action" to promote hiring of blacks and other minorities. It did not state how to take affirmative action.

In May 1968, administrative regulations regarding "affirmative action" were issued by the Department of Labor's Office of Federal Contract Compliance (OFCC). A written affirmative action compliance program was required from every major contractor and subcontractor with more than 50 employees and contract of $50,000 or more (Glazer, 1975: 46). Gradually, organizations were required to identify and count minority workers and compare them with the respective minority labor force available in that area. If there were large discrepancies, "goals and timetables" had to be developed to close any gaps between, say, black workers employed and black workers available. Employers were supposed to demonstrate "good faith efforts" in meeting goals and timetables.

The burden of proof in discrimination disputes began to shift. EEOC and OFCC began to argue that a disparity between minorities in the work force and minorities available in the surrounding labor pools was prima facie evidence of discrimination, regardless of intent. In other words, employers could be found guilty by the numbers unless they could prove otherwise, such as by having pre-existing, vigorous affirmative action programs. Therefore, starting and maintaining affirmative action quotas became the best defense against keeping at bay EEOC, OFCC, civil rights groups, and employee discrimination lawsuits.

The struggle to impose affirmative action generated court contests. Charles Murray (1984b) has argued that the 1971 case of *Griggs v. Duke Power* was a decisive turning point. The argument here centered upon whether an employer could impose minimum credentials (such as a high school diploma) to obtain employment. The Supreme Court denied the legality of such practices unless credentials or tests could be directly related to the job. The Court accepted the Equal Employment Opportunity Commission's position that tests must be discarded if they had an adverse impact on minority groups, that is, if they screened out a disproportionately large share of minorities as compared to whites. Thus, in a case cited in the next chapter, Prudential Insurance Company's use of a basic reading-skills test for employees was ruled invalid by a court. It was ruled that Prudential's practices had a definite adverse impact upon blacks because many more blacks than whites could not meet Prudential's required ninth-grade reading level. Prudential agreed to try to locate the rejected applicants and provide remedial-reading classes for them.

A number of cases involving admissions to higher education and professional schools began to work their way up to the Supreme Court during the 1970s. The first was that of *Defunis v. Odegaard* (1974). Marco Defunis had graduated magna cum laude in 1970 from the University of Washington and applied to that university's law school. The school was at that time running a dual admissions system. There was one admissions pool for white applicants and another, far less competitive, pool for minorities. The school rejected Defunis's application though the ranking system used by the law school placed him higher than all but four minority students. By the time Defunis's case was argued before the Supreme Court, he had graduated from another law school and the Court used this fact to dodge the issue and declare the entire case moot.

The next major case to be both heard and decided by the U. S. Supreme Court on affirmative action was, perhaps, the most famous one: *Regents of the University of California v. Bakke* (1978). Bakke had originally received an undergraduate degree in engineering, but his Marine Corps service in the Vietnam War convinced him he wanted to go into medicine. He completed the requisite science courses and applied to the U.C. Davis Medical School at the age of thirty-two. Like the University of Washington Law School, Davis was operating a two-track system. Sixteen of one hundred entry positions had been set aside for minorities, nearly all blacks and Hispanics. Bakke applied twice to the U.C. Davis Medical School. On each occasion, his grades and test scores were much higher than those of minorities who were admitted. When he was refused a second time, he sued, claiming denial of the equal protection clause of the Fourteenth Amendment. He won in the California courts, the most significant victory being a 7–1 decision in the liberal California State Supreme Court. The University decided to appeal the case to the U. S. Supreme Court, a move that angered leaders of civil rights organizations. The latter argued that the Bakke case did not show affirmative action at its best and that the univeristy simply wished to torpedo affirmative action programs altogether. The resulting 5–4 U. S. Supreme Court decision was fragmented and complex. But the controlling opinion, written by Justice Powell, held that race could be used as one of many criteria, but not as the main criterion of selection.

The following year the Court handed down a decision in the case of *United Steelworkers v. Weber* (1979). The Court ruled 5–2 (with two of the pro-Bakke justices not participating) that a private employer (Kaiser Steel in an agreement with the United Steelworkers) may conduct special training programs and reserve half the positions for minorities, even if the minorities have less experience or ability than whites who also apply. Unlike the Bakke case, the Weber case was appealed to the Court on Title VII of the 1964 Civil Rights Act, specifically Section 703(j), which reads:

Nothing contained in this title shall be interpreted to require any employer . . . to grant preferential treatment to any individual or to any group because of the race, color, religion, sex or national origin of such individual or group on account of an imbalance which may exist with respect to the total number or percentage of persons of any race, color, religion, sex or national origin employed by an employer.

In the Weber decision, the court majority got around the precise anti-preference wording of Title VII by saying that the language did not explicitly forbid such practices and that the overall spirit of the Civil Rights Act was congruent with voluntary preference programs. In a sharp dissent, Justice William Rehnquist termed such thinking "Orwellian."

Two cases taken up by the Supreme Court in the mid-1980s involved the issue of seniority versus affirmative action during lay-offs. The question in such cases as *Memphis Firefighters v. Stotts* (1984) and *Wygant v. Jackson Board of Education* (1986) was whether minorities recently hired under affirmative action plans should be laid off before whites with more senority. In these cases, the court held that, since no minority individuals could prove that they were individual victims of past discrimination by the municipal entities involved, then the seniority systems could take precedence over affirmative action programs. Whites with more seniority could not be laid off in favor of minorities with less seniority.

In *Local 93 of the International Association of Firefighters v. City of Cleveland* (1986) and *Local 28 of the Sheet Metal Workers v. Equal Employment Opportunity Commission* (1986), the Court approved one agreement and one court order (respectively) to settle discrimination lawsuits that involved preferential hiring or promotion of minority groups.

In all of the above cases, the Court was narrowly divided in 5–4 or 6–3 decisions. The decisions were also closely reasoned on a case-by-case basis. General legal principles had to be extracted carefully.

Another closely divided decision, but one which some legal scholars have argued can be interpreted broadly, was *Johnson v. Transportation Department of Santa Clara* (1987). The case involved preferential treatment in promotions and the use of statistical workforce data as justification for affirmative action programs. Diane Joyce and Paul Johnson were competing for the position of road dispatcher with the Department of Transportation, County of Santa Clara, California. Johnson had more seniority and scored slightly better on the oral part of the exam: Johnson obtained a 75, while Joyce obtained a 73. The local supervisor chose Johnson, but he was overruled by superiors who were more mindful of the county affirmative action plan, which was designed to achieve goals of proportional representation of women and minorities in the county workforce as compared with their percentage in the overall workforce in the area. Johnson sued under Title VII of the Civil Rights Act, as had Brian Weber in 1979. In a 6–3 decision the Court ruled against Johnson. Since Chief Justice Rehnquist was in the dissenting minority, the task of writing the majority opinion went to the most senior and most liberal justice, William Brennen. Justice Brennen wrote that manifest imbalances in the workforce with regard to women or minorities permit voluntary action to redress such imbalances. This was permissible so long as such plans do not "unncessarily trammel the interests of white employees," since it did not require the discharge of white males and their replacement with members of underrepresented groups. Sandra Day O'Connor wrote a separate, more narrowly construed concurring opinion.

Antonin Scalia, the newest justice on the Court, wrote a stinging dissent.

The court today completes the process of converting [Title VII] from a guarantee that race or sex will not be the basis for employment determinations to a guarantee that it often will. Ever so subtly . . . we effectively replace the goal of a discrimination-free society with the quite incompatible goal of proportionate representation by race and by sex in the workplace.

He complained that "this is an enormous expansion, undertaken without the slightest justification or analysis." Scalia was also blunt as to who would bear the burden of preferential treatment schemes:

The only losers in the process are the Johnsons of the country for whom Title VII has been not merely repealed but inverted. The irony is that these individuals—predominantly unknown, unaffluent, unorganized—suffer this injustice at the hands of a court fond of thinking itself the champion of the politically impotent. (*The New York Times*, March 25, 1987: 10)

In 1988, the Court took another step towards permitting the use of statistical imbalances in proving discrimination in the work place. In *Watson v. Fort Worth Bank and Trust* (1988), the Court held that statistical data could be used to support claims of sex discrimination in promotions. However, four of the eight justices participating in the case indicated that they would change the rules to make it easier for an employer to rebut a statistical study showing discrimination.

Throughout the 1980s, the Court proceeded slowly on a case-by-case basis to construct a fragile, contradictory consensus on affirmative action: race-and-gender preferences might be used in hiring and promotion—even by employers not charged with discrimination—but not in lay-offs, where seniority still takes precedence. Statistical data might be used to prove discrimination and proportional representation may be a goal of an employment program.

Much of that consensus, however, may have been shattered by what appears to be a new Court majority on affirmative action. Eighteen months after the *Johnson* decision, a 6–3 Court majority struck down a 30 percent set-aside provision for minority contractors in Richmond, Virginia. In *Richmond v. Croson* (1989), the Court majority held that, without prior findings of intentional discrimination, state and local set-aside programs violated the Equal Protection clause of the Fourteenth Amendment. "Benign" racial categories that favored blacks over whites would hereafter be considered "constitutionally suspect." Writing for the majority, Justice Sandra Day O'Connor stated:

The Equal Protection Clause of the 14th Amendment provides that "No State shall . . . deny to any person within its jurisdiction the equal protection of the laws." . . . As this Court has noted in the past, the "rights created by the first section of the 14th Amendment are, by its terms, guaranteed to the individual. The rights established are personal rights." . . . The Richmond Plan denies certain citizens the opportunity to compete for a fixed percentage of public contracts based solely upon their race. To whatever racial group these citizens belong, their "personal rights" to be treated with equal dignity and respect are implicated by the rigid rule erecting race as the sole criterion in an aspect of public decision-making.

Absent searching judicial inquiry into the justification for such race-based measures, there is simply no way of determining what classifications are "benign" or "remedial" and what classifications are in fact motivated by illegitimate notions of racial inferiority or simple racial politics. Indeed, the purpose of strict scrutiny is to "smoke out" illegitimate uses of race. . . .

Classifications based on race carry a danger of stigmatic harm. *Unless they are strictly reserved for remedial settings, they may in fact promote notions of racial inferiority and lead to a politics of racial hostility.* (*The New York Times*, April 24, 1989: A18; italics added)

The Wall Street Journal observed that, "For the first time, a majority of the justices said that all affirmative action programs alleged to discriminate against whites should be analyzed by the same tough constitutional standard that has been applied to strike down laws that minorities say discriminate against them" (January 24, 1989: A12). The *Journal* article also noted that the Court majority criticized the inclusion of many other minority groups in the set-aside program who have not suffered discrimination in Richmond (see discussion in Chapter 10).

The major targets of the decision were state and local government set-aside programs. Federal minority-contractor programs were held by O'Connor to be unaffected by the ruling. Nor were affirmative action programs undertaken in the private sector.

Within a few months, however, the new Court majority expanded the scope of its equal-protection, color-blind interpretation of affirmative action. In *Croson,* the Court held that whites were protected by the Fourteenth Amendment. In *Martin v. Wilks* (June 12, 1989), the Court majority extended to whites the protection of the non-discrimination provisions of Title VII of the 1964 Civil Rights Act. Specifically, the Court ruled that white firefighters in Birmingham, Alabama, could sue their employer for reverse discrimination resulting from an affirmative action agreement entered into by the department in the late 1970s.

One week before the *Martin* decision, the Court effectively reversed the 1971 *Griggs v. Duke Power* decision. In *Wards Cove v. Atonio* (June 5, 1989), the Court majority ruled that plaintiffs (not employers) must assume the burden of proof in demonstrating that a specific employer procedure (and not the sum total of all practices) has a disparate impact upon minorities. If plaintiffs successfully challenge a practice, the employer must produce reasonable "business justification" for use of an employment practice. Extensive "validation" tests of personnel procedures by employers need not be conducted.

Critics of the Court maintained that the recent decisions have turned back the clock on civil rights and totally reversed earlier decisions. Robert Bork countered that "all the Supreme Court has held is that discrimination must be proved rather than assumed" (*Wall Street Journal*, June 30, 1989: A12).

Some Congresspersons may seek legislation which would nullify the Court's recent interpretations. If so, it would be the first time Congress has acted decisively on the use of racial preferences since such means were all but prohibited in Title VII of the 1964 Civil Rights Act.

As the next section demonstrates, for most of the past twenty years, neither the Court nor Congress heeded public opinion on affirmative action—until the Court's *Richmond* decision. Both institutions avoided the controversy and permitted bureaucrats and lower court judges to impose affirmative action policies over and against the will of the people.

PUBLIC OPINION AND AFFIRMATIVE ACTION

White opposition to affirmative action-as-quotas has been strong and consistent ever since polling on the issue began in the 1970s. Whites have favored the idea of government help for people as long as it was compensatory and did not include quotas. For example, a Gallup poll in April 1979 asked the following question: "Would you favor or oppose the federal government offering special educational or vocational courses, free of charge, to enable members of minority groups to do better in tests?" The response in percentages (Source: Bunzel, 1986: 47–48):

	Favor	**Oppose**	**No opinion**
National	60	29	11
Men	55	34	11
Women	65	24	11
Whites	56	33	11
Nonwhites	82	7	11

On the other hand, whites' typical response to what is now standard affirmative action can be seen in the following Gallup poll: "Some people say that to make up for past discrimination, women and members of minority groups should be given preferential treatment in getting jobs and places in college. Others say that ability, as determined by test scores, should be the main consideration. Which point of view comes closer to how you feel on this subject?" The response in percentages (source: *Gallup Reports*, June 1984: 29):

	Give Preference	Ability Main Consideration	No Opinion
National	10	84	6
Men	9	85	6
Women	10	84	5
Whites	8	87	5
Nonwhites	27	64	9
Blacks	28	63	9

This pattern of responses amongst whites has been duplicated repeatedly. Polls conducted for an ABC special "Satellite Town Meeting" (June 16, 1985) found 82 percent of respondents opposed to quotas for promotions, and 71 percent opposed preferential treatment in any form. On the other hand, most respondents favored protecting minority civil rights and thought racial discrimination was still a problem.

A Gallup poll for *Newsweek* (March 7, 1988) found that 80 percent of whites and 50 percent of blacks disagreed with the statement: "Because of past discrimination should qualified blacks receive preference over equally qualified whites in such matters as getting into college or getting jobs or not?" These results, similar to past findings, are significant because the idea of affirmative action was put in the best possible light through careful phrasing. Note the use of the terms "qualified blacks" and "equally qualified whites." As has already been seen—and will be seen again—one of the major objections to real-world affirmative action is that unqualified minorities have been hired or promoted over better qualified whites. Though the *Newsweek* question tried to by-pass this problem, the strongly negative response by whites (the same as that accorded to questions which were not as carefully worded) indicates people may now automatically equate affirmative action with lowered standards or quotas.

An October 1977 CBS/*The New York Times* poll managed to elicit somewhat more white support with even more careful phrasing. Asked if college or graduate schools should give "special consideration" to the "best minority applicants," 59 percent of whites approved and 83 percent of blacks assented. A similar pattern was obtained in the same poll regarding a question regarding corporations' setting up special training programs for members of minority groups (Bunzel, 1986: 47).

In studying polling on affirmative action, John Bunzel remarked that the Louis Harris organization "has repeatedly demonstrated that if the pollsters say 'quotas,' the public says 'No,' but that if they say 'affirmative action' (and nothing more), the public says 'Yes.' As already indicated, however, if they say 'preferential treatment' the public also says 'No'" (p. 46). "Special consideration" forms of affirmative action may generate moderate support among whites, if such consideration is restricted to fully qualified or "the best" minority applicants. Strong majorities emerge across racial boundaries in support of compensatory or remedial programs that do not adversely affect other groups.

Attitudes on the Effectiveness of Affirmative Action

Sharper divisions between races emerge in polls on attitudes towards the effectiveness of affirmative action policies. In a 1978 Harris poll, 75.1 percent of blacks agreed that "in business and education, without set quotas there will be a slowing down in the hiring of blacks and other minorities," and 73.6 percent agreed with the statement "unless quotas are used blacks and other minorities just won't get a fair shake." Yet nonquota proposals obtained an even higher percentage of agreement: 89.5 percent said yes to the statement, "All in all, do you favor affirmative action programs in industry for blacks provided there are no rigid quotas?" and 91.3 percent agreed with the statement, "Do you favor or oppose affirmative action programs in higher education for blacks provided there are no rigid quotas?" (Bunzell, 1986: 46).

According to telephone survey data collected by James Kluegel (1985), whites tend to acknowledge the existence of discrimination barriers to blacks that existed in the past. However, whites now feel that such barriers no longer exist or are more than compensated for by preferential treatment programs. According to Kluegel's data, whites view racial inequalities not as the result of structural discrimination and inequality, but rather as the result of a lack of individual motivation.

By the mid-1970s, whites tended to perceive that there was reverse discrimination against whites in favor of blacks. In polling data published in Jacobson (1983), 41 percent of white respondents indicated in 1976 that they felt that blacks are "frequently" given special consideration and hired before whites. (In 1978, the figure was 35.7 percent.) A September 1984 survey for *USA Today* by Gordon Black Associates found that 10 percent of a sample of white registered voters answered "yes" to the question: "Have you, yourself, ever lost a job opportunity or educational opportunity at least partially as a result of policies and programs aimed at promoting equal opportunities for minorities?"

Data from the 1986 National Election Study (Institute for Social Research, University of Michigan) indicate that a majority of white Americans (60.8 percent) believe that affirmative action programs for blacks have reduced whites' prospects in hiring and school admissions. Whites were asked if a white person would be refused admission to a school while an equally or less qualified black was accepted; 27.6 percent believed that was "very likely," and 41.4 percent believed it was "somewhat likely." A similar question was asked about hiring; 26.6 percent of whites thought it was "very likely" and 48.3 percent thought it "somewhat likely" that a white would lose out.

The National Election Study also asked whites what they thought chances were that they or someone in their family would directly suffer this form of discrimination. In school admissions, 12.5 percent thought this very likely, and 30 percent thought it somewhat likely; in hiring and promotions the percentages were 12.4 and 28.7 respectively, for a total of more than 40 percent.

Problems with Public-Opinion Surveys

Public-opinion polls on affirmative action provide us with a basic barometer of how numbers of Americans feel as individuals about the issue. Unfortunately, survey data does not tell us how well informed people are about affirmative action. Do they really understand what it is and how it operates? Furthermore, we know little about how Americans think others feel about affirmative action and whether individuals polled feel constrained about speaking their mind on the topic. As we shall see in Chapter 8, such data would be valuable in assessing the extent to which a "spiral of silence" has operated with regard to affirmative action. Do Americans keep silent on anti–affirmative action beliefs because they feel that the majority of public opinion supports affirmative action? Interviews conducted for this study suggest the possibility, and the pro–affirmative action bias in the mass media [Chapter 7] would make it easy for individuals to believe that the majority of Americans support affirmative action.

Qualitative Approaches to Public Opinion

The most explosive findings on affirmative action attitudes stem from studies of white voters funded by labor unions and the Michigan Democratic party and conducted by political scientist Stanley Greenberg. *Report on Democratic Defection* (1985) was designed to study white male blue-collar voter defection from the Democratic party in Michigan during two previous presidential elections.

Some statements obtained from Greenberg's white, blue-collar subjects were introduced in the previous chapter. The results embarrassed the Democratic leadership and were something of a surprise to Greenberg and his associates. The issue simply "burst out" during discussions on questions on inequality asked of four "focus groups" of white Democratic defectors: union members age thirty to forty-five, non-union male age thirty to forty-five, union and non-union males age forty-six to sixty, and wives of union men, age thirty to forty-five.

Greenberg and his associates noted that

discrimination against whites has become a well-assimilated and ready explanation for their status, vulnerability and failures. When applying or taking a test for a job or school, blacks have a structured advantage. If the blacks fail, they will lower the standards to "get the minorities inside." The tests in any case are rigged. . . . Indeed, white middle-class children, when they attempt to break into the labor market, will find a black preference operating there too, blocking the way.

Thus, no participant anticipated that their children would in the future identify with the Democratic Party (1985: p. 24).

Greenberg's 1985 study and a 1987 replication were ignored by the media and temporarily suppressed by the Democratic party and unions which sponsored it. Affirmative action programs had already been steamrollered into place.

Chapter 3

AN AFFIRMATIVE ACTION SAMPLER

In writing this book, I have discovered that most professionals and lay-persons are largely unfamiliar with the problems and complexities of affirmative action policies. Therefore, I would like to provide the reader with a direct sense of the diversity and range of affirmative action programs and with the problems and contradictions involved with such policies.

The reader may choose to read this chapter carefully or skim the contents and, perhaps, return to it after reading other parts of the book. Those who consider themselves more familiar with affirmative action law and policy may be tempted to skip this sampler. I hope they will forgo the temptation and will at least skim the contents. Many of these accounts deal not only with court decisions and policy announcements but the actual behavior and organizational consequences wrought by such edicts. In addition, I shall be making references to some of these items later in the book. The reports below lend considerable support to individual data contained in the next two chapters.

In the interests of accuracy, I have quoted these accounts directly from news sources, mostly from the *Los Angeles Times*. The selection of examples is, admittedly, somewhat arbitrary, though probably no more so than affirmative action reporting by the press itself. Press coverage has been uneven and, as documented later in the book, the mass media ignored affirmative action developments until the late 1970s. Except for important court cases, affirmative action accounts were seldom accorded page one treatment until the mid-1980s. The sampler reflects this coverage; most of the items are from the 1979–86 period.

The sampler is organized under three headings: Public Sector Affirmative Action; Affirmative Action in Education; and Private Sector Affirmative Action. Within these three categories, I have arranged the items by sub-topic. Reports on the same topic (e.g., court cases, controversies over testing for teachers, law school admissions, and examinations for the federal government) are arranged sequentially as well.

Reports on court cases and other more visible public decisions represent the more manifest side of affirmative action, the obvious and intended consequences of the drive for greater intergroup equality. So are the reports on the race/ethnic composition of the state of California and U.S. government workforces and the item on the quadrupling of women managers in banking. Except for the items on the Michigan school teachers and the Memphis firefighters, I have not made reference below to decisions later handed down by the U.S. Supreme Court.

There are other items which deal with the latent or unintended consequences of such policies, such as the reports in the education section that deal with the impact of affirmative action on meritocracy and educational standards.

There is, admittedly, a strong California bias in the listings below. That is because California has the largest state population and certainly one of the most ethnically diverse; California has typically been defined as a bellwether or trend-setter state; state government officials, especially two-term governor Edmund G. "Jerry" Brown, have been aggressive advocates of affirmative action, resulting in a great many administrative and court cases involving these policies; the *Los Angeles Times* has become one of the major newspapers of record in the nation; all but two of the white males interviewed for the core chapters of this book resided in California; and I live in California.

Again, the aim of this chapter is for the reader to get a taste of the complex, contradictory, and controversial consequences generated by affirmative action, while keeping in mind that what follows is merely the tip of the iceberg. Most affirmative action processes have gone unpublicized and unreported.

PUBLIC SECTOR AFFIRMATIVE ACTION

"Texas and the U.S. Justice Department have settled discrimination suits against seven state agencies with agreements a black legislator called 'the most significant stride towards true equal employment opportunity ever taken by this state. . . . '

"Essentially each state agency agreed to hire minorities and women in proportion to their share of the "relevant labor force" for various occupations in the areas where it normally recruits—statewide in some cases, locally in others. . . .

"'It's a can of worms. . . . It will be extremely difficult, extremely costly,' said one agency personnel officer. He said there is no central source of information on minority percentages in various occupations.

"He said it would be easier to administer hiring goals keyed to the percentages of blacks, Mexican-Americans and women in the population at large than in dozens of separate job categories.

"'Maybe administratively it would be easier to pull them out of the air, but they (hiring goals) have to have meaning,' Bickerstaff said.

"Bickerstaff said the chief advantage of the settlement was avoiding expensive trials of the federal suits. 'The cost of failure would have been unparalleled. It would have involved several years of costly litigation and problems of disruption within the agencies with Justice interviewing every employee they could find,' he said."
Fort Worth Star-Telegram, December 22, 1978.

"The president of the **Public Broadcasting Service** concurred Thursday with a task force conclusion that public television is 'seriously deficient' in programming for ethnic minorities.

"Lawrence K. Grossman, PBS president, said he is uneasy about one task force proposal that would require PBS and other public broadcasters to set the amount of their minority programming according to the percentage of minorities in the overall populations."
Los Angeles Times, November 18, 1978.

"**The Equal Employment Opportunity Commission** Monday issued guidelines to protect employers from reverse discrimination charges when they institute voluntary affirmative action programs for minority workers. . . . Commission officials acknowledged that the ardor for voluntary programs among government and private employers had waned somewhat in the face of recent legal challenges brought by white males who charged that they had been discriminated against in favor of women and minorities."
Los Angeles Times, December 12, 1978.

"A federal judge has ruled that a government agency responsible for enforcing antidiscrimination laws, the **Equal Employment Opportunity Commission**, was itself guilty of discrimination in refusing to promote a woman because she was a Puerto Rican."
Los Angeles Times, January 6, 1979.

"The chairman of the U.S. **Equal Employment Opportunity Commission** inflamed a mounting civil rights controversy Friday by telling a House subcommittee that his agency has been 'misusing' racial statistics to justify forcing employers to hire larger proportions of minorities."
Fort Worth Star-Telegram, December 15, 1984.

"A retired Navy captain recently changed his name from Robert Earl Lee to Roberto Eduardo Leon and is now eligible—as a minority member—for preferential treatment under an affirmative action program in **Montgomery County, Md**.

"Leon, 56, a former Naval Academy classmate of President Carter who works in the county's **Environmental Protection Department**, legally changed his name February 21. He immediately requested that he be reclassified as a minority member and the request was granted last week. Under county guidelines, Leon's Spanish surname makes him eligible for promotion over other white males.

"'He has a knack for figuring out loopholes in things,' Eric Mendelsohn, Leon's boss, said. "Bob, I mean Roberto, is a highly regarded professional, a little eccentric in some ways. It's nice to have a Hispanic on our staff.'"
Los Angeles Times, March 11, 1979.

Police and Fire Department Cases

"A sex-bias suit filed by the Department of Justice against **Philadelphia** has resulted in a back-pay award of $700,000 to 96 women—the most extensive relief granted so far in a sex-discrimination suit against a police department. The department also must hire women for 30 percent of its officer corps."
U.S. News and World Report, August 4, 1980.

"The Supreme Court Tuesday overturned the lower court order that during the past six years has required **Los Angeles County** to hire at least one black and one Mexican-American for every three whites in the **Fire Department**.

"The justices did so for procedural reasons without ruling on any of the broad legal questions concerning racial quotas and employment discrimination that had been raised in the dispute. . . .

"According to figures gathered last June and submitted to the high court, the county has hired 170 whites, 112 blacks and 106 Mexican-Americans in the Fire Department since the court order was imposed."
Los Angeles Times, March 26, 1979.

"Released only seven months ago from a court-sponsored hiring quota that had existed for five years, the **Los Angeles County Fire Department** was sued again in federal court Thursday for allegedly discriminating against blacks and Mexican-Americans.

"A class-action lawsuit was filed on behalf of minority members in the department and unsuccessful applicants for [**Los Angeles County**] fire fighter positions by the Center for Law in the Public Interest which in 1973 won a court order requiring the county to fill 40% of all vacancies with minority applicants to make up for past discrimination. . . .

"A. Thomas Hunt, attorney for the center . . . said the new suit was brought because the county had reinstituted a written test the center believes discriminates against minorities.

"Only about 25% of those applicants accepted for Fire Department positions as a result of the last test were minority members, Hunt said, and the percentage is expected to drop to 15% for the class scheduled to start later this month."
Los Angeles Times, October 5, 1979

"Heeding pleas from Latino activists, the **Los Angeles Police Commission** on Tuesday unanimously agreed to increase by one-third the number of Latino recruits entering the police Academy.

"In the same vote, the commission also directed Police Chief Daryl F. Gates to adopt a more flexible method to select officers for promotion but Gates said afterward that he would not.

"Some Latinos believe that the Police Department's present system, in which applicants are tested, then ranked numerically on a list and promoted in strict order is often subjective and discriminates against them.

"The more flexible promotional system was approved as an affirmative action measure by Los Angeles' voters in 1983 and was later adopted by other city agencies. In essence, it would allow Gates to promote officers who do not necessarily finish at the very top of the promotional lists.

"Gates, however, said after the commission's vote that he will not change the manner in which Los Angeles' police officers win promotion. The system endorsed by the commission is subject to 'favoritism and manipulation, political or otherwise. . . . I could promote my friends. . . . ' he noted."
Los Angeles Times, March 11, 1987.

"A federal judge gave preliminary approval Thursday to a landmark discrimination case settlement requiring that minorities receive 50% and women 20% of all the **[San Francisco]** city **Police Officer** appointments for the next ten years.

"The out-of-court settlement was signed and submitted to chief U.S. Dist. Judge Robert F. Peckam, climaxing a six year struggle over a controversial lawsuit charging the city police department with employment discrimination."
Los Angeles Times, April 8, 1979

"The federal government sued the **City of San Francisco** on Tuesday, charging discrimination against blacks, Hispanics and Asians in the **Fire Department**.

"The suit by the Civil Rights Division of the Justice Department said the city had 80 blacks, 88 Hispanics, and 36 Asians among 1,472 uniformed Fire Department officers as of August, 1983. . . .

"The suit asked for a court order requiring the Fire Department to hire blacks, Hispanics, and Asians 'on an equal basis with whites' and to eliminate discriminatory hiring procedures.'"
Los Angeles Times, November 14, 1984

"Michael T. Farrell, a 25-year veteran, took over as interim chief of the **San Francisco Fire Department**, replacing Edward Phipps who quit in the midst of discrimination problems in the city's station house. Farrell, 51, a deputy chief since March, will direct the department until a permanent chief is appointed by Mayor Art Agnos. Last week, a U.S. District Court judge told Phipps, 57, that his department was torn by racial problems and was "out of control." The department is conducting an investigation into the discovery of a swastika in the office of an Asian and black fire inspector in the Financial District."
Los Angeles Times, January 14, 1988

"The **California Highway Patrol** has reached into Mexico to beef up its minority recruitment programs. An advertisement for job candidates appeared in the Tijuana-based "El mexicano," a Spanish-language newspaper that also circulates in the United States. CHP spokesman Dan Parker said a person does not have to be an American citizen to be in the patrol, but must be a legal resident of California. "'We are under-represented in Hispanic patrol persons,'" he said.
Los Angeles Times, July 12, 1981

"An **Evanston, Ill., Fire Chief** refused to promote three blacks to the rank of captain because only blacks had been permitted to take the promotional test. He was fired."
NBC Nightly News, November 29, 1980

"White firefighters who challenged court-ordered remedies imposed on the **Bridgeport, Conn., Fire Department** in a discrimination suit by blacks and Hispanics failed to have the remedies overturned. The Supreme Court left intact a lower-court decision that 73 minority persons be hired so that the number on the force would mirror the minority population of the city. The Court also ruled that a written examination developed by the city and a consulting firm not be used, since it was found to be discriminatory."
U.S. News and World Report, March 15, 1982.

"Siding with whites in the latest 'reverse discrimination' case, the Supreme Court rekindled the debate over affirmative action with a decision that is likely to have wide repercussions on both races. . . .

"The Court's new ruling stemmed from a struggle between blacks and whites over **firefighting jobs** in **Memphis** when city budget problems forced layoffs three years ago. A year earlier, the city had settled a race-discrimination suit by agreeing to fill half the vacancies in the Fire Department with blacks.

"When layoffs became necessary, a judge agreed with minorities that some of their gains would be wiped out if jobs were eliminated in seniority order. He issued an order protecting blacks at the expense of several whites with less seniority.

"In overturning that ruling, Justice Byron White declared for the Court majority that 'mere membership in the disadvantaged class is insufficient to warrant a seniority award . . . ' White added, only 'those who have been actual victims of illegal discrimination' can win a job-bias claim."
U.S. News and World Report, June 25, 1984.

"Black **police officers** laid off by the city of **Detroit** in 1979 and 1980 must be recalled and given seniority rights, a federal judge holds. He says the city violated its affirmative action duty under the 14th amendment by conducting the layoffs in a manner that reduced black representation on the force. He also finds the Detroit Police Officers Association breached its duty to represent black officers."
U.S. News and World Report, August 20, 1984

"Promotion of minority **firefighters** on a one-for-one basis with white firefighters is upheld by a U.S. appeals court in **Cleveland**. It finds the city can enter into a consent decree to this effect to redress admitted past discrimination. The court rejects a claim that a recent Supreme Court ruling prevents court-ordered affirmative action for individuals who are not actual bias victims. It notes the agreement will not require the hiring of unqualified candidates or interfere with seniority rights."[1]
U.S. News and World Report, February 18, 1985.

"The Supreme Court, rejecting claims by white job seekers of "reverse discrimination," Monday let stand an appellate ruling allowing state agencies to unilaterally raise the test scores of minority applicants without a court finding of previous racial bias.

"The justices, over three dissents, refused without comment to hear a case brought by a group of 15 white **New York State correctional officers** who protested that they were unfairly bumped down a job-promotion list when the state civil service commission adjusted test results to give more minority candidates passing scores. . . .

"In a written test, administered to 275 candidates in 1982, only 25% of the minorities passed, compared to 48% of the whites. State officials weighed the test results' adverse impact on minorities and the likelihood of a suit by minorities—and decided to adjust the scores to raise the minority 'pass' rate to about 50%. The white job applicants then brought suit, charging 'blatant' discrimination."
Los Angeles Times, January 8, 1985

"A federal judge ruled Monday that the **District of Columbia Fire Department** promotion policies under its affirmative action plan are unconstitutional.

"The plan's promotion features clearly violate the Constitution, U.S. District Judge Charles R. Richey said, 'as that portion of the plan unnecessarily trammels on the rights and interests of white firefighters. As such, the promotion aspects must be struck down."
Los Angeles Times, April 2, 1985.

"A top Latino **FBI** official who is leading a class-action lawsuit accusing the FBI of racial discrimination charged Thursday that "bigots" are in power at the highest levels of the nation's top law enforcement agency. . . .

"Perez, transferred to El Paso in early 1984 after a two-year feud with the head of the FBI's Los Angeles office, Richard T. Bretzing, filed his lawsuit in El Paso in early 1987 and it has since been certified as a class-action case for about 280 of the FBI's 400 Latino agents."
Los Angeles Times, April 8, 1988

"After the **Boston fire department** rejected them because of poor exam scores in 1975, identical twins Philip and Paul Malone did not think of giving up. Back they went in 1977 with a new application and a new strategy: they declared they were black. As such, the Malones were hired by the department, which was under pressure to take on more minority firemen. Under a court-ordered affirmative action plan, it no longer mattered that the brothers, with exam scores of 57% and 69%, fell far short of the passing grade of 82% required for whites.

"For ten years, no one officially questioned the Malones's self-proclaimed blackness. Then in February 1988, the twins were put on a list of blacks among firemen proposed for promotion to lieutenant. The list went to fire commissioner Leo Stapleton. He knew the Malones were the department's only identical twins, and if they weren't white, it was news to him. Stapelton asked the state's department of personnel administration to check out the twins' status.

"Eventually the twins, now 33, claimed that they did not learn they were black until 1976, when, they say, their mother discovered a sepia photograph of a pale-looking woman she said was their black great-grandmother. After an investigation of their claim, they were fired.

"The dismissal, which the Malone's have appealed to the State Supreme Judicial Court, has Boston churning. Amid rumors that there have been other phony claims of minority status, mayor Ray Flynn ordered a review of the hiring practices in the fire and school departments. Two weeks ago, Flynn disclosed that at least five other fire fighters will be asked to prove they are not white."
Time, October 31, 1988

Federal Workers and the Conflict Over Civil Service Exams

A profile of **federal workers** done by *U.S. News and World Report* revealed that "minorities are heavily represented—21.6 percent—compared with about 14.8 percent in the private labor force."
U.S. News and World Report, August 4, 1980

"The **U. S. Government** abandoned the old **Federal Civil Service Entrance Examination** because not enough blacks and minorities passed and because exam questions were not job related. That's why the government finally abandoned the entrance exam and instituted the career exam. But even with it the pass rate for minorities still lagged behind the rate for whites (42% of white applicants pass the career exam, compared with only 13% of Latinos and 5% of blacks).

"Two years ago, a group of blacks and Latinos who had failed the test sued the **Office of Personnel Management** on the grounds that the test was manifestly unfair. They alleged further that the exam tested for general knowledge not required for the 118 job categories for which it was used.

"The case never came to trial. What the attorneys for the government and the lawyers committee are working out now is a consent decree mandating a test that will produce the right numerical results."
Columnist William Raspberry, *Los Angeles Times*, January 2, 1981

"Ten days ago, Associate Attorney General John H. Shenefield, on the Administration's behalf, signed a consent decree designed to settle an affirmative action suit charging racial discrimination against the federal government's own **Office of Personnel Management**. Under the terms of the agreement, which Reagan transition officials vainly sought to delay until they took office, the federal government is committed to abolish the Professional and Administrative Career Examination (PACE). PACE will be replaced with some method of assessment aimed at ensuring that the numbers of Hispanics and blacks getting jobs is roughly proportionate to those applying: in other words, a quota."
Barron's, January 19, 1981

"The **federal government,** under pressure from discrimination lawsuits to change its hiring procedures for entry-level jobs, plans a new system emphasizing college grades and tests geared to specific jobs.

"The new procedures will officially end the traditional written examination for such jobs. Director of the Office of Personnel Management, Constance Horner, said the new system, expected to be in place by next April, will permit the government to compete more efficiently with the private sector for 'high-quality' college graduates seeking entry level professional or administrative positions.

"'It will also permit the government to attract a more racially and ethnically diverse work force,' she said. . . .

"The government hasn't had any entrance test for more than 100 types of jobs since 1982, when the Professional and Administrative Career Examination, known as PACE, was discarded as racially discriminatory after a lawsuit. Hiring since then has been based on what was to be a temporary process of interviews, recommendations, and college grades. A federal judge here also threw out that process last year, calling it 'arbitrary and capricious,' but the government has continued using it while appealing the case. . . .

"The proposal must still be reviewed by the courts."
The Wall Street Journal, June 24, 1988

"A white federal employee who charged that he was denied promotion for 10 years because of reverse discrimination was promoted by his superiors Thursday after a judge threatened to use federal marshals to ensure the promotion. . . .

"U.S. District Judge Robert Vining ordered the **[Department of Housing and Urban Development]** Wednesday to promote Charles Mayson to director of the agency's regional compliance division.

"The order resulted from a suit in which Mayson asked the court to force HUD compliance with two findings by the EEOC that Mayson, who is white, was a victim of reverse discrimination.

"Judge Vining accused HUD officials of stalling and told them to promote Mayson by 9 a.m. on Thursday or face federal marshals. . . .

"In ordering the promotion Wednesday, Vining said that HUD's refusal to promote Mayson was a 'flagrant . . . willful and callous' disregard of EEOC orders and added that, if it were up to him, he would fire the HUD officials who were reponsible."
Los Angeles Times, May 10, 1985

"'The time is approaching to again pick **federal judges** strictly on individual merit and to stop giving special consideration to blacks, Hispanics, and women,' out-going Att. Gen. Griffin B. Bell said Wednesday. . . . Bell, who has drawn fire from some interest groups for not recommending more women and members of minorities, said that when President Carter finishes filling the new judgeships created by Congress, $7\frac{1}{2}$% of the judges will be black, 3% Hispanic and $6\frac{1}{2}$% women.

"These percentages contrasted with 'virtually nothing' in the way of representation for these groups when the Administration took office, Bell said.

"'Related to the percentage of each in the lawyer population, this is substantial representation,' he said."
Los Angeles Times, June 15, 1979

Affirmative Action in State Agencies

"The [California] state Supreme Court, taking a stand on minority preference programs, Friday upheld the use of racial quotas in affirmative action plans for hiring **public employees**.

"A sharply divided court ruled constitutional what it called 'race conscious' hiring programs designed to correct racial imbalances resulting from past discrimination. . . .

"The case the state court decided Friday involved a "minority preference appointment' plan adopted by the Sacramento County Civil Service Commission.

"The Commission found that there was only one minority among the 65 lawyers in the county district attorney's office—a number it called 'disproportionately low' to the 19.5% minority population of Sacramento County.

"The commission found that the racial imbalance was the result of unintentional discriminatory practices—such as the use of unvalidated oral exams for job applicants and inadequate minority recruitment efforts. As a result, the district attorney's office was ordered to hire at least one minority attorney for every two non-minority attorneys hired until 8% of all attorneys were minority.

"The district attorney, James M. Price, resisted the order and took the case to court, contending that the hiring quotas unfairly discriminated against non-minorities, violating state and federal statutes and the equal protection guarantees of the California and United States constitutions.

"The district attorney won in both a trial court and a state court of appeals. . . .

"The [state Supreme Court] majority drew a sharp rebuke from Mosk, author of the court's 1976 ruling in Bakke . . . 'we must not give carte blanche approval to every proposal, however undemocratic, made in the name of purportedy improving race relations. . . . For every person quotaed in, another is quotaed out,' he observed."
Los Angeles Times, January 25, 1980

In 1975, when Robert Boggs "was ordered to fill 10 [**State of California Health Department**] clerk-typist positions with minorities and told not to worry about whether they could type, he refused and was shuffled off, after a 15-year state career, to a do-nothing job."
Los Angeles Times, July 3, 1977

"Of the total number of appointments the governor has made [**Governor Jerry Brown of California**] more than half are women, blacks, Latinos and Asians. No other governor can match that record."
Los Angeles Times, April 8, 1982

A story reporting Latino protests for more state jobs noted that: "The percentage of state employees who are black and Asian (10.1% and 5.2%, respectively) is higher than those group's representation in the state's overall work force, **[California] Personnel Board** statistics show." [Among younger workers the minority percentages are approximately double these rates—FRL]
Los Angeles Times, February 3, 1983

"A director of the **Bay Area Rapid Transit District** charged 'reverse discrimination' in that a disproportionate number of jobs in the system are presently held by blacks. BART Director John Glenn said only 52.2% of the transit district's 2,400 employees are white, while whites make up 68.4% of the population of the three-county area served by the system. He called the situation 'terrible' and said the district should set up its own 'affirmative action' program favoring white hiring. Glenn represents a district of high unemployment caused by the shutdown of a General Motors plant."
Los Angeles Times, January 31, 1983

"An affirmative action manual that contends 'all white individuals are racists' was denounced Sunday by state officials and one assemblyman called it 'inflammatory and hate-filled.'

"The 38-page manual was used by the **[New York] State Insurance Fund**, a state agency that handles workmen's compensation cases, at three recent employee training seminars, but officials recalled it and canceled further seminars after they became aware of its contents.

"The manual defines racism as 'different from racial prejudice, hatred or discrimination. Racism involves having the power to carry out systematic discriminatory practices through the major institutions of our society.

"'In the United States, at present, only whites can be racists since whites dominate and control the institutions that create and enforce American cultural norms and values,' the manual reads.

"It concludes that 'all white individuals in our society are racist,' even those who have no conscious prejudice because they receive 'benefits distributed by a white, racist society through its institutions.'

"'Our institutional and cultural processes are so arranged as to automatically benefit whites, just because they are white,' it said. . . .

"The manual was compiled by Carolyn Pitts, a $39,872-a-year affirmative action officer who has worked for the State Insurance Fund since 1985. . . . Pitts, who is black, could not be reached for comment Sunday."
Los Angeles Times, April 4, 1987

AFFIRMATIVE ACTION IN EDUCATION

Controversies Over Testing and Quality Control:
Law Schools and Universities

"A **National Academy of Sciences' Research Council** report strongly discounted 'cultural bias' in standardized testing."
Los Angeles Times, February 3, 1982.

A report on college admission procedures co-sponsored by the **College Entrance Examination Board** and the **Educational Testing Service** found that "minority status is, on average, the most influential personal credential in determining admissions preference, indicating 'strong affirmative action programs.' . . . The study said other factors that positively affect selections are alumni ties and geographic location."
Los Angeles Times, April 7, 1982

AT **UCLA** "last November a group of law students staged a protest over a plan to abolish the **law school**'s 25% minority quota in favor of a plan to allocate 60% of the admissions on the basis of grades and test scores and 40% on such factors as academic potential, career goals, work experience and race."
Los Angeles Times, March 11, 1979

"Members of minority races—particularly blacks—scored considerably lower than whites on the **California Bar Examination** in the fall of 1978, according to a study of test scores conducted by the California State Bar Journal.

"Among first-time takers of the fall 1978 exmination, the latest for which statistics have been completed, 67.8% of the whites passed, while only 19% of the blacks did. Latinos had a 30.9% pass rate, Asians, 53.4% and other minorities, 32.4%."
Los Angeles Times, March 8, 1980

"Changes designed to 'ease the physical burden' of the **California Bar Examination** will go into effect with the next test to be given would-be lawyers Feb. 27-March 1, the State Bar has announced. . . . By placing less emphasis on writing ability, the changes can be expected to help minority applicants who may have language difficulties. Chicanos, blacks and other minority groups have complained that the examination has discriminated against them."
Los Angeles Times, February 8, 1979

"Scores on last July's **California Bar Exam** showed their biggest one-year drop in 21 years, and the pass rate was the lowest in many decades, according to new figures from the State Bar.

"The decline was especially severe among minorities, the figures show. Just 11.6% of the blacks who took the exam passed, compared to 48.3% of the whites, the report said. The passage rate was 18.1% for Latinos and 30% for Asians."
Los Angeles Times, January 9, 1985

Arthur N. Frakt, dean of **Loyola University School of Law,** was interviewed in the *Los Angeles Times,* about the above test results: "Most disturbing about his analysis, Frakt said, is the realization that minorities enrolled in the school under affirmative action policies have the least chance of practicing law. His findings mirror those made as long ago as 1979 by the state Bar showing that minorities have the lowest pass rate on the Bar just as they have the lowest entry scores and grades in law school.

"'You will find most of the minorities at the C or C− level, so for many of them it may be a real exercise in frustration that, yes, they can get through law school, but if the Bar pegs its exam to a higher level, their chances of passing are very limited.'"
Los Angeles Times, January 20, 1985

"Troubled by minority students' dismal failure rate on the California Bar examinations, the **UCLA Law School faculty** has voted to toughen its graduate standards and improve the school's academic support systems.

"The changes, which were approved at a meeting of the faculty Friday evening, were adamantly opposed by various student organizations on the grounds that such changes would reduce minority groups' chances of entering and graduating from the Law School. . . .

"A recent study showed, [UCLA Law School Dean Susan Westerberg Prager] said, that while nearly 90% of regularly admitted UCLA students now pass the California Bar exam, the passage rate is only about 30% for those who are admitted under a special program designed to attract minority and other educationally disadvantaged students.

"'That information was sufficiently dramatic that I did not feel we should let another year go by without addressing at least some of the issues it raised,'" Prager said in a recent letter addressed to the schools' approximately 900 law students.

"UCLA's admissions program was designed in 1978 after the California Supreme Court's decision in the Bakke case, which prohibited schools from setting aside special admissions slots exclusively on the basis of race. In fact, however, UCLA's program, like similar programs at other universities, has been the school's 'primary tool' in admitting racial minority students, most of whom could not qualify under regular admissions standards, said Michael D. Rappaport, UCLA's assistant dean of Law School admissions.

"In recent years between 24% and 40% of the entering classes have been members of minority groups, and the majority of them have been admitted

through the diversity program, Rappaport said."
Los Angeles Times, May 3, 1987

"The **California State University** campuses at Los Angeles and Dominguez Hills have the dubious honor of being the only colleges or universities in the state where fewer than half of the graduates who took the new basic skills test for prospective teachers have passed. Only 33% of the Dominguez Hills graduates who have taken the test passed. . . . About 47% of the candidates who earned their degrees at Cal State Los Angeles passed. . . .

[Statewide] only 26% of blacks and 38% of the Latino candidates passed. . . . Both Cal State Los Angeles and Cal State Dominguez Hills have a majority of minority students, university officials noted."
Los Angeles Times, August 9, 1983

"Despite a high failure rate among minorities who have taken California's new teacher's exam, state officials say they have no evidence that it is racially or culturally biased, and have no plans to change it. . . . Meanwhile, state officials and **California State University** education deans are moving independently to require students to take the test before they enter teacher-training programs rather than after completing them."
Los Angeles Times, March 16, 1983

"Beginning next year, **California State University** students will have to be in the top half of their college class to enter upper-level teacher training programs. . . .

"'We don't attract greater numbers of successful teaching candidates by "dumbing down" our preparation program,' said Cal State Chancellor W. Ann Reynolds.

" . . . Several campuses were embarrassed in 1983 when the state began publishing passing rates on the new basic skills test for teachers. . . . In response, the Legislature demanded that college students take the test before beginning their education courses, usually in their junior or senior years. . . .

"As the rules were being formulated several education deans and members of the Cal State Board of Trustees complained that the standards could screen out black and Latino teachers who are in short supply in California's schools. In what Jones called a 'negotiated compromise,' the final rules say that up to 15% of the students may be admitted to education departments if they fall below one of the standards but have other 'compensating strengths.'"
Los Angeles Times, May 17, 1985

"The **California State [University] Board of Trustees** last week tentatively approved new standards for admission beginning in 1988. The requirements include 16 academic courses in high school, including four years of English, three each of mathematics and social studies, two years of science and foreign language and one year of fine arts. . . .

"The move towards higher standards raises legitimate concerns about whether minorities will continue to have equal access to higher education."
Los Angeles Times, (editorial page) November 19, 1984

"The grades and test scores needed for freshman admission to the Cal State system are being lowered slightly and, as a result, several thousand more high school seniors may be accepted this fall than would have been under previous rules, officials announced Wednesday.

". . . Cal State officials said they are worried that Latino and black applicants appear to have more trouble than other students in finishing those [required] high school courses. . . .

"A recent study by the California Postsecondary Education Commission was the main impetus to the Cal State admissions changes. That study showed that only 27.5% of 1986 high school graduates were eligible for Cal State admissions even though the goal under the state's Master Plan for Higher Education calls for Cal State to accept students from the top 33.3%.

"The study, released last month, showed a wide range of Cal State eligibility among ethnic groups. Fifty percent of Asian high school seniors were eligible, 31.6% of whites, 13.3% of Latinos and 10.8% of blacks."[2]
Los Angeles Times, April 10, 1988

The following is an account of the California State University's female/minority set-aside forgivable grant program for doctoral studies:

"Oralia Gonzales is one of 100 women and minorities who are benefitting from the **California State University**'s unique effort to get more underrepresented individuals into the pipeline leading to the doctoral degree. Under this program, eligible women and minorities may receive up to $10,000 per year for three years to study for a doctorate.

"On completion of the program, the loans will be converted to grants at the rate of 20 percent for each year the participant teaches in the CSU system. Thus, the entire loan will be 'forgiven' after a recipient has taught full-time for five years.

"'The **Forgivable Loan Doctoral Incentive Program** is one of the few programs of its kind in the nation,' said CSU Chancellor W. Ann Reynolds. . . . 'We cannot sit back and hope that we will be the beneficiaries of harvests sown by others. We must "grow" our own generation of women and minority academicians who will in turn assist future generations in developing to their fullest potential.'

"Because of the overwhelming success of the program, Reynolds will request at the March Board of Trustees meeting that an additional $1 million be added to the 1989–90 CSU lottery budget to extend the loans to another

100 students annually. Currently, the Forgivable Loan Doctoral Incentive Program, financed by lottery funds, provides for 100 loans at a cost of $1 million."
CSU, Stateline, January, 1989

NEA and Standardized Testing

"While many Americans, as measured by opinion polls, believe that the quality of public education has gone down in the last decade, NEA officials rarely discuss the issue, except when quality is equated with additional revenue for education.

"'The **NEA** has been opposed to every effort to raise the quality of education, unless by that you only mean giving more money to teachers or giving them more control over the system,' charged Chester Finn, a Vanderbilt University education professor and former education aide to Sen. Daniel P. Moynihan (D-NY).

"As an example, Finn cited the NEA's attempt to abolish all standardized tests for students and teachers.

"'They've been against any kind of educational standard for kids or for teachers,' he said, 'and I don't think you can have quality education without some standard of knowledge or performance.'

"The NEA has said standardized tests for students are biased against minorities and succeed only in stigmatizing those who are not learning as fast as the 'average' child."
Los Angeles Times, July 4, 1982

Affirmative Action for College Faculty[3]

A United Professor of California union newsletter (January, 1983) described the results of an early retirement program offered by the **California State University and College System**: "In terms of affirmative action gains, while 60 percent of the early retirees were white males, preliminary data shows that two-thirds of their replacements, hired during the first three quarters of 1980–81, were women and minorities."

[From "Will Colleges' Mission Be Sabotaged?" by John H. Bunzel, *Los Angeles Times*, Op Ed page, January 22, 1980.]

Six years ago, the trustees of the California State University and Colleges adopted a policy obliging each of the 19 campuses and the chancellor's office to "treat all persons in employment without regard to their race, color, religion, sex or national origin."

Beyond assurances of nondiscrimination, this affirmative action policy required that "specific, good-faith, positive efforts" be made to increase the opportunities of qualified women and minorities to be hired. Despite only a few years' experinece with this policy, the trustees are considering adopting a new policy that will permit what one top administrator calls "a little discrimination for good affirmative action purposes."

The new policy is a numbers-oriented strategy of affirmative action that, if adopted, will serve to sabotage the primary mission of higher education, which is to provide quality education to all eligible students on the basis of equal access and treatment.

To understand just what the new policy would do, let us examine sections and language of the present policy, which the new policy would delete.

• Regarding affirmative action recruitment, the present policy states that no faculty or staff position "is limited or reserved to or set aside for persons of any particular sex or minority status, nor shall any such restrictions, reservations, or set-asides be made." This specifically confirms the trustees' mandate to provide everyone with a genuinely equal chance to be selected.

New draft proposal: Deleted.

• The present policy states that equal opportunities shall be provided to any qualified person "to compete for and attain employment and advancement on the basis of ability." This specifically underscores the trustees' commitment to open, fair and nondiscriminatory competition for all job openings.

New draft proposal: Deleted.

• The present policy states in its preamble that all persons shall be distinguished "on the basis only of merit—their abilities, knowledge and achievements." It is an irreducible criterion purposely included to leave no doubt about the intent of the trustees to award positions on the basis of individual competence.

New draft proposal: The principle of "only merit" has been deleted.

• On the subject of goals and timetables, the present policy includes these carefully considered comments: "The goals shall be numerical only if supported by adequate data as to the availability in the labor market of qualified minorities and women in the discipline or assignment for which the goal is established," and "It must be emphasized that the use of goals and timetables does not imply quotas or preferential treatment. Quotas and preferential hiring are not in accordance with national, state, or trustee policy."

New draft proposal: Deleted.

• The present policy commands that "those judged to be best qualified" should be selected, retained and advanced "without regard to race, color, religion, sex or national origin." By stressing the concept of merit and prohibiting preferential treatment of any kind (a prohibition that has also been completely eliminated in the proposed new policy, the trustees are declaring openly that the highest intellectual and academic standards shall not be diluted with irrelevant criteria in, say, the selection of faculty.

New draft proposal: The trustees' unambiguous support of the "best qualified" principle has been deleted. . . .

No euphemism or uncertainty of meaning can conceal the fact that the trustees' current clear policy of nondiscrimination is now being refashioned. Affirmative efforts to eliminate discriminatory practices, to recruit broadly, to make sure that the evaluation of a person's peformance is not "racially infected"—these are the necessary forms of affirmative action on which the present trustee policy rests. The question that the trustees must now decide is whether they wish to depart from their present position and adopt instead a new view of discrimination that, among other things, does not expressly prohibit preferential treatment and relies heavily on numbers as ends in themselves.

"The faculty of **Occidental College** has overwhelmingly voted its support for a proposal to bring more minority students and teachers to the Eagle Rock campus.

"The proposal, resulting from two years' work by a Committee on Minority Issues appointed by President Richard C. Gilman, recommends measures to ensure that at least one-third of each entering class is minority by 1987 and to build minority representation on the faculty to 15% by 1990. . . .

"To solve the problems, the committee recommended. . . .

"Revision of the college Equal Opportunity statement on hiring to make minority status 'one of the various factors to be considered in determining which candidates are best qualified.'

"More aggressive recruitment of minority faculty through flexibility in salary and rank offerings. . . .

"Rejection of hiring searches which produce less than an adequate number of minority applicants."[4]
Los Angeles Times, April 22, 1984

"**Miami University of Ohio** has increased the number of blacks on its faculty from seven to 28 through an aggressive campaign openly billed as 'minority-preference hiring.' Under the plan, instituted in 1986, departments can hire blacks without a full search if the candidate is approved by a majority vote of the department. In other words, a black candidate doesn't have to be the best person for the job; he or she has just to be minimally qualified."
The New Republic, June 6, 1988

Affirmative Action for Teachers

"U.S. Supreme Court turned back an attempt by **Boston Teachers Union** for review of court-ordered hiring quotas for black teachers that have resulted in massive layoffs of white teachers."
San Francisco Chronicle, October 5, 1982

"A collective bargaining pact that alters last-hired, first-fired teacher layoffs to protect minority-employment gains is legal, declares a U.S. district court. White **teachers** laid off in **Jackson, Michigan**, argued that such preference violates the Constitution in the absence of proved past discrimination. The court, noting underrepresentation of black faculty, finds teaching is more than a job and that minority teachers are key role models for minority students, who have often been deprived of other role models through discrimination."[5]
U.S. News and World Report, October 11, 1982

"The demotions of seven former administrators, all white, in the predominantly black **Compton Unified School District** constituted a violation of the educator's civil rights, a federal judge rules in Los Angeles Friday."
Los Angeles Times, November 21, 1981

"The **Los Angeles Unified School District** Monday settled a five-year-old federal lawsuit alleging the district illegally discriminated in the hiring, promotion and assignment of Hispanic teachers. . . . The key provision of the settlement provides that the suit will be dismissed in 1982 if the district has hired 80% or more of the qualified Hispanic applicants who apply for teaching positions."
Los Angeles Times, March 30, 1979

"The **Los Angeles Board of Education** adopted a more flexible affirmative action plan for Latinos than for women because women have allegedly suffered more discrimination, district officials said this weekend.

"In an agreement filed in federal court last week, the board pledged to promote the same ratio of women as those who apply. In April, 1979, the board pledged to hire Latinos at only 80% of the rate at which they apply."
Los Angeles Times, August 4, 1980

"The percentage of women appointed to administrative posts in the **Los Angeles Unified School District** has far exceeded the long-range goals set by the district, according to a new report. . . .

"Since July 1, 1980, women have been promoted to 80 of 117 elementary school principal posts, or 68%. The settlement set a goal that 60% of grade school principals be women. . . .

"When the lawsuit was filed in 1979, 17% of secondary high school principals and about 38% of elementary principals were women."
Los Angeles Times, October 1, 1985

From the **Constitution of the National Education Association**:
Article IV, Executive Officers
"Section 4. Ethnic Minority Guarantee:
"If, after eleven (11) years, no member of an ethnic minority group has served as President, nominations at the subsequent Representative assembly shall be restricted to members of such groups."

Article VIII
"Section 2. Ethnic-Minority Representation
"Affiliates of the Association shall take all reasonable and legally permissible steps to achieve on their elective and appointive bodies ethnic minority representation that is at least proportionate to the ethnic minority membership of the affiliate."

Affirmative Action for Students

"A federal appeals court ruled Monday that the **University of North Carolina** had violated the rights of white students by trying to assure minority representation on the student council and honor court. . . . The student constitution of the university's Chapel Hill campus provides that if two of the 18 council members are not minority students the council president must name two who are."
Los Angeles Times, February 6, 1979

"**Cleveland** public school officials have mandated that all basketball teams must have 20 percent white players, 'tokenism in reverse.' "
CBS News, November 29, 1980

"The **Los Angeles Unified School District** has ordered the coaches of high school academic decathlon teams to see to it that their squads 'reflect the sex and ethnic makeup' of the student body, a requirement that one coach labeled a quota system.

"'I think it's outrageous,' said Rose Gilbert, whose team at Palisades High School has won all four of the annual citywide academic contests. 'They don't do this for the football team or the basketball team or the debate squad. Why single us out?' . . .

"Last week, district officials told Gilbert and other high school coaches that they would disqualify teams in next November's competition if they do not have a 'reasonable representation' of females and minorities.

"'I'm going to do a visual review on the day of the competition, and teams which don't comply will not be permitted to compete,' said Paul Possemato, director of the senior high division.

"District officials said the guidelines for the 4-year-old academic contest have always called for a team to be 'representative' of its school. Moreover, two of the six members must be 'A' students, two must be 'B' students and two must have a 'C' average. According to several accounts the new enforcement action stems from several complaints that the winners have tended to be predominantly white teams from the west San Fernando Valley."[6]
Los Angeles Times, May 15, 1985

"**Los Angeles school officials** said Thursday they will pull back from an order requiring high school academic teams to reflect the ethnic makeup of their schools and instead will urge coaches to encourage more female and minority students to compete. . . .The final policy will not have 'any language that has an implication of or suggests a quota,' School Supt. Harry Handler said.

"District officials have been under pressure from both the school board and the U.S. Department of Justice to retreat on the directive issued earlier this month."
Los Angeles Times, May 31, 1985

However, after the initial furor died down, the **Los Angeles School Board** eventually issued an edict which was largely similar to the original: "This year the 53 teams are competing under controversial new guidelines. Previously, the teams were chosen on the basis of test scores and teacher recommendations and had to include two A students, two B students and two C students. Those rules still apply. But in June the Los Angeles school board added a new policy stating that the teams 'should reflect' the composition of the school's bodies by race and sex.

"The policy was formulated in response to criticism that the decathlon was dominated by mostly white male teams from Westside and West San Fernando Valley schools—schools, the critics noted, that are 40% to 50% minority.

"The policy is more lenient than an earlier one adopted by the board that would have *required* teams to be representative by sex and race. The earlier version came under attack for appearing to establish a quota system and was protested most loudly at top-rank Palisades, the decathlon winner for four straight years.

"But all of this year's teams passed a review conducted by the senior high school division, according to Assistant Supt. Dan Isacs. Although no school was asked to specify the composition of its team, each principal had to submit a written report describing efforts made to include all ethnic groups and both sexes. Isacs said he is satisfied that the schools made 'efforts of a sincere nature' to abide by the new policy.

"Although school district officials denied that Palisades was being targeted, members of the Palisades team bristled. . . . 'It's reverse racism,' said one member, a white female who did not want to be identified. . . . This year's squad has three girls and one black."
Los Angeles Times, November 16, 1985

"With its first resident students, who will begin moving into new dormitories on Sunday, **California State University, Los Angeles,** is shifting into a new age and toward a new mission. . . .

"The dormitories were built to attract 18-year-old high school graduates who will take full course loads with the aim of graduating in four years. . . . They signify a countercurrent to the constantly shifting masses of minorities and part-time students who, administration officials say, are draining the university's resources and turning serious students to other campuses. Administrators candidly admit that the public sees it as rapidly declining to a second-rate institution.

"'We want more Anglo students,' said Edward Kormondy, vice president for academic affairs. 'We are perceived as a school for minorities.'

"'I think we've been off course,' said Raymond Terrell, dean of the School of Education. 'We don't demand much. This feeds the white community's perception that 'minorities' means 'inferior.'

"Ten years ago, Cal State L. A.'s non-Latino white enrollment was 47%. Now it is 33% and that includes many Middle Easterners and others seeking remedial education. . . .

"The new dormitories are a first counteractive step, Kormondy said. He expects that they will attract good students. There are no racial quotas for dormitory living. In fact, the question of race is not asked on the dormitory applications."
Los Angeles Times (San Gabriel Valley Section), September 13, 1984

PRIVATE SECTOR AFFIRMATIVE ACTION

Court Settlements: Back Pay, Quotas

"**General Electric** settled an Equal Employment Opportunity Commission complaint by agreeing to spend 32 million to upgrade women and minority workers."
U.S. News and World Report, December 4, 1978

As part of a consent judgement sought by the Justice Department and the Equal Employment Opportunities Commission, **Lee Way Motor Freight Inc.** in Oklahoma City, after losing a decision in the U.S. 10th Circuit Court of Appeals, agreed to hiring quotas. "Under these goals, the company will make from 15% to 50% of its truck driver openings available to blacks and Hispanics. From 15% to 25% of the office workers openings and 15% to 20% of the mechanics openings will similarly be made available."
Los Angeles Times, January 10, 1980

"**Motorola Inc.** agreed to spend $13 million on back pay, expanded affirmative action efforts and legal fees to settle five job bias suits, according to the Equal Employment Opportunity Commission. The suits had been brought by the EEOC and individual job applicants. . . .

"The consent decree, approved by a federal court in Chicago, also sets up a 'placement goal formula' for hiring and promoting women and minorities between 1981 and 1986. The EEOC staff lawyer said this means Motorola agreed to fill 20% of its semiskilled job vacancies with blacks, 11.2% of its sales positions with women and 3.5% of its sales jobs with Hispanic individuals."
The Wall Street Journal, September 24, 1980

"In one of the largest job discrimination settlements ever, **Ford Motor Company** has agreed to pay 13 million dollars in damages and spend 10 million to recruit and train minority-group and women workers. The settlements end a nationwide investigation that the Equal Opportunity Commission began in 1973.
U.S. News and World Report, December 9, 1980

"**Lockheed California Corp.**, the subsidiary of Lockheed Corp. that last week settled a sex-discrimination case by agreeing to provide hundreds of middle-management jobs for women during the next five years, hasn't exactly been buried under an avalanche of job applications. But there have been inquiries, a spokesman said. . . . The number of job applications probably will increase after Lockheed notifies 7,000 past and present employees and past job applicants of the consent decree, Stadler said. . . . Because the job targets are expressed in percentages, the number of jobs will depend upon total employment."
Los Angeles Times, September 18, 1983

"During the past six years, about 8,000 members of minority groups were turned down for jobs at **Prudential Insurance**, in part because they could not meet minimal standards for reading or math. Though most were high school graduates, scores of 3 or lower were common on math-competency tests, where the scale runs to 9. Last week Prudential revealed that it was going into the business of remedial education. In a precedent-setting agreement with the U.S. Department of Labor, the company promised to spend an estimated $3 million to offer 260 classroom hours of training to the same people it had rejected for jobs. At least 600 graduates will be offered full-time employment. . . .

"Newark-based Prudential's endeavor . . . followed a five-year Labor Department investigation of the company's hiring practices. Prudential, wary of a potential government suit and mindful of its $50 million worth of business with federal agencies and their employees, agreed to the compromise settlement.

"The investigation began after a routine review by the Labor Department's Office of Federal Contract Compliance Programs, which enforces a 1965 presidential order barring racial discrimination by federal contractors. The findings suggested that Prudential was rejecting a disproportionate number of minority applicants."
Time, September 3, 1984

"After nine months of negotiations, the National Assn. for the Advancement of Colored People has reached an agreement with **McDonald's** restaurants that is expected to increase substantially the number of minority franchise owners and funnel an additional $110 million or more into the black community over the next five years.

"Negotiations on the agreement were spearheaded by leaders of the Los Angeles NAACP, which called for a boycott of McDonald's products in April, contending the fast-food chain discriminated against blacks in its hiring, purchasing and franchising policies. The boycott was lifted after three days when McDonald's officials—meeting with top NAACP representatives in Mayor Tom Bradley's office—agreed to discuss the civil rights group's concerns.

"Unlike other agreements negotiated by the NAACP, the McDonald's pact benefits other minorities by increasing employment and franchise-ownership opportunities for Latinos and Asians as well as blacks.

"Under terms of the five-year agreement, McDonald's will: Seek qualified minorities and prepare them to purchase and manage franchises, until the pool of franchise applicants is at least 25% to 30% minority. (There is often a waiting list two or three years long for franchise ownership.)

"Establish 100 new black-owned restaurants over the next four years. (There currently are about 300 black-owned McDonald's restaurants, Beavers said.)

"Increase the number of minority employees and appoint more minorities to management and administrative positions.

"Establish a minority purchasing program to increase opportunities for minority vendors to supply the restaurants with food, packaging and services.

"Increase expenditures with black-owned professional firms, such as advertising agencies, insurance companies, law firms, and banks."
Los Angeles Times, February 17, 1985

"Race-bias claims by the Equal Employment Opportunity Commission against **International Business Machines** are rejected by a U.S. district court. It finds the EEOC "utterly failed" to prove its case and that class-action members in the case, at best, testified only about isolated incidents of perceived discrimination. 'Many seemed intent on self-destructing careers, that, if anything, were enhanced rather than limited by their race,' says the court. It adds that IBM's safeguards against bias are the standard for its industry and for private business nationwide."
U.S. News and World Report, April 23, 1985

Sears, Roebuck & Co. Case

Sears Roebuck & Co., the nation's largest retailer, has been contesting a suit brought by the EEOC, which charges Sears with discriminating against women. "It is the last of several celebrated cases brought by a liberal, activist EEOC in the 1970s against corporate giants such as AT&T, General Motors, General Electric and the steel industry.

"While the other big firms settled the cases with back pay awards and hiring plans for women and minorities, Sears braved the fire from the Carter Administration. Now it has a friendlier opponent: the Reagan administration. . . .

"EEOC Chairman Clarence Thomas has repeatedly criticized the case in public. 'I personally have problems with cases that rely on statistical evidence of discrimination (in large firms),' Thomas told a congressional hearing . . . 'The EEOC should not rely solely on statistics to process these (class action) cases,' Thomas said. . . . 'I do not believe that every statistical disparity between races or ethnic (groups) or the sexes in the work force results from discrimination.' . . .

"According to EEOC officials, the case has cost at least $2.5 million and at times has taken up more than a third of the agency's litigation budget. Yet the Sears case is only one of more than 300 cases that the agency has brought in the last year.

"That's not all. If Sears wins the case, the company may ask the court to pay its legal fees—which could run as high as $20 million, according to some estimates.

"The potential damage to the agency as well as his own philosophical opposition to the case has put Thomas in a tight political spot. 'I've been trying to get out of this since I've been here,' he said in an interview. 'It's a case brought by my predecessor during the Carter administration and even those people had doubts about it.'

" . . . EEOC's case is statistical: While 60% of applicants for sales jobs at Sears from 1973 to 1980 were women, about 27% of the persons hired were women. In 1972, before Sears began an affirmative-action plan, 9.9% of such jobs went to women.

"The EEOC's study of the women applying for the jobs also found that 40% of them had experience in the types of sales job that they sought.

"The government is also charging Sears with not promoting women on its sales staff to commissioned sales jobs, which are potentially more lucrative. . . .

"The EEOC also contends that 72% of Sears noncommissioned sales staff was female but that fewer than half of the promotions to commissioned sales jobs—about 40%—went to women.

"Sears has responded with testimony from economists and with polls showing that women were not interested in commissioned sales jobs, which often are in fields such as house siding, plumbing and auto parts.

"'Statistics can be helpful in the proof of some lawsuits,' said Charles Morgan, the former head of the Washington office of the American Civil Liberties Union who now represents Sears. '(The statistics) must relate to the real world, however, and have relevance to what is being measured. Men and women are not equally interested in selling men's clothes and women's clothes. Men and women are not equally interested in selling drapes, plumbing, heaters, auto parts and truck tires.'"

"The legal fight has generated animosity between Sears' senior managers and the EEOC. According to both sides, Sears officials have not wanted to settle the case but would rather defeat the EEOC and 'celebrate'—a Sears' official's word—in return for being dragged by the EEOC through a decade of charges of racial and sex discrimination.

"The animus between the two sides spilled into public light in 1979 when Sears filed suit against the federal government, charging it with creating a work force dominated by white males and thereby forcing Sears to hire white males.

"Sears said that government created that white male work force with veteran's preferences and GI bill benefits. It contended that Social Security and welfare payments induced women not to work. It charged that federal age-discrimination laws had slowed the exit of white men from the company and thus the entrance of women and minorities.

"The suit was dismissed.

"Since the Reagan Administration took office, Sears has been on the offensive. The government has backtracked on race-discrimination charges filed against Sears during the Carter years.

"Although Sears settled that suit, it has allowed the sex discrimination charges to drag on.

"'They don't want to settle,' said an EEOC official. 'They want to win, and they want to rub our noses in it.'

"Sears officials note that they have had an affirmative action plan requiring that women and minorities fill one of every two job openings—a quota —at the same time that the Reagan administration is suing to halt the use of quotas around the nation."
Los Angeles Times, July 15, 1985[7]

Supply and Demand

In a story on "Electronics Firms Ask Reagan to Alter Affirmative Action Goals," William Endicott reported, "Essentially, electronics industry leaders contend the current rules bog them down in paperwork and discriminate against their highly technical industry by requiring them to hire according to the racial and sexual makeup of the population in their communities rather than by the available—and presumably skilled—work force.

"As a result, thousands of jobs in the industry are going unfilled because of the necessity of hiring women and minorities to meet affirmative action quotas.

"'Clearly, we're not meeting specific quotas and goals in some areas,' said Gary Fazzino of the giant **Hewlett-Packard Co.** in Palo Alto. 'The technical nature of the jobs make it difficult to fill them. . . .

"'We want a program that truly penalizes people who are doing a poor job and doesn't hassle those making a good-faith effort. . . . Our great fear is that this is a motherhood, apple pie issue. We have to prove our credentials.'"
Los Angeles Times, February 20, 1981 (*Times* deletions)

"A **banking industry** official cites the quadrupling of women and minorities in bank management jobs since 1970."
The Wall Street Journal, July 29, 1980

"The major problem in retaining black managers is higher outside salary offers, say 47% of the 155 chief personnel executives polled by Hendrick and Stuggles."
The Wall Street Journal, February 26, 1980

Non-Preferred Groups

"A federal appeals court ruled in New Orleans that whites must sometimes suffer 'disadvantages' in order to remedy injustices against blacks. The ruling came in a suit filed by three white workers at a **Texas rubber plant** who contended that they were victims of reverse discrimination. They said the company's granting of 'remedial seniority' to black employees in their department amounted to displacing whites from their jobs. But the appeals court, reversing a lower court, said the whites were not actually displaced, but only suffered some disadvantages."
Los Angeles Times, February 22, 1980

"A federal judge this week upheld a verdict that awarded a **Topeka** woman $50,000 in what appears to be one of the few successful reverse discrimination lawsuits filed by a white person in the United States and the first such lawsuit won by a white plaintiff in Kansas.

"U.S. District Judge Earl E. O'Connor, ruling in Topeka on a posttrial motion and other questions in the case said Betty Commons was the victim of reverse discrimination when her employer, the Topeka **Montgomery Ward** store, demoted her in 1983 in order to promote a black woman with less seniority and experience.

"During the [earlier] trial, Commons said she had been employed for 15 years as the manager of the credit department at the Topeka Montgomery Ward store, where she supervised six to eight employees.

"In April, 1983, Commons said, store manager Jim Fleshman told her that the catalog and credit departments would be combined and that the job of supervisor would be given to a 29-year-old black woman who had been with the company for six years.

"Fleshman offered Commons her choice of two clerical positions, each of which paid $3,000 less a year, but said Commons would have to train the younger black woman to assume what was essentially Commons' former position as a condition of her continued employment. Commons refused and was fired.

"Judge O'Connor noted that when Fleshman offered Commons the demotion, 'Grace Patterson, the store personnel manager, had already been requested by Fleshman to prepare plaintiff's severance papers.'

"'. . . Both economic and personal pressures were exerted upon store managers to meet minority requirements. Supervisors were told to promote blacks over whites regardless of their qualifications,' O'Connor said."
Topeka Capital-Journal, August 1, 1985

NOTES

1. This decision was upheld by the U.S. Supreme Court in 1986.

2. The article failed to point out that a legislative resolution has required the Cal State student body to reflect the ethnic representation of the state's high school graduating seniors by 1990. The new high school course requirements obviously hindered that goal.

3. See Appendix 6 for additional documentation.

4. The article mentioned that Occidental currently had 4 percent minority faculty. Given the low rates of turnover for faculty in the 1980s, a goal of 15 percent by 1990 would necessitate nearly complete rejection of white male applicants.

5. The U.S. Supreme Court overturned this ruling in 1986.

6. The *Los Angeles Times* ran approximately a full page of its "letters to the editor" column on the decathlon quota plan. Most of the writers were strongly opposed.

7. For additional discussion of the Sears case, see Chapter 10.

Chapter 4

INVISIBLE VICTIMS: INDIVIDUAL REACTIONS

The previous chapter illustrated the collective complications wrought by race-and-gender-conscious policies in organizational settings. As stated in Chapter 1, no one knows how widespread reverse discrimination has been. One telephone survey of white males suggests a one-out-of-ten figure (Gordon Black Associates, September 1984).

Also largely unknown is how individual white males responded to actual encounters with reverse discrimination. As William Beer has pointed out in his review of sociological literature on affirmative action, there is only one small-scale, laboratory social scientific study of the reactions of white males to reverse discrimination situations.

Stephen Johnson tested reverse discrimination reactions of thirty-two white undergraduate students in a university laboratory setting. Each of the subjects was asked to solve a puzzle. The subjects were told that their responses would be judged against that of a competitor, who was actually non-existent. Half of the subjects were told they had lost to the competitor because the latter's solution of the puzzle was better. The other half were told after solving the puzzle that the competitor had been assigned a bonus score based upon the other's economic deprivation. Half of the subjects were told the competitor was black; the other half were told their competition was white.

Attitude measurements taken before and after the experiment indicated that, of the subjects who were told they had lost because of the "economic deprivation" factor, there was more aggression and perceived injustice towards black competitors than whites. On the other hand, "When the S's loss resulted from the other's superior performance . . . the white S's were less aggressive toward the black other than toward the white other'' (Johnson, 1980b: 15). In other words, the subjects perceived reverse discrimination when told they had lost in competition to a black person because the experimenter added an arbitrary bonus for economic deprivation. No such reaction occurred when they were told they had lost to the competitor's superior performance.

While Johnson's study was cast in the classic experimental paradigm, the results, nonetheless, are of limited depth and generality because of the use of student subjects in a laboratory setting at a university.

Attitude surveys on affirmative action also provide an artificial and highly superficial feel for white males' true feelings on affirmative action. As was seen in Chapter 2, attitude surveys on this topic are highly dependent upon the wording of the questions asked respondents. Chapter 8 shows that an atmosphere akin to 1950s McCarthyism has thwarted open criticism of affirmative action.

Thus, though attitude surveys are amenable to quantitative techniques championed by many leading sociologists, affirmative action realities are resistant to count-and-prove approaches. Institutions and individuals are very sensitive and guarded about this issue.

When studying white males' reactions to reverse discrimination, the researcher must deal with the subjects' strong feelings of self-censorship, pride, shame, pain and blame.

"I don't think I can talk to you today," rasped a weary Mike Grant[1] on the other end of the telephone line. "This [reverse discrimination] lawsuit is really getting to me. I've been on the phone all day. I didn't know it would be this much hassle. It's really gotten dirty. Two of my friends—former friends, I should say— have turned on me. They're giving me a real hard time. Let's set another date."

"Hey," Jack Smith called to me when I saw him some months after his interview, "I've found some more guys who'd like to talk with you. But they're scared. They're still in the system and this is sensitive stuff."

Some subjects had blocked feelings and memories about reverse discrimination incidents:

"You know," said Bob Allen interrupting himself," I just remembered, this wasn't the first time I'd run into reverse discrimination. I remember several years ago I was told flat-out by a couple of banks where I'd applied for jobs that I was the wrong race and sex. Funny, 'till now, I'd forgot all about that."

White males' reaction to affirmative action is relatively new and neglected psychological terrain. A more flexible, case-study, "logic of discovery" must be employed. Affirmative action might be seen as squarely in the "underground" area of inquiry probed by anthropologist Alan Dundes, who has stated: "The oral tradition has no censorship. . . . That's what makes it so valuable to study. It brings you very close to the cutting edge of what people are thinking . . . People will say a lot of things to each other that they won't commit to paper" (*Los Angeles Times*, April 27, 1986). As was seen in Chapter 3, and will be seen further in this chapter, affirmative action decisions are often informally or orally made with only vague (if any) reference to written policies.

Therefore, the two interviewers and I used more flexible "open-ended" interviewing formats (see Appendix 5) in our case-study approach to reactions of white males to reverse discrimination situations. We especially wanted to elicit the subjects' reactions *in their own words* whenever possible.

LOCATING INVISIBLE VICTIMS

From late 1984 to the spring of 1986, two researchers and I sought white, male subjects through networks of friends, acquaintances, co-workers, and a few students. We networked our way to thirty-four subjects and interviewed each in depth utilizing an interview format of open-ended questions. In locating our subjects, we initiated "referral chains" in a manner outlined by Patrick Biernacki (1986: 200–220). The first contact in a network of six school teachers was obtained from a newspaper report on affirmative action preferences in teacher assignments. One of the research assistants worked in a large state bureaucracy—thus, he began a referral chain into that organization. Some subjects were acquaintances or acquaintances of acquaintances who, in turn, suggested others they knew who had confronted reverse discrimination situations. Three individuals who had taken legal action in the courts were obtained from newspaper accounts.

In selecting subjects, we tried to determine to the best of our abilities that the only or primary reason for a subject losing a job or promotion was due to race or gender. We eliminated two cases after the interviews were concluded because it could not be clearly determined whether affirmative action was the key factor in a job loss. We also tried to obtain a balance of white-collar/blue-collar and private/public employees—though corporate employees were ultimately underrepresented. Approximately one-third of the interviews were conducted by telephone.

Direct interview data were supplemented with subsequent informal interview data with students and others who heard about the project—usually after the formal interviewing had been completed. Interviews with primary subjects were also supplemented with background interviewing of ten affirmative action or personnel officers, about half of whom worked for major corporations. More recently, I was able to supplement directly gathered data with reports on reverse discrimination accounts published in newspapers

(May and Houston, 1985) and in political scientist Stanley Greenberg's studies of disaffected, white Democrats (1985).

Attempts to sample respondents randomly simply made no sense. Reverse discrimination was not been a randomly distributed phenomenon. My research in this area has led me to believe that reverse discrimination has occurred primarily in public-sector employment in states with large minority populations or liberal political traditions. (That affirmative action has operated very strongly in the public sector is suggested by the following statistic: "Fully half of all black managers and professionals are government workers" *The New Republic*, February 6, 1989: 18). Corporations that are government contractors have also been subjected to affirmative action reviews by the Office of Federal Contract Compliance. Such reviews have led to somewhat greater gains for minorities (Leonard, 1984a; 1984b) and, hence, may have led to more reverse discrimination situations than in non-monitored corporations (Jencks, 1985b).

The interviewers and I sought subjects who were "reasonably sure" that they'd been excluded from a job or a promotion because of their race or gender. Approximately one-third of the subjects were interviewed by telephone. Most interviews lasted approximately ninety minutes, though some ran as long as three hours. We promised the subjects full confidentiality. Therefore, in this study all names of individuals are pseudonyms, and no employer is identified by name. In the cases of some subjects, I was able to obtain some degree of external validation of their accounts through accounts of others familiar with the case or through statistics on changes in race-and-gender composition of work forces. In most subjects' cases, however, I went no further than the individual accounts of reverse discrimination.

It might be argued that the study would have been a stronger one if my interviewers and I had been able to obtain greater external confirmation of subjects' accounts. Yet in terms of the study's focus upon the subjects' social psychological reactions, external validation was not of utmost importance. Following the old dictum of the symbolic interactionist perspective in sociology: if the subjects perceived the situation as real, then their responses to it were real.

The search for corroborating evidence would have immediately compromised the confidentiality of the subjects. Even if this had not been the case, there would have been the time-consuming and logistical problem of locating former employers or administrators and trying to confirm the experience of a single employee, which might have occurred several years before. Furthermore, it seemed ludicrous to assume that corporate or government officials would readily admit that they had, in fact, openly and deliberately discriminated against a specific white male. The legal implications were obvious.[2]

SOCIAL CHARACTERISTICS OF THE SUBJECTS

Fourteen of those formally interviewed[3] claimed to have been denied promotions primarily or exclusively for reasons having to do with affirmative action. Eight persons asserted that they had lost jobs for similar reasons, and four persons claimed to have been "ambushed" in the name of affirmative action during job reclassification procedures. The six teachers were caught up in various mandatory teacher transfer programs conducted by the Los Angeles Public School District to provide city-wide racial balance in its teaching force.

Twenty-nine subjects were located and interviewed during 1985 and the spring of 1986. Three pre-test subjects, interviewed in 1982, were also included in the total sample, since their responses were comparable to those in the 1985–86 interviewing period. The average age at time of interview for all subjects was 41.4, with a range of 27 to 58 years of age. However, it should be remembered that most subjects were five to ten years younger when the incidents of reverse discrimination took place, during the 1970s, for the most part. Furthermore, the social characteristics of a distinct subgroup—six teachers and a community college instructor—were somewhat different from the rest. As a group they were older, more liberal (registered Democrats), wealthier, and better educated. Thus, if we factor out this teacher subgroup in terms of age, the median age for the rest of the sample dropped to 38.2.

Average individual income for those interviewed was $28,812, considerably above the average individual income for a single resident of California ($18,000). If the community college instructor and six teachers are factored out, that figure drops to $26,960. Joint income of husbands and wives, for those respondents who were married, averaged $46,578; it is in this figure, especially, that the subgroup of teachers is distinct. Four of the teachers interviewed were two-teacher families, with both husband and wife having accumulated many years in that profession. Without the subgroup of teachers and the community college instructor, the average joint income for married respondents drops to $41,307, not far from the $36,000 median income of families in California.

All the subjects had finished high school, and twenty-two were college graduates, some with graduate degrees. Most were in middle-level white-collar occupations, such as administration or teaching, while others were in sales or crafts occupations (e.g., the subgroup of cameramen). One was a truck driver, and one was a law student. Note that these were not necessarily the occupations in which the respondents had experienced discrimination. (Those data can be found in Appendix 1.)

Twelve were single or divorced, while the remainder were married. In terms of social origins, it is interesting to observe that few had fathers in high-level professions. Only one was the son of a doctor, and another was the son of a dentist. One had a mother who had been a lawyer. Much more typical was the blue-collar, craftsman, or lower-level white-collar father. Many of the subjects in this study have experienced upward mobility in their occupational history. Some have maintained that direction of movement while others, through affirmative action or other problems, have lost ground.

About half of the subjects had mothers who were full-time housewives, but this pattern did not continue in subjects' own marriages. Only three of those who were married had wives who were primarily housewives; the remaining fifteen wives had full-time jobs outside the home.

Eighteen of the subjects were Protestant, seven were Catholic, two were of "mixed" or no religious background, and five were Jewish, primarily in terms of "ethnicity" rather than formal religious training or practice. Indeed, only three persons were at all active in religious organizations.

AFFIRMATIVE ACTION DEFINED; CLASSIFICATION OF REPONSES

I shall use the terms affirmative action and reverse discrimination somewhat interchangeably throughout this study. By affirmative action, I shall be referring primarily to those policies which allegedly attempt to remedy past discrimination again minorities and women through the use of numerical quotas and preferential group treatment (i.e., "goals and timetables"). I am primarily concerned with minority quotas, and somewhat less with quotas for women. Quotas for minorities seem to have had more emotional and political bite than the latter.

Until a few years ago, social scientists and proponents of affirmative action tended to ignore or simply dismissed the probability that reverse discrimination against whites might even exist. The same was true of the mass media. Therefore, professional and popular literature simply has had no place for such social realities.

There have been numerous studies of how other groups have reacted to race or sex discrimination. The following list of possible responses can be culled from this literature: acceptance, avoidance, aggression, deviance, negative self-image, increased in-group solidarity, assimilation, denial of membership in the affected group, or the "vicious circle" in which discrimination causes negative behavior among members of the affected group, which, in turn, reinforces stereotypes leading to discrimination (Allport, 1958; Vander Zanden, 1980; Parello, 1985). A problem with such categorization schemes is that classifications are not necessarily mutually exclusive; that is, there can be combinations such as "acceptance-anger," or "acceptance-avoidance," "acceptance with self-hatred," etc.

For purposes of classifying white males' responses to discrimination, the categories such as "assimilation" or "denial of membership in the affected group" really made no sense. Instead, I have classified the thirty-two subjects' responses into five categories: (1) Acquiescence, (2) Acquiescence/Anger, (3) Acquiescence/Departure, (4) Defiance/Protest, and (5) Circumvention. (See Table 1.) Brief summaries of all subjects' accounts of reverse discrimination are in Appendix 1.

Table 1
Classification of White Males' Responses to Reverse Discrimination

Acquiesce	Anger/Acquiesce	Acquies/Depart	Defiance/Protest	Circumvent
F. Sanders	J. Smith	G. Gordon	S. Grey	S. Clark
B. Allen	S. Mulligan	P. Elton	D. Brown	T. Tuperman
S. Huddles	T. O'Neil+	B. Watson	F. Nunn	
A. McWhirter	R. Oakes+	D. Loftis	M. Grant	
G. Mann	G. White	H. Overton+		
E. Mathis	E. Coles+	L. McCall		
S. Schwartz	D. Hathaway+			
D. Elliot	F. Goldberg+			
N. Garfano	M. Greene			
	S. Falkner			
	G. Miller			

+ Indicates extreme anger, ususally with verbal protests, less often with written (usually ineffective) protest.

ACQUIESCENCE

The men who acquiesced usually did so with a measure of quit resignation. "There was nothing I could do," was a common refrain. Most felt they had no alternative job opportunity at the time or in the foreseeable future. Nearly all sensed—or were told by superiors or co-workers—that they should keep their mouths shut. One or two felt that setbacks were temporary and expressed optimism that "they would get their chance eventually." Such persons usually felt that the goals of affirmative action were worthy and were willing to endure the sacrifice.

Bob Allen

Allen (age forty at the time of interview) was one of those who passively and optimistically acquiesced. He was a supervisor in a personnel department of a large California financial corporation. During the mid-1970s, he and other co-workers began to wryly observe that you "had to wear a skirt to get ahead here." Allen was passed over for promotions on three consecutive occasions. All three individuals promoted over Allen were females, two of whom he felt were much less qualified than he; in fact, he had hired one in an entry-level position only the year before. (Data obtained from this corporation indicate that, during the 1970s, the percentage of female managerial personnel jumped sharply from 8 to 36 percent.) Though there was some grumbling, Allen viewed the situation as temporary and felt he would eventually be promoted. Generally, he favored affirmative action as it is practiced in his corporation, "though he wouldn't want them to go any further." He opposed strict quotas and feels that the only long-run solution is selection by merit. He classified himself as a liberal and continued to vote for liberal Democratic candidates.

Allen was one of the first interviews conducted for this study, part of an initial pilot sample conducted in 1981. In 1985, he was re-interviewed. He had, indeed, been promoted. He maintained that he was glad he kept silent concerning earlier episodes of reverse discrimination because "it would have been more damaging to my career to have complained rather than maintain silence." He felt affirmative action pressures at his corporation climaxed in the early 1980s "when there was sort of a revolt among black employees in one division who felt they were being discriminated against. . . . Everyone was accusing everyone else of being racist." The matter was finally settled. Allen worked on labor-force statistics to determine if the corporation was utilizing representative numbers of minorities, a task he found difficult to carry out because the corporation was spread throughout the state but concentrated in two large urban areas. "We didn't know which statistics to use."

Sol Schwartz

Sol Schwartz (forty-seven at interview) was one of the few teachers who simply accepted being transferred to another school under the racial balancing program of the Los Angeles Unified School District. This was largely because Schwartz was a solid liberal Democrat and "believed strongly in affirmative action." Schwartz was notified two weeks before the school year began in 1980 that he would be laid off. (At least two minority faculty with less seniority than he remained.) Fifteen minutes later he received a call from a predominantly minority junior high school that he could have a position there. His friends, and especially his wife, were furious. "I had to forcibly restrain my wife from picking up the phone and calling the principal." But while she was angry at affirmative action, Schwartz directed his anger at the administration. He had been a union activist and felt the principal chose Schwartz for transfer, in part, because of this.

The next two years were a terrible strain on both Schwartz and his family. He had to rise at five in the morning in order to commute to his new school, which was thirty-five miles from his home. After two years, however, he managed to be transferred back to a school nearer his home.

Upon reflection, Schwartz firmly believed he was better off for the experience. He had become "too comfortable" and came to realize that "everyone needs a kick in the butt once in a while." He continued to feel that the public "misunderstands" affirmative action and equates such programs "with hiring incompetents."

ACQUIESCENCE/ANGER

This response category contained the largest number of persons who simply felt they could do nothing about a reverse discrimination episode but were nonetheless angry or very angry. The very angry persons often complained to co-workers or friends and sometimes to supervisors. One or two wrote letters to superiors, but no one took the incident to outside agencies such as the courts or the Equal Employment Opportunity Commission.

Ed Coles

When he was thirty-one, Ed Coles took the loss of an academic position at a California liberal arts college in 1980 as a "real defeat." He had taught part-time at the school and, when a faculty member died in 1980, he filled the vacated position full-time for a semester while the faculty went through formal search procedures to fill the position on a more permanent, tenure-track basis. Much to his surprise, Coles was not even interviewed for the spot in that process, "not really considered at all." The position went to a black candidate who was just completing his doctorate from a school far less prestigious than the institution where Coles obtained his. The chairperson of the department, according to Coles, was a radical feminist much concerned about the plight of South Africa. (The political leanings of the chair and the race and degree of Coles's competitor were independently confirmed.)

When he lost the position, Coles's marriage plans also fell through. His financee earned little as a lay teacher in a Catholic school. She had a child by a previous marriage and Ed Coles's job opportunities seemed limited indeed.

Coles found work as a hospital clerk for ten months and began to drink heavily. He then taught part-time at a state university in California and finally obtained a tenure-track slot at a small Midwestern university in 1983. Though still deeply committed to academic life, he has also honed his computer skills and is obtaining a master's degree in that area because he sees that future opportunities in the humanities are limited.

Robert Oakes and George Mann

Robert Oakes (fifty-six at interview) had been working as a cameraman in a pool used by local television stations during the late 1960s and 1970s. He began to notice that more and more minority (and a few female) apprentice/trainees were being hired on and, eventually, sent out with teams of more experienced cameramen. He also observed that, in the wake of the 1965 Watts riots, more and more news assignments were minority-oriented. "I began to wonder if there was any other news in this town besides minority-concerned stuff."

As opposed to a specific jolt or event, Robert Oaks and a fellow cameraman, George Mann, began to notice affirmative action as an unfolding pattern of events, but they didn't think it would affect them. For one thing, the quality of the trainees, they both claimed, was extremely poor.

But, in the late 1970s, the stations converted from film equipment to videotape cameras. The stations made all cameramen and apprentices reapply for videotape cameraman credentials. When they did so, the older white male veterans were screened out while the young minority trainees were given the jobs. Robert Oakes recalled:

The transition from film to tape involved making the veterans apply for their own jobs. You had to get a Number One ticket from the F. C. C. Guys went through a lot to get those tickets—it cost some of them $700 to do it—and they still couldn't get their old jobs back. They had to try and buy their own jobs and they couldn't do it.

Oakes was angry, in part, because "he saw it coming too late" and was resentful that the union did nothing about it. He also sustained greater financial injuries than did his friend George Mann, who was ten years younger. Mann admitted that "I knew they'd sell us out—the stations and the union . . . and the studios wanted to eliminate the high seniority people."

Fred Goldberg

Late in the summer of 1978, high school teacher Fred Goldberg discovered that his social security number had "come up" in a lottery system used by the L.A. School District to transfer teachers to achieve racial balance. He was not pleased. "My reaction was one step short of violence . . . I didn't commit murder, though," he said. Some four hundred teachers in the L.A. School District were "lotterized" that year.

The lottery system was ended after a year. Forty percent of those teachers lotterized simply quit. But Goldberg and six teachers from his school did not. They "were still sentenced to three years in schools far from our homes."

"It was one of the most stressful and worst experiences that my wife and I have ever had to endure," Goldberg stated. "I lost almost all my sick leave during those years. Stress led to physical problems." Goldberg might have taken legal action himself, but a class action suit filed by other teachers was lost at the district court level.

"I still find it hard to talk about."

ACQUIESCENCE/DEPARTURE

A natural response to an injury would be to withdraw from the situation as soon as possible. That is what six of the respondents did.

Lloyd McCall

McCall had migrated to California from the Upper Peninsula of Michigan with a master's degree in mathematics. He took a part-time position in a community college and then became a full-time temporary instructor. Mathematics was a high-demand field, and McCall had high hopes for a tenure-line position. Affirmative action had not been a factor in his native, rural Michigan, and he only gradually became aware of quota-like pressures. At the end of the year of his stint as a part-timer, a minority president was imposed on the college by the trustees over and against the will of the faculty.

In 1983, an opening for a tenure-line position in the physics department occurred. McCall interviewed for the position, but a woman just out of graduate school, with no experience, was hired instead. Another tenure-line position the following year was filled by an Asian woman, again with equal credentials but less experience than McCall.

In 1985 a third tenure-line slot became available. McCall again went through the entire application process and emerged as one of two finalists. McCall's competitor took a position elsewhere. McCall himself received an offer from another institution, but waited to see the outcome at his current institution. The chair of the department informed McCall that the campus president had told the chair to hire a Filipino female candidate screened out during initial interviews with the mathematics department. McCall took the position he had been offered at another campus.

Hal Overton

In the fall of 1983, Hal Overton had moved into an "acting administrator" position with a large public university when the former administrator retired. Overton had worked in that department for years and claimed to be well regarded. He had even hired subordinates according to the dictates of the university's affirmative action office. ("We got all kinds of paperwork problems if we didn't," he said.) The university, in fact, had a region-wide reputation for being "very strong on affirmative action."

Nevertheless, Overton, his colleagues, and friends assumed that he would be the one chosen to fill the administrative slot on a permanent basis after a year-long formal search. They assumed that affirmative action meant that women or minorities were given preference only if they were equally or better qualified for the job. And things looked promising indeed, when Overton was one of the three finalists. But he was not chosen. Instead, in May of 1984, a female with poorer qualifications and less experience and who did not completely meet the stated job specification was brought in from a private university. Overton would work under her in his old position.

Overton was "totally devastated." For months, he claimed that he "forgot what it was like to be happy" in spite of a three-week trip to Europe and additional time he took off for sick leave. He reported drinking heavily and going to the beach—anything to avoid going to the university. His close friends, also furious, urged him to quit. Instead, he filed charges with the California Fair Housing and Employment Commission.

Overton did not pursue the complaint with the Fair Housing and Employment Commission, so they dropped the case after a year. Nor did Overton take the matter to the courts. Instead, he quit. About the time his new superior was to arrive, Overton was offered a new position at another institution of higher education, which he gladly accepted.

Gary Gordon

Some twelve years earlier, in 1972, Gary Gordon, a mid-level correctional officer with the state of California, was informed by his superiors that the department intended to implement affirmative action "all the way" and that future promotions would depend, in large part, upon officers' affirmative action records. Besides supervising other correctional officers, Gordon was sometimes involved in the interviewing and hiring processes. He began to notice that, no matter what recommendations the interviewing panels made, the departmental authorities usually hired minority candidates. "I was told that basically we were looking for minorities. If there was a minority applicant who was anywhere near equal to the others, then he would get the job regardless of the interviewing panel's recommendation."

Gordon also discovered problems in disciplining or writing up minority subordinates. Rather than talking with a troublesome subordinate, the authorities would call in Gordon. He reported that one black probationary employee finally was fired at Gordon's facility but was immediately hired at another unit in the correctional system.

The white correctional officers filed a reverse discrimination suit, which they won in the California Supreme Court in 1978. While Gordon had heard about the movement of the suit through the courts, he was not optimistic about the results of a victory. At a personnel management seminar held about the time the suit was decided, "a white Department of Corrections personnel officer said there were seventeen ways around the state personnel board's rules on hiring by merit and in promoting minorities." As he suspected, the victory in the reverse discrimination suit did no good. "Sacramento did what they damn well pleased, anyway. . . . A lot of people quit in disgust. Morale went right down the tubes.'' (The problems in affirmative action in the California Department of Corrections were profiled in a segment of the first television news special on affirmative action, *The Equality Debate* [ABC, August 27, 1977]. When the director of the system was asked about the complaints of reverse discrimination by white correctional officers, he simply smirked and stated, ''It's your turn now.'')

Gordon watched the department's affirmative action program operate not only with regard to new-hires but upon his supervisors. He claimed to have seen well-qualified white supervisors lose promotions to less qualified women or minorities, in one case to a woman who had not even worked in the correctional department.

Gordon gave up on any promotions for himself. ''There were some jobs I would have applied for—I was good at my job—but I didn't put in for them because there wasn't a ghost of a chance. You could look at who was applying and getting the jobs.''

Gordon was able to opt out of the system when he was injured in a prison disturbance. He was urged to take a disability pension and he did. He did not especially regret leaving. ''If you work around those slammers, you come out with a jaundiced view of society anyway. And that affirmative action business sure didn't help.''

DEFIANCE/PROTEST

Three persons interviewed for this study filed lawsuits against employers on charges of discrimination: Mike Grant, Frank Nunn, and Samuel Gray. A fourth subject, teacher David Brown, tried to seek redress through his teacher's union (to no avail) and took more colorful steps to publicly protect his fate (also to no avail).

Mike Grant

Until 1983, Grant had not had a promotion in the large state administrative agency for which he had worked since 1968. In 1973, he wrote a mild letter of protest to the head of the agency, stating that, while he was sympathetic to affirmative action goals, he felt that unqualified persons were being hired and promoted. He claims to have received a ''non-response response'' filled with rhetoric.

Grant remained silent on the issue for the rest of the 1970s. Though he claimed that he was repeatedly bypassed for promotion in favor of less qualified minority persons, he ''went along.'' He claimed he did not bring up the matter in private conversations unless others did. A devout Christian, he felt some sympathy for affirmative action and is sympathetic to the less fortunate.

In August 1983, Grant stated that he was asked to apply for a high-level job as aide to one of the persons overseeing the entire state divison. He asked if affirmative action might be a factor and was told that the particular position fell outside of affirmative action guidelines. Besides, of the other nine similar positions, seven were filled by minority persons. In September, Grant was informally notified that he had been appointed. His superior announced the decision within the governing board. Grant completed the appropriate forms and began training assignments in mid-September.

Word was passed informally throughout the state and, as he made his rounds in his new position, Grant received many calls and notes of congratulations. But in early October, his superior called him in and told Grant that he would not have the job after all and that the supervisor had been told to hire a minority. "Let's face it, Mike, you're not the right color."

Grant filled in for his former superior, who was on vacation, then was returned to his old job. Colleagues and friends assumed Grant had somehow "screwed up" in the new job.

Grant resigned his job and filed suit in state court.

The outcome of Grant's legal actions is uncertain. Grant relocated and attempts to re-establish contact with him were unsuccessful.

Frank Nunn

By his own admission, forty-six-year-old Frank Nunn has always been a "classic Jewish liberal." He was active in the civil rights movement and suffered a back injury during a police beating, which has hospitalized him twice since that time. He believed in affirmative action and still does, though he admits he still hasn't sorted out his feelings on the matter. ("I agree with Justice Powell in the Bakke decision that race can be *a* factor, but not *the* factor.")

While involved in the civil rights movement and other social causes, Nunn obtained bachelor's and master's degrees in social science and, in the 1970s, became actively involved in the administration of a popular black mayor. Because of his background and training in public administration, Nunn obtained a rather high-level job, though he did notice that he was the only white at that level in that particular agency.

The agency for which he worked for two years was not covered by the city civil-service system until 1977, when plans were made to convert the agency positions to civil-service status. The agency employees had to take the civil service examination and be merged with civil service employees already on the list seeking promotions. Nunn claims to have been at the top of the merged list, but the next six highest scores went to persons already in city government in other agencies. There were eight new positions. Two minority administrators in Nunn's agency were not high enough on the list to retain their positions in the transformed agency, unless Nunn was removed from the list.

Therefore, according to Nunn, he was abruptly and without warning fired from his position two weeks before it was to come under civil service rules. By law, his name was automatically removed from the list, and the two minority administrators retained their positions in the "new" agency. (Nunn obtained internal memoranda detailing these intentions, and these documents were the basis of his legal proceedings.)

Nunn filed charges with the Equal Employment Opportunity Commission and the Civil Service Board. The latter voted unanimously to restore Frank to two civil service lists and he was offered another job at $8,000 a year less than he had previously earned. But city officials refused to follow through on the other recommendations of the board, and Nunn again filed charges with the Equal Employment Opportunity Commission and other federal agencies. He claimed to have been harrassed in his new position to such an extent that he was forced to seek psychiatric counseling for the first time in his life. The conflicts on the job compounded problems in his social life, and Nunn wound up taking two short disability leaves and a final long-term disability leave.

Since the EEOC had a huge backlog of cases and since the city was reneging on promises made to him, Nunn filed a reverse discrimination case against the city in 1979. Nunn reached a settlement with the city regarding the job in which he was harrassed (after the reverse discrimination event) and he enrolled in law school in another city.

Looking back on the situation in which he eventually suffered reverse discrimination, he admits

I should have seen it coming. . . . I was the only white male at that level in the entire agency. There were various slights and slurs that I took because I wanted to work in the administration of a black mayor. So I turned the other cheek and got the shit slapped out of me. . . . It was a twenty-four-hour-a-day battle. . . . It shot my personal life to hell.

Nunn lost his reverse discrimination lawsuit against the city in 1986.

Samuel Gray

Filing reverse discrimination charges was not nearly as traumatic for Samuel Gray, a forty-nine-year-old college physics professor. Gray had been passed over for a deanship for which he'd been ranked number one through an entire process (screenings by faculty, student, and administration committees and by the president of the campus). He had remained number one until a new step was suddenly added—an interview with the head of the entire district—who was a minority and appointed "one of his own" further down the list.

I'm mad as hell and I'm not going to take it any more," Gray quipped, when he was interviewed in 1986. "I really expected to get the position after I was first on the list. But when the chancellor's interview came up, I knew I was sunk."

He admitted the timing of his suit may have made things different for him than Bakke and others (such as Frank Nunn) who filed in the 1970s. He claimed that the entire college community had been in turmoil for years over hiring processes and that "every single hiring they've had has been a fight for years." The recently appointed Latino president of his campus, he reported, had simply been "imposed" upon the college community—over their expressed opposition—by the district administration.

"My major goal," stated Gray "is to stop this sort of hiring in the future. . . . It won't help me much. If I got the position through a lawsuit, there'd be no way of working things out anyway."

Upon hearing he had not been chosen, Gray immediately wrote to the Board of Supervisors. This action turned out to be futile and gave the faculty union an excuse to stay out of the dispute. The union claimed that by writing directly to the Board of Supervisors, he had "used up" the formal grievance process.

Gray checked out the Equal Employment Opportunity Commission, but they seemed cool and wanted to examine the matter on an individual case basis. But in contrast to EEOC's usual procedures, the agency did not want to look at past patterns of hiring and promotion in the community college district. So Gray approached a large law firm, which took his case on a contingency basis. Gray was delighted to find he had the full support of his colleagues, who donated $6,000 to cover his initial court costs.

THE FRUSTRATING COURSE OF LEGAL ACTION

I re-interviewed Gray just as this book went to production in March 1989. By that time, Gray's case had been tried before a jury in federal district court. Gray's frustrating, time-consuming experience seems typical of while males who take legal action in reverse discrimination cases.

Much to the surprise of Gray and his lawyer, they lost the charge of conspiracy and monetary damage award. An even greater frustration was the judge's refusal to allow any consideration of whether the college's affirmative action plan was constitutional. On several other aspects of the case, however, the jury remained deadlocked. Since the all-important, constitutional question had been ignored, Gray's lawyer tried to move the case directly to the federal appellate court. But the appellate court, according to Gray, had a huge backlog of reverse discrimination cases, which it appeared reluctant to confront. Gray's lawyer was told to ask for a complete retrial on all charges. In November 1988, the district judge informed Gray's lawyer that he would set a new date for retrial—but had not done so by March 1989.

The law firm conducting Gray's case was a large one and, feeling that the chances for victory were quite favorable, had accepted the case on a contingency basis. The case had cost the firm more than $300,000. Though he'd received financial contributions from fellow faculty, Gray had spent money of his own and was emotionally exhausted.

"It's really taken it out of me," he admitted. "It's been one hell of a strain on me, my family, work relationships. . . . The legal system grinds you into the ground. The courts are a real crap shoot. We were really surprised by the verdict. . . . It's going to take about five more years before this thing is settled. If anyone were to ask me to take these things to court—knowing what I do now—I think I might say 'no.'"

Gray's remarks parallel those of a potential subject whom I contacted but who refused to be interviewed for the study. He, too, had sued the public agency for which he worked. After a five-year battle, he won. His struggle, however, had taken an enormous toll on his personal life, his family relationships, and his career. He did not care to relive the ordeal through an interview.

As mentioned in Chapter 1, legal redress through administrative agencies or the courts has not been perceived as a viable option by most white males interviewed for this study. Most seemed to feel that filing a complaint with EEOC or taking action in the courts would do them little good. Legal action against current employers was seen as producing more harm than good. These attitudes of mistrust or futility toward the legal system parallel similar views among female and minority victims of discrimination interviewed by Kristen Bumiller. Her conclusions very much apply to the findings in this book.

People who have experienced discriminatory treatment resist engagement in legal tactics because they stand in awe of the power of the law to disrupt their daily lives. At the same time, they are cynical about the power of the law actually to help them secure jobs, housing, and other opportunities they lay claim to. They fear that, if they seek a legal resolution, they will not improve their position but will lose control of a hostile situation. These respondents also feel that asserting their legal rights could not enable them to express their sense of dignity but would force them to justify their worthiness against a more powerful opponent. Injured persons reluctantly employ the label of discrimination because they shun the role of the victim. Therefore, they choose to rely on strategies for economic and personal survival that perpetuate their victimization but are seen as more desirable than submitting to the terms of legal discourse. (1988: 109)

The experiences of those white males in this study who attempted to resolve reverse discrimination through legal channels indicate that the price of justice—if obtained at all—is very high.

David Brown

Just before the school year opened in 1980, David Brown called the principal to ask about pre-school duties. He was told he was being laid off and that the art program was being shut down. The reasons given were racial and ethnic balance requirements and cutbacks necessitated by Proposition 13.

Since Brown's program and activities had won awards, there was a general clamor from the students and the community, with limited results, which did not benefit Brown. The art program was partically restored, but a less experienced black female teacher was brought in to run it. A woman of Indian heritage with less experience and seniority than Brown was also permitted to stay.

Meanwhile, for the first six weeks of school, Brown sat in the library and performed substitute teaching duties. He reported being depressed because "I couldn't understand why things were happening as they were." His feelings of depression and alienation were not dampened when he was asked to do clerical work. He refused. Instead, when not substituting, he engaged in solitary picketing with a sign which read "This administration is corrupt and morally bankrupt." He was cheered on by the majority of other teachers (two of whom confirmed his account). The vice principal took photographs.

Brown simultaneously filed grievance and unfair labor practices charges. The union dropped the grievance at an appeals level as the major defense of the school—ethnic balance—had been triumphant in most other cases. Such procedures took more than a year.

After several weeks, Brown took a position in another school where he taught subjects for which he was not prepared. After several months, he complained bitterly to the principal and was transferred to an art position in a junior high school. He reported there for two days and was appalled by the overcrowding and lack of supplies. "I asked myself 'what the hell am I doing here?' So I quit."

Brown left teaching entirely, went into business for himself, and now feels that "getting bumped was probably one of the better things that happened to me. I couldn't be happier than doing what I'm doing."

CIRCUMVENTION

The three men in this category usually preferred manipulation and perseverence rather than challenge and open confrontation. They did not have especially strong views on the topic of affirmative action. They just attempted to "beat the system" quietly and get around such barriers.

Thomas Tuperman

Like Sol Schwartz, Thomas Tuperman was also selected by his principal for transfer to a distant school both for reasons of fiscal cutbacks and ethnic balance. Unlike Sol Schwartz, Thomas Tuperman wouldn't cooperate. He refused reassignment to another school and took, instead, the option of serving in the substitute teacher pool for six to seven weeks. Meanwhile, the principal hired three new minority teachers with less seniority than Tuperman. The latter filed a grievance with the union. According to Tuperman, the principal countered the union's charge that he was hiring teachers after dismissing Tuperman by stating that Tuperman's return would have jeopardized the school's "ethnic balance." Nevertheless, the district ordered Tuperman's reinstatement a month after the new school year began, but with the contingency that Tuperman's return would not truly jeopardize ethnic balance. Evidently, it did not, and Tuperman was triumphant.

A self-described socialist, Tuperman felt that affirmative action in some forms is permissable or necessary. In the case of the L.A. School District, "The goals were all right, but the timetable was unrealistic." Tuperman, like Schwartz, felt that ethnic balance orders were employed by principals to intimidate, manipulate, and get rid of teachers they did not like.

Tuperman's resistance proved successful. He beat the system. However, as seen above, David Brown's protests were for naught. A front-page story in the *Los Angeles Times* (October 1, 1980) on the issue found few teachers who successfully resisted being transferred. (As previously mentioned, lawsuits against such transfers were unsuccessful.)

Steven Clark

Another individual who beat the system worked as a middle-management bureaucrat for a division of the state of California. Steven Clark found promotional opportunities in several geographical locations blocked in 1977 because of affirmative action pressures. A supervisor he knew learned from his superiors that Clark "didn't have a snowball's chance in hell of getting the promotional positions he'd applied for because those positions had been targeted for members of 'protected classes.'"

But Clark applied for yet another promotional opportunity in another location. The manager there (who was black) selected Clark but had to face down a challenge from the division's equal opportunity section because Clark was white.

Because Clark was able to obtain a promotion rather quickly in spite of affirmative action barriers, he did not feel the anger expressed by many others in this study. "I was able to circumvent the problem that was forced upon me. Still, I would have preferred non-circumvention."

Clark was aware that affirmative action was a very sensitive issue in the division and that by loudly protesting "I could have won the battle but lost the war. . . . One of the things I considered was what effect a grievance would have upon my future career . . . the repercussions." This was a common theme among all subjects. And not without good reason: society was likely to blame the victim of affirmative action quotas rather than criticize the policies.

NOTES

1. All names are fictitious.

2. Sociologist Laurel Richardson chose to investigate a semi-hidden, sensitive social phenomenon in her research on single women who have affairs with married men: *The New Other Woman* (1985; 1986). In gathering subjects for her study, Richardson stated that she traveled a great deal and simply "announced my research interest to everyone I met—conferees, salesclerks, travel acquaintances. Women I met either volunteered to be interviewed or put me in contact with women they knew to be involved with married men." Through these methods, Richardson obtained hundreds of contacts, though ultimately her research was based primarily upon "in-depth interviews with 55 women who were having or had once had a long-term relationship with a married man" (1986: 26).

However, I did not travel as widely as Richardson. Nor did I feel I could be as open about my study as she was about hers. As will be explained in Chapter 9 in the section "Doing Affirmative Action Research in California," studying the impact of affirmative action on white males—especially in the late 1970s and early 1980s—was a politically/professionally risky venture.

3. See Appendix 2.

Chapter 5

INVISIBLE VICTIMS: REACTIONS OF CO-WORKERS, FRIENDS, AND RELATIVES

The previous chapter dealt with the individual responses of white males to reverse discrimination situations. This chapter deals with how others responded to those accounts of discrimination. (For more information, see Appendix 3.)

Historically, women and minorities who have encountered discrimination have usually been able to find solace and understanding within their own groups. Depending upon historical circumstances, other victimized groups, the mass media, and society at large might also at least recognize such injuries.

Minorities, women, the poor, and other disadvantaged groups have also benefitted from a recent intellectual imperative in the social sciences and in the mass media against "blaming the victim." Before the late 1960s and early 1970s, Americans tended to judge individuals as responsible for their own fates in a "world of just deserts." The blame for social problems such as poverty lay not with social arrangements, but with flaws in individual character or, perhaps, because "deviant values" had been internalized by groups or individuals. Any remedial action was designed to change the individual, not society. Social programs to help such persons were premised upon the philosophy of "a hand, not a handout."

In 1970, William Ryan's influential *Blaming the Victim* appeared. The book vigorously attacked the "blaming the victim" philosophy and placed the blame for most social ills on inequitable social and economic arrangements. This book, and others like it, were responsible for what Charles Murray has described as a fundamental shift in (liberal) "elite wisdom" of the 1960s and 1970s. Blaming the victim was rejected; blaming the system was accepted (1984b). Social science, social policy, and mass-media elites saw institutional racism, sexism, inequality, and other forms of oppression as the causes of social ills. Hence, the need for vast compensatory policies and programs for redistributing wealth, opportunities, and power.

But how to deal with those who were injured or victimized by such redistribution programs? Can one blame the system? Blame the individual? Or simply pretend that no one is hurt at all?

We shall see in this chapter that white males have not been accorded the status of victims of unjust social policies. Instead, their accounts of reverse discrimination, if voiced, have been met with awkwardness, disbelief, skepticism, or a discouraging "there's nothing you can do" response. Only half the subjects have been offered social support by friends and co-workers. The mass media have preferred to ignore the issue or belittle the complaints of white males. Corporate employers have responded with blaming-the-victim affirmative action seminars designed to demonstrate that white males have been wrong to resent discrimination.

CO-WORKERS, FRIENDS, AND RELATIVES

As data in Table 2 indicate, about half of the co-workers and friends of those interviewed for this study provided some degree of social support. They commiserated, were sympathetic, or at least listened to and believed

Table 2
Responses of Co-Workers, Relatives, and Friends to White Males' Accounts of Reverse Discrimination (N = 32)

	Co-Workers	Relatives	Friends[1]
Support	14	18	16
Support/No Support[2]	4		
Mixed Support	6		3
No Support	3	1	2
Not Discussed	5	12	11
Not Applicable		1	
TOTAL	32	32	32

1. Five subjects indicated friends who were also co-workers.
2. Category refers to split or polarized support, often along the lines of sex or race of co-workers.

the subject's account of reverse discrimination. Much of the support appears to have been token or simply polite, but at least it was offered.

Six subjects reported "mixed" support from co-workers. This category covered either lukewarm or equivocal responses or situations in which some were supportive and some were not. An additional four subjects indicated that responses from co-workers were polarized, often split along race and sex lines, with women and minorities offering mild verbal condolences but also holding that preferential treatment was necessary or long overdue. On the other hand, the correctional officers reported that some of their minority co-workers were embarrassed by preferential treatment, especially when such treatment was accorded to incompetent minority employees. They feared that qualified minority employees might be stigmatized as having got their positions solely by virtue of their race or ethnicity.

This level of support was better than I—and probably most of the subjects—would have suspected. Still, most men in this study were wary of discussing their true feelings regarding reverse discrimination, at times, even with the interviewers. Fear was the reason: fear of not being believed, fear of being perceived as racist, fear of appearing a complainer or unmanly.

This wariness accounts, in large part, for eleven men not discussing the reverse discrimination incident at all with their friends, while twelve men did not discuss it with relatives. The situation was harder to avoid with co-workers. Five subjects avoided mention of the incident with co-workers.

Teachers caught in the teacher-transfer program were especially bitter about the lack of support by co-workers and friends. Fred Goldberg declared his friends responded to him as a "victim" whom they did not wish to see or think about:

You really found out who your friends were. I expected people to call and give support, but they never did. People have their own problems. People were really on the warpath when the lottery was instituted. But when it passed them by, things returned to normal—for them.

By and large, it was an interesting experience to see how people respond to victims. That's what the six of us who got lotterized were. As victims, we had a common outrage. But the others were happy the lottery had passed them by and didn't want to have to deal with us. When I ran into teaching friends at restaurants, grocery stores, and the like, we avoided one another. It was just like in the famous short story, "The Lottery," by Shirley Jackson.

People who were selected to be stoned in that story were told they had no right to complain because "everyone had had an equal chance."

Teacher David Brown voiced similar sentiments: "You find out who your friends are. I found out I didn't have as many as I thought I did. . . . I was treated as though I had an illness." "Being selected for the lottery was like a form of rape," stated teacher Dwight Hathaway. "When one teacher found out she'd been lotterized, the whole room went silent. Everyone was thinking, 'There but for the grace of God go I.'"

The lottery system was dropped after a year. Under subsequent transfer arrangements, Hathaway feared he would be "bumped" if he did not volunteer to go to another heavily minority school for three years, after which time he supposedly would be allowed to return to his home school. When he attempted to return after teaching three years at a school thirty-five miles from his home, he was shocked and saddened that some of his former friends tried to sabotage his return. "White males were trying to hang on any way they could."

Friendship, Ideology, and Social Support

Those who found mixed or no support from friends were somewhat more likely to be liberals or to have liberal friends. Liberals who confronted a friend's affirmative action injury were in the awkward position of having to criticize either the policy or their friend.

Schoolteachers' bitter reaction to being ignored or labeled as outcasts by friends and co-workers was undoubtedly due to the fact that most had liberal friends. Said Manning Greene: "My friends and co-workers didn't know how to handle this. They wanted to empathize but felt cognitive dissonance. And I was afaid of being called racist."

University administrator Hal Overton's friends initially sympathized with his attacks on affirmative action. But they seemed embarrassed by his continued attacks on those policies; they soon greeted such attacks with silence. Overton sensed that they simply wanted to assume that their friend's was a deviant case of affirmative action gone wrong. As stated earlier, Democratic or liberal victims and friends were faced with a dilemma: affirmative action was supposed to be good, but something terrible had happened to a friend as a result of such policies.

But many with moderate or conservative friends—especially male friends —also reported problems with sympathy or support. Conservatives were more likely to simply not believe the account or to blame the victim.

"My friends outside the system just didn't understand why I wasn't getting on full-time right away and getting promotions," said Jack Smith. "They just didn't understand the situation." All three ex-correctional officers interviewed for this study emphatically held that "outsiders" couldn't comprehend how vigorously affirmative action quotas were being applied. They, too, feared either being thought of as racist, or—even more unmanly—of making excuses.

Only college professor Samuel Gray reported near unanimous support, emotional and financial, from colleagues and friends in his lawsuit against the college. (Indeed, colleagues and friends contributed nearly $6 thousand of the $10 thousand needed for initial legal fees.) But this, as Gray admitted, may have been a result of timing. His colleagues had long been fed up with nearly twenty years of affirmative action abuses, and Gray sensed a turning point in public thought on the matter. (The two other persons in this study who filed lawsuits became isolated from co-workers and friends.)

Though more than half of the subjects experienced support from friends, co-workers, and relatives, with the exception of Samuel Gray, no one reported co-workers or friends who actually urged protest or legal action. No one wanted to do anything on behalf of their injured colleague or friend. On the contrary, some co-workers and friends counseled the reverse-discrimination victim to quietly accept his fate and "not rock the boat." Men in this study were generally encouraged to adopt sex-role appropriate attitudes and behavior ("Take it like a man"), to be discussed in greater detail in the following chapter.

This largely token or mixed social reception, sometimes accompanied by skepticism or outright disbelief, sets apart discrimination against white males from discrimination against women and minorities. Unlike minorities and women, white males feared that their accounts of reverse discrimination might not be given credence by their own kind.

Fortunately, most of these men's best friends were not other men.

"My Wife Is Mad as Hell; She's Angrier Than I Am" (Samuel Gray)

Those who were married were almost always strongly supported by their wives. Indeed, in some cases, wives were angrier over reverse discrimination than husbands. Three of the wives of those interviewed for this study specifically asked to be interviewed themselves: "Do you want to know what I think?" called Bob Allen's wife from another room.

"It hurts us, too," complained Dustin Loftis's wife. "It's hurting the family structure."

Loftis's wife went on to argue a point made by few laypersons and no experts on affirmative action: discrimination against married white males not only has the potential to injure them but also any wives who do not work outside the home. When the husband loses a job or promotion, the impact is doubly felt in such traditional households. This "hidden" or latent conflict generated by affirmative action between career women versus homemaker wives has gone virtually unnoticed in the affirmative action literature.

Parents were also indirectly affected, especially those who had had aspirations for their sons and, perhaps, had paid graduate or professional-school expenses. Most subjects indicated that their parents "understood" the roadblocks posed by affirmative action. But there was bitterness for those most deeply hurt by affirmative action, such as would-be academics Loftis and Coles, who eventually dropped out of academic careers altogether. Coles's parents had helped with graduate school expenses. Loftis's father-in-law was a former college dean who only dimly perceived affirmative action difficulties.

Correctional officer Gary Gordon's wife was supportive, but partly because she had other relatives in the corrections department and knew what was going on. Some other officers were not so lucky. Gordon mentioned that some of his subordinates did not receive emotional support from spouses. "At parties, or barbeques, and so on," Gordon remembered, "some of the wives of my subordinates would come up to me and ask if it were really true that their husbands weren't being promoted because of reverse discrimination. They just didn't believe it."

Ex-correctional officers Jack Smith and Pete Elton also confirmed such accounts and added that some marriages ended, partly as a result of frustrated career ambitions, compounded by wives' failure to comprehend the force of affirmative action barriers.

Timothy O'Neil and Steve Clark, both state employees, had somewhat unusual cases. At the time of his affirmative action troubles, O'Neil was engaged to (and subsequently married) a black nurse. "We discussed the situation and the Bakke case. Her feelings about it were different than mine, so we dropped it then. Now, she's aware of the problem for whites and is supportive and sympathetic. But she's seen discrimination from a different side of the fence, too."

Clark's wife was Filipino and worked in a job in the same state government division as her husband. "She knew I was upset," recalled Clark. "She bought me a television to try and ease the fact that she was promoting and I wasn't. But she wouldn't admit that she was promoting because she was female/minority. Yet she was promoting over better-qualified whites."

CHANGES IN SELF-CONCEPT, POLITICS, AND VIEW OF SOCIETY

In Chapter 4, I addressed the general psychological reactions of white males to reverse discrimination situations. Here, I should like to deal with the deeper, more reflective changes regarding the sense of self-worth and views of social institutions and society.

Social psychologists have long recognized that a person's identity is considerably influenced by the responses of others toward him. How, then, did others' understanding of reverse discrimination—or the lack thereof—affect these men? Did an encounter with reverse discrimination have a lasting impact? Was the experience traumatic?

Eight of the thirty-two individuals interviewed flatly denied any damage to self-worth or self-esteem. About half of these men simply forged ahead and "toughed it out" with little change in their own self-concept or their ideas of the system. Robert Oakes, a displaced camerman, pointedly directed his anger outwards towards the system rather than blame himself. So did Samuel Gray, who launched a lawsuit. Bob Allen claimed that his bouts with reverse discrimination in banking had affected his self-conception or self-esteem "not at all." Yet statements elsewhere in Allen's interview, and those of some others as well, contradicted such quick, positive assessments.

Nine individuals had minimal damage done to their self-esteem, usually temporary. At the "minimal" end of the damage spectrum were camera-man George Mann and middle-management state government employee Steven Clark. Both Mann and Clark claimed they were "less motivated" as a result of their encounters with reverse discrimination. They were no longer sure that hard work paid off. Others in this category were momentarily stunned or set back by loss of a job or failure to move beyond the interview stage. Alan McWhirter claimed that he "got tired of chasing and losing out on [firefighting] jobs." Frank Sanders also mentioned that occupational immobility bothered him.

Affirmative action setbacks damaged more deeply those who thought they were in relatively secure careers in government, teaching, or university work. Most of the teacher-transfer victims were in the "moderate" to "severe" range. The shock of relocation after years of presumably secure employment caused massive doubt and dismay, as did different teaching environments and students. David Hathaway remembered,

On the second day in my new school, I was supervising playground activities. Suddenly, fire trucks pulled out of a nearby station and took off roaring down the street, their sirens screaming. My kids in the suburbs would have watched in awe. But these kids didn't miss a beat of their play activities. It was just background noise to them. That's when I knew things were really different.

Discipline problems in the new school in combination with the long commute thoroughly depressed and exhausted Hathaway. Transferred teacher Fred Goldberg lost "all of my sick time" and experienced severe "anguish and hardship." Even Sol Schwartz, an ardent supporter of affirmative action, admitted to "shock, depression, and self-doubt. I now knew I was dispensible." Manning Greene admitted that losing his position caused "about a month in the doldrums. It was a real blow."

In classifying some of the teachers' answers to questions on self-esteem, it was sometimes difficult to separate actual damage to self-esteem from the sheer toll of the transfer experience in terms of shock and fatigue. Yet most admitted to some degree of deep questioning; indeed, two left the profession. The teachers' emphatically expressed debt of gratitude to their wives ("my wife was *wonderful*") also indicated the degree of personal trial and anguish the men had experienced.

Correctional officer Jack Smith absorbed a moderate amount of self-concept or self-esteem damage in his frustration at being stranded in part-time duties while, he claimed, less-qualified minorities were moved by him to full-time positions. He was content, he said, to "let it ride" for a while. As he became angrier and more depressed, he engaged in more "general bitching" to co-workers and superiors (one of whom warned him to "keep quiet"). Such pressures made him "internalize things more," though he and his new wife began to quarrel over affirmative action, among other things. They were divorced after a year of marriage.

Ed Coles and Frank Nunn sustained more severe damage to self-concept and self-esteem.

As outlined in the previous chapter, Coles was not even interviewed for a humanities position at a liberal arts college after he had filled similar positions on a part-time, then full-time basis. He claims a less-qualified black male was hired. Coles and his fiancee had pinned their hopes on his getting the job and the financial security it would bring. Coles claimed the relationship ended on very nearly the same day he was refused the job. After working as a clerk in a hospital for a time, he finally obtained a full-time position at a small, midwestern college.

Frank Nunn claimed he was fired to make way for minorities who had not scored as high as he on the civil service exams. In subsequent wrangling with the city (and, Nunn reported, harrassment) he sought psychiatric help and claimed his "personal life was shot to hell."

This turmoil affected his relationship with a woman he lived with and whom he planned to marry. "On the night of July 15, 1977—a few hours after my discharge became effective—I accompanied the woman I loved and lived with to the West Los Angeles Women's Center for an abortion. This decision probably wouldn't have been made under different circumstances, and it profoundly altered our relationship."

Nunn's girlfriend subsequently married another man. Nunn himself negotiated a stress disability leave from the city. He lost his lawsuit against the city in 1986.

Changes in Political, Societal, or Philosophical Outlooks

As a whole, most men interviewed for this study were moderate to conservative. Nearly all subjects were registered voters. About half of those who chose to identify themselves as Democrats, were moderate to conservative. The schoolteachers were something of a liberal minority, while those affiliated with law-enforcement jobs (or who had aspirations for such careers) were the most cynical and jaded. In a sample of men who tended to stress realistic or cynical views, it is not surprising that a negative encounter with affirmative action produced no long-term changes in political outlook, or that a third indicated that affirmative action incidents simply confirmed previous views of a corrupt system. Most mentioned becoming more disillusioned with society as a whole or its major political institutions, especially the courts, the executive branch, or unions.

Tables 3 and 4 show the responses in more detail. Nearly half experienced no change in political views, while more than a third of the others had their political views confirmed. Frank Sanders, Tim O'Neill, Ed Coles, Hal Overton, Samuel Gray, Fred Goldberg, David Brown, Steve Falkner, and Frank Nunn all reported varying degrees of rightward shifts in their political outlooks. Goldberg admitted that his vote for Reagan in 1980 was a "gesture of anger," and that he gradually returned to liberalism. But both Sanders and Goldberg said they were now "estranged" from the Democratic party because of its pro-quota stand. Tim O'Neil "switched parties because of affirmative action." Others said affirmative action setbacks merely added to a conservative drift. No one became more liberal or moderate than they had been.

When asked if they believed that individuals were responsible for their own successes or failures, one-third generally agreed, one-third agreed with major qualifications ("it's who you know"), and a third disagreed. As shown in Table 4, there was no particular variation in response to this question by political affiliation.

The tabulations may appear somewhat bland, but many of the politically related comments were not:

Tim O'Neil: A lot of us were sold a bill of goods. We were told if you went to college, you could write your own ticket. But for the Baby Boom generation, it's no longer true. And, on top of that, affirmative action has lowered standards to the point where education almost counts against you. . . . I've gone from being a liberal to very conservative, even reactionary. It's sad. I want revenge.

Greg Miller: I'm bitter over the way they did it—as well as what was done. I loved my job, I really did. I'd never heard of this happening to anyone else. It's wrong.

Jack Smith: Regular folks are fed up with this stuff. Chuck the whole (affirmative action) thing. Equal opportunity and merit should be the sole criteria.

David Brown: I'd like to see people treated as individuals rather than groups. Merit should determine everything.

Ed Coles : A woman who wants to settle down and have a traditional family is going to be hurt by affirmative action.

Robert Oakes: What color you are influences very much whether you get ahead. Artificial opportunities are being created and many good people are not able to get ahead because of this.

Samuel Gray quipped that he would "wait until the following year"(when his lawsuit was to go to court) to see how he felt. And Mike Grant was simply "confused" as to his views on society or social institutions. Grant was a devout Christian who felt torn between guilt over the past plight of minorities (especially blacks) and the equally strong desire to right the wrong done to him.

Compare the above responses to those obtained in Greenberg's study of Michigan white, blue-collar focus groups. The moderator asked, "Who do you think gets the raw deal?" Answers:

Table 3
Changes in Political/Philosophical Views Among White Males as a Result of Reverse Discrimination Experiences (By Self-Identified Political Affiliation) (N = 32)

	No Change	Confirmed Previous Views*	More Conservative	Confused	Total
Repub.	8	6	2	1	17
Demo.	6	5	3	0	14
Independ.	1	0	0	0	1
TOTAL	15	11	5	1	32

Table 4
Responses of White Males to Question Asking Whether the Individual Is Responsible for His/Her Own Success or Failure (By Self-Identified Political Affiliation) (N = 32)

	True	Partly True	Not True	Total
Republican	6	4	6	16
Democrat	5	5	3	13
Independent	0	1	0	1
Total	11	9	9	30*

*Two individuals (Democrats) gave answers that were vague or unclear.

We do. . . .

The middle class white guy.

We do. . . .

The average working man, male.

'Cause women get advantages, blacks get advantages, the Hispanics get advantages, Orientals get advantages. Everybody but the white male race gets advantages now. (1985: 72)

There are certainly parallels in the responses of the two groups. (See also the responses from Greenberg's subjects in Chapter 1.) As a whole, however, the thirty-two subjects interviewed for this study were more passive and philosophical in their response. They were less outraged and more disillusioned, alienated, bewildered, and confused. Though all but two adamantly rejected quotas, many indicated that they were aware of the societal problems posed by the disproprotionate numbers of black and Hispanic poor. Greenberg's subjects expressed less sympathy for minorities and were less concerned with being perceived as "racist."

Other Reactions

There were many individual reflections on the operation of affirmative action policies. Those of liberal or moderate political orientation sometimes sought to reconcile their lingering views that some forms of affirmative action might be desirable with the negative consequences of such programs' operation.

For example, in both scholarly and public discourse, arguments for affirmative action are advanced at the "macrosociological" level—that is, in terms of statistics demonstrating gross inequalities—especially between blacks/whites and males/females. Critics counter arguments on the large-scale level, but have also sought to buttress their case by citing gross injustices stemming from the operation of affirmative action in small-scale or "microsociological" settings (Sowell, 1981; Sowell, 1984; Jencks, 1985b; Glazer, 1985).

State worker Steven Clark had discussed this apparent macro-micro disjunction in depth with his wife who, as Clark stated, "came at it from a different perspective" because she was black.

It all depends upon whether you look at it from what I call the big picture or the little picture.

My wife, for example, points to the big picture in that history has dictated us to be in a position where we have this [large-scale] problem. Events of history have caused this. Something must be done. In theory . . . affirmative action is valid . . . as long as it is practiced the way it's supposed to be.

The problem is that the way it is actually practiced involves human beings who have ambitions and preferences. But practices will be less than optimum design. This is the big picture my wife points to.

But, by the same token, the little picture is that the realities of the theory of affirmative action as it is applied in the real world have resulted in the replacement of one form of discrimination with another.

Another major theme in affirmative action debate has been the policy's apparent threat to meritocratic criteria, especially as measured by education and test scores. Those who saw women and minorities with less education or lower scores being moved by the policies were upset and disillusioned.

Public employees in this study repeatedly commented upon hiring and promotion of "incompetent" minorities or females. Several men in this study had been involved in hiring others. They recalled pressures to hire women and minorities regardless of whether they were as qualified as white applicants, sometimes regardless of qualifications at all. (The accounts in the Chapter 3 "Sampler" give credence to such views.) California state employee Timothy O'Neil even recalled seeing a "Form 1308." This document, he and one other state worker maintained, was to be used as a defensive device when hiring or promoting less qualified minorities over more qualified white males. Though it was attempted, we were unable to obtain a copy of the document for this book.

Chapter 6

INVISIBLE VICTIMS:
INSTITUTIONAL RESPONSES

We have seen that nearly all of the men in this study either explicitly or implicitly indicated that they feared being thought unmanly if they complained about a reverse discrimination situation. No one wanted to be perceived as a crybaby. And, as we shall see, if they failed to act out this gender-prescribed behavior, the mass media and other institutions were quick to remind them. Sex-role behavior has had a decisive impact upon how men responded to reverse discrimination and upon how others responded as well.

Traditional sex-role norms have long denigrated male expressions of weakness, powerlessness, or individual failure. Traditional inhibitions against viewing males as powerless have been reinforced today by what Warren Farrell terms a "new sexism," a product of women's liberation. The new sexism, with its emphasis on women's victimization by society, refuses to acknowledge men's vulnerability to pain and injury produced by the same social constraints. Contemporary "male bashing" in popular culture furthers a dehumanized, insensitive image of males. Under both old and new sexism, men cannot be seen as victims (Farrell, 1989: 189-236).

We have seen this victim-denial process illustrated in the previous chapter. Interestingly, the data indicated that this denial process was strongest among men; wives were often the most sympathetic source of support. We must examine further the social and cultural sources of silence or self-blame among men who have encountered affirmative action obstacles.

AMERICAN MEN AND FRIENDSHIP

During the past ten years, an increasing number of scholars have begun to focus on "men's studies." Amongst the most significant findings have been that males in contemporary America have few close friends and have problems with emotional bonding outside of marriage (Goldberg, 1976; Stearns, 1979; Pleck, 1981; Doyle, 1983; Miller, 1983; McGill, 1985). Miller writes:

> The differences in the intimate behavior of men and women are never more apparent than in the area of friendship. . . . Even the most intimate of male friendships (of which there are very few) rarely approach the depth of disclosure a woman commonly has with many other women. We know that very few men reveal anything of their private and personal selves even to their spouses; fewer still make these intimate disclosures to other men.
>
> One man in ten has a friend with whom he discusses work, money, marriage; only one in more than twenty has a friendship where he discloses his feelings about himself or his sexual feelings. (1983: 157)

Elliott Engel observed that "the typical male friendship, unfortunately, comes in one climate only: fair weather." In American culture, he argues, "we've been raised with positive male images that only sanction either standing alone or standing together as a team." Competition, not closeness, is nearly always dominant in the male bond and "the very stuff that intensifies an acquaintanceship into a devoted friendship seems reserved in our society for women only. . . . Men nurture their feelings only inwardly and later harvest ulcers or heart attacks" (1982: 13).

A pioneer in men's studies, Herb Goldberg, observed, "Many men I interviewed admitted to not having one intimate male friend whom they totally trusted and confided in. However, most of them seemed to accept this as being a normal and acceptable condition" (1976: 127).

A decade later, Lillian Rubin stated the same findings in almost identical words. She noted that in survey data, "In sharp contrast to the women, over two-thirds of the single men could not name a best friend. Equally interesting, this was not something that seemed troubling to most of them" (Rubin, 1985: 63). Rubin found it was much the same for married men. She echoed Engel's above remarks on competitiveness and lack of feeling.

> But given the wariness with which men approach each other, given their fear of displaying vulnerability or dependency to another man, there's not much incentive to find time for friends. . . Men who claimed years of close friendship failed to confide to each other their distress at any number of conflicts, *especially those that touched their personal or work lives in ways they feared would diminish their stature.* (P. 66; italics added)

Friendship and Response to Reverse Discrimination

The above findings on men and friendship were vividly illustrated time and again during the interviewing for this study. Though most interviews went smoothly, there was sometimes a sense of "drawing out" buried feelings and emotions. "God, I'd forgot about so much of this," groaned Fred Goldberg in mid-sentence. "Maybe this interview wasn't such a good idea after all." On the other hand, approximately one-third of the subjects seemed glad to air feelings they had never discussed, with the possible exceptions of talking to wives. Some were surprised that anyone was doing a study on this topic.

Whether or not the men eventually obtained any measure of social support, there were deep inhibitions about saying anything at all.

"Why didn't I say anything about it [reverse discrimination incident]? Gee, I hadn't thought about it," mused Dan Elliott. "Pride, I guess. I didn't want to make excuses."

"When it hits you," said Lloyd McCall, "you don't want to admit it at first. Instead, you think it must be something in you. You doubt yourself. Your repress it, try to forget it."

The interviewers and I stumbled into this aspect of male behavior when at least half of the subjects paused or hesitated when asked about how friends responded to accounts of reverse discrimination.

"What do you mean by 'friends'?" was often the response.

What we were encountering was the relative absence of close, personal friendships amongst American males. Most married men's best friends were their wives. Most married or single men had few or no really close friends with whom they could or would confide deep, personal feelings, especially disappointment over a career setback. What friends many respondents had were also co-workers. The overlap between these two categories made responses difficult to classify in some instances. (At least four of the sixteen friends who indicated support in Table 2 were also co-workers.)

Therefore, the seemingly positive data contained in Table 2 of the previous chapter must be read with some caution. To judge by Table 2 alone, half of the men interviewed received support from friends. On the surface, that appears fairly positive. But the "support" was often token or transitory. Correctional officers indicated a cynical, tough solidarity with their colleagues. Community-college teacher Samuel Gray reported the most intense level of solidarity in his court battle against the administration. But these were the exceptions. Most "supportive" friends and relatives simply and briefly acknowledged the problem, then went on their way. Deep or lasting commiseration simply wasn't there.

"People have their own problems," Fred Goldberg dryly concluded.

These men, typical of males in contemporary America, have been conditioned against the communication of deep feelings, especially such taboo areas as failure on the job. Thus, American males neither individually nor collectively can cope very well with systematic discrimination directed against them.

Karl Marx insisted that for an any sort of class consciousness to arise, there must be communication of a common sense of oppression. But imbued with the doctrines of individual achievement, individual responsibility, competitiveness, "silent but strong," and "take it like a man," there has been no chance of collective awareness, much less organized action by class-conscious white males. Hence, most lawsuits are lonely struggles.

In more traditional settings where more stereotypical thinking still prevails (see Greenberg, 1985), the loss of a job to a minority or female may be doubly damning. Without widespread, collective awareness of affirmative action barriers, a man who loses a job to a minority or female might be opened to double scorn, first, for having lost the job in the first place and, second, for having lost it to a minority or female—who is presumably less qualified. (Indeed, such stereotypical thought styles may have been reinforced, in some instances, by the promotion of less-qualified—or unqualified—persons under the more aggressive forms of affirmative action—see Chapter 12.)

With the mass media and the social sciences rarely recognizing the phenomenon, much less portraying it sympathetically, white males have been easily and silently victimized one by one. Many men have been quick to blame themselves for their own failure. However, if they have recognized affirmative action problems, they have felt constrained about complaining at all or "carrying on" because this would be a violation of the masculine code of "strong and silent." Thus, white males have been prevented from linking personal problems with public issues, the core of sociological understanding of self and society (Mills, 1959).

The lack of ability to link private problems with public issues was strikingly confirmed with regard to a question on what the subject knew about public-opinion polls on affirmative action. Only two subjects were at all aware that the public had been polled on the issue of affirmative action. Only one subject knew that polls showed massive public opposition to affirmative action as preference. In fact, the subjects' views were very much in line with public opinion. Nearly all of the white males interviewed opposed outright preferential treatment and group-based quotas. Some favored "affirmative action" of some sort, though they did not know how to define it. Many favored some sort of remedial training or education.

BLAMING THE VICTIM: CORPORATIONS

The "silent-but-strong" norms of American male sex roles were reinforced by corporations, the mass media, and other institutions. Blaming the victim fused with "take it like a man" in both small group and larger organization settings.

A *Wall Street Journal* report on corporate attempts to neutralize white male anger over reverse discrimination illuminates management's approach to white male resentment of affirmative action policies.

A special supplement to the regular March 24, 1986, edition of the paper was devoted to a report on *Corporate Women*. One story was entitled "The Last Angry Men: Some Companies Begin Confronting Men's Resentment of Successful Women" (p. 18D).

According to reporter David Wessel, a consequence of white males' competing with women and minorities is an "inevitable backlash." Corporate managers have allowed men to blame affirmative action barriers for their own failures and have permitted resentment to "smolder unchecked." Therefore, "now a few big employers are trying the only remedy they can think of. They're attempting to bring the anger out of the closet on the theory that resentment that's exposed can be defused." The rest of the report and some others like it (see the *Newsweek* item below) make clear that "defused" means "neutralized," if not "brainwashed."

Merck & Co. of Rahway, N.J., was one of the first companies to require large number of employees to attend carefully structured discussions of affirmative action. The all-day sessions included a video of a white male executive warning a white male middle manager about his persistent failure to meet company affirmative action goals. The subordinate responded with a diatribe on affirmative action that was supposed to ignite a discussion among the viewers.

And it did, says Lawrence Branch, Merck's director of equal employment affairs. . . . Of the 17,000 company employees who participated, 69% said they had a more positive attitude toward affirmative action. An additional 28% said they hadn't changed their minds. . . .

Mead Corp. sent all 6,000 of its salaried workers to half-day affirmative action seminars between November 1983 and last July. "In the event a position I want is offered to a woman, I may be somewhat more understanding about the company's need to be progressive," says Jerry Josselyn, 27, a financial analyst who attended a Mead seminar. (1986: 180)

To grasp what is going on here one might ask, would corporations sponsor similar sessions for women and minorities to help rationalize discrimination against them? Of course not.

The entire article reeks of the assumption that white males lose out only in "fair competition" to women and minorities. At times, perhaps, they do. Other times, however, the game has been rigged and white males have lost opportunities to less qualified minorities or women. Reporter Wessel ignored that possibility and the legitimacy of frustration which must accompany such setbacks.

What we have here is a kind of play-within-a-play: an article describing how corporations rationalize preferential treatment and blame the victims for being angry while the article itself implicitly does the same thing. Both the reporter and those he reports upon blame the victim.

Similar strategies have been employed by corporate management to deal with more general racial tensions. *Newsweek* (March 7, 1988) carried an article on a racial "awareness" seminar utilized by corporations such as Bell Laboratories, AT&T and Mead Corp. also have had employees attend two-day seminars on white racism. Using confrontational techniques, seminar leader Charles King tries to create an "atmosphere of oppression" that will convince participants that white institutions are inherently racist.

Los Angeles Times reporters Lee May and Paul Houston claimed that "affirmative action has won grudging acceptance in the work place" and that "despite continued sharp criticism from the Reagan administration, the anxieties created when minorities and women first received preferential treatment in hiring have begun to fade away" (1985: 1).

Yet the data in their report indicate a clear management-worker split in the "acceptance" of affirmative action. Many white and black corporate managers do appear to accept such programs. Female and minority persons quoted in May and Houston's article also accept affirmative action.

Virtually none of the white male workers quoted in the May and Houston article accept affirmative action. On the contrary, the white workers expressed anger, bitterness, or grim resignation about quotas in both hiring and promotion. The reporters describe one person whose wounds have obviously not healed: a Boston policeman who was thrice injured.

To white officer William McCarthy, the special advantage given blacks on Boston's new sergeant's exam is grossly unfair and demoralizing. McCarthy, who like Eversley holds a college degree in criminal justice, already considers himself a two-time "victim" of affirmative action. His hiring was delayed for five years and he was laid off once despite having more seniority than blacks who were kept on the job. (1985: 15)

May and Houston also indicate a differential acceptance of affirmative action in the private sector as opposed to the public sector: "If affirmative action has proceeded smoothly at private employers such as Monsanto—it continues to generate ill will elsewhere" (p. 15).

The headline and initial positive thrust of May and Houston's article sought to reinforce the corporate management party line of "everything's fine" on affirmative action. But the data in their article indicated otherwise. Indeed, problems in reporting on the story—related by Houston in a telephone conversation—suggest this possibility. In some settings, notably police and fire departments, workers were instructed not to talk to outsiders about affirmative action operations. But May and Houston found white workers nonetheless cooperative, even eager, to discuss affirmative action. Houston mentioned that he and his co-reporter were "shooed away" from employees in a company cafeteria. Therefore, they interviewed many workers off-premises or off-duty.

BLAMING THE VICTIMS: THE MASS MEDIA

I am, perhaps, getting ahead of the plan of the book in discussing the media in this chapter when more detailed examination is in the next. However, the media are crucial in molding people's perceptions of reality, especially with regard to social issues. Therefore, what sort of response was offered by the media to white males who had encountered reverse discrimination? The same response provided by some co-workers, friends, and corporations: denial or blaming-the-victim.

The mass media basically ignored affirmative action. When they did portray a reverse discrimination situation, the message was that white males should simply "take it like a man." In 1975, an "All in the Family" episode was the first commercial situation comedy to broach the issue. Archie Bunker's "meathead" son-in-law was competing with a slightly less qualified black student for a graduate fellowship. The black student got the award, and the dean explained to Mike that "we sometimes have to tip the scales a little bit to make up for past discrimination." Mike was still somewhat frustrated but took the black student and his wife out to dinner in a gesture of reconciliation. No real harm was done and Mike later in the series obtained a position at the University of California, Santa Barbara.

A textbook model of blaming the victim was offered white males by *Newsweek* magazine's "My Turn" column. Frank Lovelock had been reduced to day labor because of a glutted job market for Ph.D.s and by quotas. Lovelock commented on his attempts to commiserate with a fellow day-laborer, a black male named Charlie:

I didn't tell him [Charlie] how cheated I felt for spending so much time pursuing a Ph.D., only to enjoy a permanent sabbatical without pay. I didn't tell him about the rage I'd known when a female friend confided that I was wasting my time applying for a position at a local college because word was out that the department had to hire a woman. I didn't tell him that I had begun to buy into the ideas that reverse discrimination and hiring quotas were evils that worked against the principles of fair play. And I didn't tell him that I wanted some organization—the National Association for the Advancement of White Protestant Males Who've Never Made It—to carry my banner, to speak out in my defense, to give me rationales for coping with personal failure.

I'm glad I didn't serve this mush to Charlie. It was stinky stuff. Cooked up in a caldron of self-pity, it wasn't fit for human consumption. Unfortunately, I had started to become addicted to it. I hope to goodness that it's out of my system now.

There were good reasons that Charlie and I had been habitually unemployed. But these reasons had more to do with us as individuals, I think, than they did with any conspiracy to keep us out of the mainstream. Neither of us had really taken control of our lives. . . . Strange, I don't hear Lee Iacoca, Jesse Jackson, or Barbara Walters advancing this doctrine. (September 16, 1985: 8)

Would *Newsweek* have printed such a column if it had been written by a black man for other blacks? To ask the question is to know the answer. The import of Lovelock's public self-flagellation was clear enough for white males: blame yourself, not the system, and especially do not criticize affirmative action. If you do, you're making excuses. Anyone can make it to the top in America if they try! Stop whining and get on with it!

Lovelock and *Newsweek* were articulating the values that reinforce blaming the victim and that underpin the American male, sex-role behavior: individualism, responsibility for self, and self-blame. Admittedly, these values have been a powerful motivating mechanism for many American males. And this sex-role orientation has also made white males vulnerable to the steamroller of affirmative action.

BLAMING THE VICTIMS: THE DEMOCRATIC PARTY

No institution has more vigorously suppressed white males' claims of injury under affirmative action than has the Democratic party and its liberal allies in the mass media and the university. I shall have much more to say concerning the possible political impact of affirmative action quotas in Chapter 12. Suffice it to say here that, after twenty years of pushing race-and-gender preferences, the Democratic party has begun to search for a way to stem the flight of white, male voters to the Republican presidential candidate. According to *Newsweek* (November 18, 1984: 58), 73 percent of the white, male vote nationwide went to Ronald Reagan in 1984, and in some regions the figure was close to 90 percent. Similar patterns prevailed in the 1988 presidential election.

Walter Mondale's landslide loss of the 1984 awakened the concerns that led to Stanley Greenberg's embarrassing research findings of anti-quota anger in *Report on Democratic Defection* in Michigan. I have already discussed in Chapters 1 and 5 the acrid denunciations of preferential-treatment programs that Greenberg and his associates obtained in their 1985 and 1987 studies. Again, the strength of the outbursts surprised Greenberg and his colleagues—and his sponsors, as well.

What is of interest here is the reception accorded Greenberg's findings by his sponsors. Greenberg presented these and other similar data to a convention of state Democratic party chairpersons. He reported that "they were not pleased." The next day, the Democratic party's national committee met and, according to scattered reports in the press, attempted to suppress Greenberg's reports—which nonetheless got some play in Michigan newspapers. Yet the findings had such profound implications that another study was commissioned in 1987. Initially, the findings were kept under tight wraps, though Greenberg admitted the findings on affirmative action were much the same.

The Democratic party has fought to render invisible the issue of affirmative action. It also has denied white males the right to legitimate complaint under such treatment—it has tried to deny the victims altogether. At least one prominent Democrat, former Secretary of Health, Education, and Welfare Joseph Califano, has directly stated that Democratic support of affirmative action, coupled with failure to understand the legitimate objections of whites to such policies, is a major reason the Democrats have not carried a majority of white voters in presidential elections since Harry Truman's election in 1948—with the sole exception of Lyndon Johnson in 1964 (Califano, 1988).

INSTITUTIONS, WHITE MALES, AND AFFIRMATIVE ACTION

There is little question that institutional responses to white males' encounters with affirmative action barriers has generated alienation and tension. More research needs to be conducted on how both white males and the institutions have dealt with these feelings. Also, what have been the human costs in terms of time, energy, and commitment lost to both the victims of reverse discrimination and the perpetrators?

The mass media might have studied such questions. But they have not.

Chapter 7

AFFIRMATIVE ACTION AND
THE MASS MEDIA

The television in the average American home is now on more than seven hours each day. More than 60 percent of Americans indicate that television is their primary source of news. This suggests that both commercial programming and television journalism have enormous power to shape perceptions of reality. As Ralph Turner and Lewis Killian have pointed out, the mass media authenticate the facts and determine which issues are important (1987: 191-202).

In determining which issues are important and real, the media determine which topics will be debated and which points of view can be legitimately expressed. The media thus influence the formation and life of "publics," groups crucial to Western capitalist democracies. Publics are groups interested in, but divided about, an issue (Turner and Killian, 1987). According to Alvin Gouldner (1976), the free and rational debate of issues in publics has been a keystone of the dynamic character of capitalist societies. The bane of such freedom, of course, is censorship. Publics thrive only with free discussion and open debate.

Elisabeth Noelle-Neumann has emphasized that the mass media provide people with the very words they use in debating an issue: "If the media fail to provide them, then there will be no words. . . . The media provide people with the words and phrases they can use to defend a point of view. If people find no current, frequently repeated expression for their point of view, they lapse into silence" (1984: 172-173).

David Altheide has suggested a strong connection between television news and perceptions of everyday reality. Citing data to support this contention, Altheide holds that there is a "relationship between what people see on the nightly news and what they regard as problems and issues—people 'watch the news' *because* that is where newsworthy events are presented'' (1976: 25-26; see also Gans, 1978).

Noelle-Neumann holds that the mass media structure individual perceptions at the unconscious level. The individual unconsciously incorporates the media information and perceptions into his or her own views: "The individual adopts the eyes of the media and acts accordingly" (1984: 169).

There is no question that the mass media pervasively affect both how people think and about what they think. Social life is increasingly structured around the mass media. Everyday conversation is full of references to what is seen or read. Forecaster Faith Popcorn has suggested that Americans are increasingly "cocooning" themselves in their homes via video equipment (*Newsweek*, June 15, 1987:46–47).

In this chapter, I shall be assuming a very close relationship between what transpires on television and the major news media and the contents of American consciousness. Specifically, I shall argue that throughout most of the 1970s and well into the 1980s, the mass media have ignored affirmative action as a major issue. By so doing, they have effectively banished the topic from individual consciousness and widespread face-to-face conversation in publics.

By the term "mass media," I shall be referring to the major television networks, the major news magazines (especially *Time*, *Newsweek*, and *U.S. News and World Report*), and, to a lesser extent, major newspapers of national stature such as *The New York Times*, *The Wall Street Journal*, and the *Los Angeles Times*. I shall also examine how affirmative action was portrayed—as little as it was—on commercial programming.

As is the case throughout this study, I am concerned with affirmative action primarily in the form of preferential treatment for race and minority groups. I am less concerned with gender preferences.

My efforts here represent a combination of the traditional "count-and-prove" sociological approach and a more interpretive, qualitative, historical perspective. The sociology of silence is a somewhat peculiar area: how does one measure what was not (but, at times, logically might have been) discussed? Who does or should determine what is or should be "news" (Gans, 1978; Lichter, et al. 1986)?

I will try to measure with some degree of quantification the frequency of reporting on affirmative action in the periodical literature included in *The Reader's Guide to Periodical Literature*. When dealing with the most popular news and entertainment medium—television—I shall make use of the *Vanderbilt University Television News Index and Abstracts*. However, as the abstracts director has admitted in personal correspondence, the data provide only a partial account of the television record during this period.

I shall become somewhat more qualitative and interpretive when I turn to commercial television's treatment of affirmative action. I shall also employ a more qualitative or historical method of focusing on significant events that may have served to center the viewing and reading public's attention on affirmative action: The U.S. Supreme Court decision on *Bakke* in 1978, the *Weber* decision made the following year, the so-called conservative revolution (marked by California's Proposition 13 and the election of Ronald Reagan as president in 1980), the Pulitzer Prize scandal involving Janet Cooke, the contentious confirmation hearings on Supreme Court nominee Robert Bork, and the 1988 Presidential campaign of Jesse Jackson.

I shall then briefly compare media coverage of affirmative action to media treatment of a highly related issue: busing. The chapter will conclude with an overview of the implications of this data and other studies on media ideologies and perceptions.

THE EVOLUTION OF AFFIRMATIVE ACTION: PRE-BAKKE, POST-BAKKE

Sociologists have tended to view social change as the cumulative product of incremental build-ups of tensions, conflicts, or other forces within the social system. Historians, on the other hand, have tended to view change as the result of the intrusion of unique or sudden, significant events (Nisbet, 1969). The following analysis of reports on affirmative action as recorded in *The Reader's Guide* and the Vanderbilt *Television News Index* lends some support to both views. Generally, there was a gradual increase in the number of articles and reports on affirmative action, which undoubtedly reflected the growth and conflict engendered by affirmative action programs. The number of entries skyrockets during 1977 and 1978, when the *Bakke* case burst upon the national scene as it was taken up by the U.S. Supreme Court.

Affirmative Action in the Print Media: What Was Mentioned

Data from *The Reader's Guide*[1] covering the period from March 1967 through February 1980 are presented in Table 5. These data indicate that there was never a total silence in the print media regarding affirmative action. However, it is important to remember that the *Guide* covers periodicals, most with highly limited circulations. Most of the articles on affirmative action were in a wide range of print media, from various business, labor, and ethnic journals to such intellectual outlets as *Commentary* and *The New Republic*.

Behind the numbers is the finding that the three major news weeklies—*Time, Newsweek,* and *U.S. News and World Report*—printed only about one article each per year on affirmative action. Most of those yearly articles (usually short ones) covered the same event or story. For example, in the

Table 5
Frequency of Affirmative Action Related Reports Cited in *Reader's Guide to Periodical Literature*, **March 1967–February 1980**

Year ending Feb.	No. of Reports	Year ending Feb.	No. of Reports
1968	21	1975	29
1969	19	1976	42
1970	17	1977*	37
1971	5	1978	60
1972	7	1979	40
1973	17	1980	82
1974	28		

*First cover story on affirmative action in a major news weekly: "Reverse Discrimination: Has It Gone Too Far?" *U.S. News and World Report*, March 29, 1976. (The next cover story in a major news magazine did not appear until about eighteen months later with the September 28, 1977, issue of *Newsweek*.

late 1960s, the news magazines' affirmative action news accounts dealt with attempts to integrate the labor unions by the "Philadelphia Plan." In the 1972–73 period, *Newsweek* and *U.S. News* carried stories on colleges' and universities' efforts to implement affirmative action; *Time* did not. The recession of 1975 produced a new focus of conflict: affirmative action demands versus seniority in layoffs. Many of the forty-two affirmative action-related pieces for that year concerned this conflict.

In March 1976, *U.S. News* became the first of the major news weeklies to run a cover story on affirmative action. The magazine thus anticipated the rush of other articles that would be written as the *Bakke* case advanced to a hearing before the U.S. Supreme Court in 1977-78. Indeed, for the March 1977–February 1978 volume of *The Reader's Guide*, there were twenty-eight articles listed under the new heading: "Bakke." In the post-*Bakke* era, other new race/ethnic/sex-related headings began to appear in the *Guide*.

In addition to the fact that, especially prior to *Bakke*, the major news magazines paid relatively scant attention to affirmative action, the reporting that was done was usually after-the-fact accounting of various administrative and judicial *faits accomplis* in the realm of affirmative action implementation and enforcement. That is, the magazine reports and commentaries usually concerned court challenges, judicial decisions, and administrative conflicts that took place after affirmative action policies had been formulated "backstage" by government and corporate authorities. The media have undoubtedly missed much of the action in affirmative action due to the way such schemes have been imposed, as the previous chapters indicate (Mansfield, 1984).

A study of "East Coast Bias" in the news media by the *Los Angeles Times* (November 17-18, 1988) suggests that most major news organizations have long followed the leadership of *The New York Times* in deciding which issues merit press attention. Thus, it is likely that the major news weeklies contained in the survey of *The Reader's Guide* were following the *Times'* lead on this topic. Barry Gross's count of editorials and letters on affirmative action in *The New York Times* through 1977 reflects patterns found in my survey of *The Reader's Guide* (Gross, 1978: 163). I do not think one would find a different pattern of coverage on affirmative action in the daily print media.

Affirmative Action as "The Other Shoe That Doesn't Drop"

Instances of intentional or unintentional avoidance of affirmative action in logically related contexts pose a nearly unsolvable methodological problem. That said, there were clearly some areas of news coverage in which affirmative action could have or should have been raised, but was not.

As items in the "Sampler" chapter indicate, the press did eventually begin to grapple with the seemingly inverse relationship between affirmative action and standards of quality via standardized tests, grades, and other meritocratic criteria. However, there were earlier rumblings on the quality of education in the late 1970s and early 1980s, but the issue of affirmative action in such problems was largely ignored.

For example, in April 1978, in a *New Times* article entitled "What's the Opposite of Education?" reporter Rob Fleder described the hiring of hundreds of incompetent or illiterate teachers in the New York City public schools. That affirmative action might have provided some of the rationale for bureaucratic shortcuts in the hiring process was not mentioned, even though most of the problem teachers were Spanish-speaking. (A year later, in a *60 Minutes* segment, the iconoclastic Mike Wallace was less charitable about bringing up affirmative action and its bearing on this same scandal.)

In the 1980s, all three major news weeklies ran cover stories on the crisis in teacher competence. All three reports ignored or quickly dismissed affirmative action's role in this. In the *Time* cover story entitled "Help! Teacher Can't Teach!" (June 16, 1980: 54-63) the magazine's writers immediately dismissed the "usual suspects" of affirmative action and busing in explaining declining standards in the teaching profession. Throughout the article, the reporters dodged the issue of affirmative action, including the obvious implications of their account of a teacher-testing program in Florida's Pinellas County: "Though all had their B.A. in hand, about one-third of the applicants (*25% of the whites, 79% of the blacks*) flunked Pinellas' test the first time they took it in 1979" (p. 58, emphasis mine). Only in the next-to-last paragraph of the eight-page article did the writers hint at the issue of affirmative action when they mentioned the fear in some circles that competency testing for teachers might discriminate against minorities.

Avoidance of linking affirmative action with declining competency in teaching was also obvious in the March 14, 1983, cover story on the subject by *U.S. News and World Report* (Pp. 37-42). The cover featured a white female teacher wearing a dunce cap. No mention was made of the low minority scores on teacher competency tests throughout the country until the final column of the final page of the story, and then the information was confined to two sentences. A similar cover story on the teaching competency crisis in *Newsweek* (September 24, 1984: 64-70) made no mention of affirmative action, race, or ethnicity, whatsoever.[2]

TELEVISION COVERAGE OF AFFIRMATIVE ACTION

The Evening Newscasts

A review of affirmative action-related items in the *Vanderbilt Television News Index and Abstracts* from the first year of its publication in 1972 through 1980 reveals a pattern remarkably similar to that in the print media.

From 1972 to 1976, few reports dealing with affirmative action appeared on the nightly half-hour news broadcasts of the three major television networks. During these years, the three major networks combined devoted approximately twelve to fifteen minutes broadcast time per year to affirmative action-related reports. As with the print media, most of these reports were basically reports of *faits accomplis*, decisions by courts, for the most part, but also of actions or reports of other government agencies such as the Justice Department or the Equal Employment Opportunity Commission (EEOC).

Television journalists, however, appear to have been slightly ahead of their colleagues in the print realm in recognizing the implications and importance of the U.S. Supreme Court's willingness to hear the *Bakke* case. Whereas *Newsweek* did not print its first cover story on affirmative action until 1977, NBC News devoted four and a half minutes of its nightly newscast on November 19, 1976, to a special segment on "reverse discrimination" and the *Bakke* case. CBS followed suit with a four-minute special on the same topic on December 14, 1976. The year 1977 saw an increasing number of reports on affirmative action, including a five-minute installment on ABC's nightly newscast on "discrimination, minority preference, school and housing desegregation" on August 24, 1977. Shortly afterward, CBS devoted nearly three and a half minutes to a clash over affirmative action politics at a steel mill.

When the *Bakke* case was argued before the Supreme Court on October 22, 1977, NBC devoted a full six minutes of its nightly newscast to the event, while CBS and ABC each gave the story about three minutes. There was very little reporting on affirmative action during the first half of 1978. By mid-June, however, the nightly newscasts were anticipating a decision on the *Bakke* case. When the decision arrived on June 28, 1978, it marked the high-water mark in television news coverage of affirmative action. ABC turned over most of its evening newscast to discussion of the decision. NBC stayed with the story for sixteen minutes; CBS, for fifteen minutes. In the following two days, NBC and CBS each took four to five minutes covering the aftermath of the decision.

During the remainder of 1978, ABC focused for more than three minutes on a Supreme Court decision sanctioning use of race in hiring and promotions. NBC later devoted four minutes to a story on the court-ordered imposition of a quota system for the Bridgeport, Connecticut, Fire Department. Each of the networks devoted at least ninety seconds to scenes of Bakke enrolling at the UC Davis Medical School. And each network devoted somewhat more than two minutes to the Supreme Court's decision in late 1978 to hear the case of the "blue-collar Bakke," Brian Weber.

But neither the *Weber* case, nor any other issue regarding affirmative action, ever again caught the interest of television journalists the way *Bakke* did. The decision in the *Weber* case, handed down on June 27, 1979, received nearly six minutes on NBC (the same as *Bakke*) but only about three minutes on both ABC and CBS. Television reporting on affirmative action fell off precipitously after that. Television was beginning to focus on another matter; just above the topic heading of "integration" in the Vanderbilt *Television Abstracts*, the number of entries under the topic of "Inflation" began to grow rapidly.

Other Television Coverage of Affirmative Action

There have been very few national news specials or public affairs programs of any consequence on the topic of affirmative action. The issue was twice debated on the PBS series *The Advocates* in the early 1970s, but the audience for these programs was minuscule. On the other hand, the normally intrepid reporters for the popular news show *60 Minutes* dealt only once with affirmative action prior to *Bakke*. This was a rather timid segment entitled "Why Me?" concerning an affirmative action program in a security guard company. In the post-*Bakke* era, *60 Minutes* has dealt more critically with affirmative action issues at least twice.

The first major (hour-long) network news special on affirmative action per se was broadcast by ABC on August 27, 1977. *The Equality Debate* opened with the *Bakke* case but moved on to explore other areas of affirmative action, such as quota programs in hiring and promotions among California correctional officers and in the Atlanta police and fire departments. The program was given a half-page "Close-Up" in *T.V. Guide*. Unfortunately, the program aired opposite a football game featuring the popular Dallas Cowboys, so few people tuned in.

In the mid-1980s, affirmative action was debated on a PBS series, *The Constitution, The Delicate Balance*. On June 16, 1985, a *Satellite Town Meeting* anchored by Ted Koppol on the topic "Racism: New Times, New Questions" aired on many, though not all, ABC affiliates. A second special appeared one year later on June 20, 1986, a PBS-sponsored *Frontline*: "Assault on Affirmative Action." The ABC and *Frontline* programs were well-balanced, though both tended to focus heavily upon effects of affirmative action upon public sector workers, notably fire department personnel and school teachers. The ABC special included a specially commissioned public opinion poll, which found the usual results: though most of those polled still thought discrimination was a problem, 82 percent rejected quotas for hiring and promotion.

Until the mid-1980s, affirmative action was not a popular topic on television talk shows and appears to have been actively avoided. Whether there were systematic efforts to suppress the affirmative action issue is difficult to determine. However, sporadic censorship of affirmative action was suggested by social critic and satirist Mort Sahl as he was discussing his own radio talk show on the NBC *Tomorrow* show. Asked by host Tom Snyder if he had ever received pressure from network executives concerning the contents of the radio show, Saul mentioned that he had received pressure on only one topic: affirmative action. Snyder did not pursue the point and the issue was never raised on *Tomorrow* until the Janet Cooke scandal (discussed below). The reconstitution of the civil rights commission and the appearance of welfare-state critiques, such as Charles Murray's *Losing Ground* (1984b), led to raising the issue of affirmative action on some talk shows such as *Donahue*, in the mid-1980s. Omission rather than comment remained the rule.

For example, in 1983 NBC broadcast a one-hour special on *America in Search of Itself*, based upon Theodore White's book of the same name. White's book contained a long section in which he critiqued the ideology of race and sex quotas. That section of the book had been heavily attacked in major reviews. But there was no mention of affirmative action or even race and ethnicity in the NBC program. In fact, there was only one black face in the entire broadcast: a quick shot of a black woman beaming at Senator Kennedy as he made a speech. Also typical of this pattern was a 1983 edition of *The David Susskind Show* devoted to a discussion of the relations between blacks and Jews. Though the four main guests tried to bring up the divisive issue of race and sex quotas, Susskind kept the focus largely on foreign affairs. Eventually, five minutes of the ninety-minute program were permitted for a quick airing of the issue.

Affirmative Action on Commercial Television

I have already described in the previous chapter the 1975 *All in the Family* episode that dealt with affirmative action. There have been few other portrayals of affirmative action in other television programs. An episode of the series *Paper Chase* showed the struggle and ultimate success of a female law-school student who had been admitted under a quota. The only hint of problems with affirmative action came in an episode of *WKRP in Cincinnati*, when a black disc jockey discovered that he had been offered a posh job with a corporation mainly because he was black.

Well into the mid-1980s, then, commercial television writers and producers avoided the issue of affirmative action. On those few occasions when such policies were acknowledged, the message was either openly sympathetic or that affirmative action was a non-controversial reality that should simply be accepted.

To my knowledge, there has never been a major television program in which a white male's life was considerably damaged because of affirmative action barriers. Indeed, those familiar with television fare would probably find the mere possibility of such a script unthinkable. Affirmative action has received satiric treatment in a 1987 film, *Soul Man*. The movie portrays a young white male who gains an affirmative action scholarship to Harvard Law School by chemically darkening the color of his skin. Some critics denounced the film as "racist."

EVENTS AND AFFIRMATIVE ACTION

In news and commercial programming, then, affirmative action has been ignored. Thus, the mass media have, to some extent, created a reality in which this issue and its attendant problems do not exist.

Yet the media do mediate. Events occur, whether the media are predisposed to cover them or not.

The evidence from *The Reader's Guide* and the Vanderbilt *Television News Abstracts* clearly indicates that the appeal of the *Bakke* case to the U.S. Supreme Court dramatically increased the tempo of affirmative action coverage by the media. The *Weber* case was another event that served to bring to the surface the many questions and problems concerning the operation of numerous affirmative action programs in corporate and government enterprises.

Two other events, one broad and one narrow, had definite implications for affirmative action and compelled media attention to the issue. The more diffuse event was the so-called conservative revolution marked by the passage of the tax-cutting Proposition 13 in California and the subsequent election of Ronald Reagan as president in 1980. In his analysis of the taxpayer revolt of the late 1970s, Daniel Yankelovich saw public doubts concerning affirmative action and other entitlement programs:

An even more potent factor bugging the taxpayer, says Yankelovich, involves the raging debate over two competing conceptions of fairness. One is the concept of need as a right, a notion that is built into much federal legislation. As Yankelovich puts it: "If I need food or education or health care, I have a right to it." From that standpoint, it is fairness when government guarantees that the need will be met. But this reasoning collides with the other concept of fairness based upon an older proposition, which in Yankelovich's words runs, "I get what I deserve. I worked hard for my pension so I deserve it. I have been here longer than anybody else, so I have earned my seniority. He is smarter than Joe so he deserves to go to college."

There is no ambiguity about where the majority stands, says Yankelovich. It backs the concept of fairness based upon getting what you deserve and opposes the notion that need constitutes a right. . . . More than 80% are against affirmative action when it is carried to the point of reverse discrimination. (*Time*, July 15, 1978)

As for the election of Ronald Reagan, the record would seem to speak for itself: in the courts and other governmental arenas, the Reagan administration has consistently opposed the most aggressive quota forms of affirmative action. The press was more than ready. It was eager for combat.

Within one year after Reagan's election, several reporters and commentators were decrying a perceived Reagan retreat on affirmative action (see, for example, "A Retreat on Civil Rights?" *Time*, September 27, 1982: 62-63). Almost an event in itself was the protracted struggle in 1984 over the Reagan-inspired reconstitution and redirection of the U.S. Civil Rights Commission. Supreme Court sanctioning of affirmative action programs has consistently been headlined as a victory over the Reagan administration. Yet neither the press nor the candidates raised the issue at all during the three presidential campaigns of the 1980s. Busing was also actively ignored.

In 1981, however, journalists had to focus on an affirmative action–tinged scandal in their own profession. In that year, a young, black, female *Washington Post* reporter, Janet Cooke, had to return the Pulitzer Prize because it was discovered that she had fabricated the story for which she had been honored. The Pulitzer governing board had overridden the recommendation of its own committees in granting Cooke the award.

Several prominent journalists immediately raised the issue of preferential treatment by both the Pulitzer governing board and by the *Post* in initially hiring Cooke. Asked by a nervous Tom Snyder ("People may accuse me of being racist for asking this") if the Pulitzer board members had bypassed their own award committees in order to give the award to a black female, Pulitzer committeewoman Judith Crist responded, "Of course they were. That's exactly what they were doing." They were overly anxious to hire Cooke in the first place because she would have qualified as a "twofer" for affirmative action purposes: She was both black and female. Indeed, in a special essay on the scandal for *U.S. News and World Report* (May 4, 1981: 80-81), author James Michener charged that this could have been the only reason for the *Post*'s failure to check out Cooke's fraudulent credentials. ABC reporter Ted Koppel pointedly criticized *Post* ombudsman Hugh Green for ignoring affirmative action implications in his (Greene's) sixteen-thousand–word analysis of the scandal.

The Cooke case is an excellent example of an event from which the media really could not turn away, even though it was apparent that the reporters and commentators did not relish discussing the obvious affirmative action implications of the scandal.

By way of contrast, most of the news media, and the academic community as well, could and did ignore a 1982 National Academy of Sciences'

Research Council report that strongly discounted "cultural bias" in standardized testing (*Los Angeles Times*, February 3, 1982). The report was clearly relevant to the debate on merit-based criteria versus affirmative action. It has rarely been cited since.

Two more recent developments that begged mention of affirmative action were the 1988 Senate confirmation hearings on the nomination of Robert Bork for the U.S. Supreme Court and Jesse Jackson's 1988 presidential campaign. Yet the issue was rarely raised in either process.

The phrase "affirmative action" or "quotas" rarely surfaced during the long and acrimonious Senate confirmation hearings on Supreme Court nomine Robert Bork. Bork's anti-quota views were a top, but largely tacit, concern of those opposing him. Senator Edward Kennedy, the leader of the anti-Bork campaign, has long been a strong supporter of affirmative action quotas. Yet few senators or witnesses specifically raised the issue. Television advertisements against Bork avoided the topic. Two persons who did confront affirmative action were Bork supporters: economist Thomas Sowell and Senator Orrin Hatch. Bork's critics preferred to question Bork on the more general and vague interpretations of the equal protection clause of the Constitution rather than confront affirmative action specifically. (Political scientist Gary McDowell followed the Bork hearings closely and was a frequent guest commentator on both PBS's *MacNeil-Lehrer Report* and ABC's *Nightline*. In a telephone interview, McDowell confirmed the invisibility of affirmative action during the Bork confirmation hearings. McDowell suggested that lack of assertiveness and organization by White House lobbyists for Bork were partly responsible for the lack of attention to this issue.)

The Jesse Jackson presidential campaign obviously raised many issues with regard to race in American society. Initially, both journalists and rival politicians were timid in their treatment of Jackson. Eventually, press and politicians grew somewhat less cautious. Nevertheless, journalists and political opponents refused to question Jackson about affirmative action. Typical of press coverage was a *Newsweek* (March 21, 1988: 18-23) cover story on Jackson that did not once mention affirmative action; nor was the topic raised when Jackson was the sole guest on a *Donahue* show (May 29, 1987). When Jackson mentioned affirmative action by name or used the broader term "social justice," he was rarely, if ever, challenged by journalists or other politicians to explain how such policies might affect middle-class whites.

Jackson's color undoubtedly linked his candidacy to racial policies (busing and affirmative action) in the minds of white voters—whether they were "racist" or not. Furthermore, Jackson had led, or had threatened to lead, boycotts against major corporations, such as Coca-Cola, Burger King, and MacDonald's, unless they signed "fair share" agreements (i.e., quotas) to give blacks a "fair share" proportion of jobs or franchises (see *The New Republic*, May 9, 1988: 10-13). By 1988, Democratic party leaders already knew that whites were decoding the Democratic campaign theme for "justice" and "fairness" as having anti-white or reverse-discrimination overtones (see Greenberg, 1985; also, *Newsweek*, December 9, 1985: 38). There can be little doubt that sizable segments of whites viewed Jackson's use of these terms with the same mistrust.

Jackson also escaped scrutiny on another race-related issue that the news media had not been able to ignore so easily: busing.

AFFIRMATIVE ACTION AND BUSING: A BRIEF COMPARISON

In suggesting that there has been a pattern of media (and, therefore, public) inattention to affirmative action, the question might well be raised: inattention as compared to what other social issues? Space does not permit detailed comparison of affirmative action treatment in the media with that accorded to a host of other issues. However, it would be highly logical and useful to compare affirmative action with a related issue concerning racial balancing and equality: court-ordered busing for school desegregation.

Court-ordered busing has unquestionably received much more play in the national news media than have voluntary or court-ordered affirmative action plans. Why?

First and foremost, busing was "box office" from a media standpoint. There were huge numbers of children affected, angry parents, vocal demonstrations, and bold, sometimes charismatic, personalities and organizations who opposed busing. For example, during the late 1970s and early 1980s, print and broadcast media in Los Angeles were kept busy covering busing battles not only in their own metropolitan area but in other areas of the state as well. The nationally known president of the Los Angeles school board was voted out of office because of his support of busing. A highly active organization opposed to busing, Busstop, elected some of its members to the school board, one of whom subsequently ran successfully for Congress. A state senator championed (successfully) a bill to weaken state constitutional criteria for desegregation. Pro-busing forces were equally vehement and school board meetings were scenes of intense verbal battles. The busing program was greeted with widespread resistance and evasion, especially by whites.

Affirmative action had none of this. Affirmative action policies have affected mainly younger workers in public-sector jobs or in large corporations with government contracts. Attempts to increase minority and female participation in an organizational work force have not necessarily been as sweeping, obvious, and up-front—especially after Bakke's lawsuit—as were practices designed to racially balance busloads of students. Aside from B'nai B'rith, there have been few well-organized groups that have openly (or even covertly) opposed affirmative action. (On the importance of organizations' ability to gain access to news organizations, see Altheide, 1976: 115-124). No personalities emerged to speak against affirmative action; even Allan Bakke pointedly refused interviews and evaded cameras.

The findings in the previous chapters should be applied here. White male victims of affirmative action programs felt reticent—and were sometimes made to feel that way—about speaking out on affirmative action. Lack of organized outcry encouraged media avoidance of the issue, which, in turn, provided little wider support for complaints of affirmative action's victims. Without media coverage of the issue, white males feared their accounts of reverse discrimination would not be believed.

What we have here, then, is a vicious cycle. As was also documented in the previous chapters, affirmative action has been a slippery, behind-the-scenes, orally directed process. Proof has been hard to come by. The nature and operation of affirmative action, then, was not made-for-news coverage. But there has been something else at work here too.

AFFIRMATIVE ACTION AND THE MASS MEDIA: LIBERAL BIAS?

Members of the mass media, especially print and television journalists, are defensive about continuing accusations of liberal bias. Nevertheless, such accusations have been confirmed in an increasing amount of scholarship and data. The evidence has become so obvious that even press insider columnist David Broder (1987) admits that the press in general shares "reformist values" with regard to civil rights, civil liberties, political reform and social legislation (Broder, 1987: 334). He refuses to acknowledge this as an ideology and maintains that it does not affect reporting of the news.

A press outsider, sociologist Herbert Gans (1978), also delineated what he termed a "paraideology" amongst the press. Like Broder, Gans identified this paraideology as reformist; he argued that the news selected by the media has tended to affirm many key reformist values in the American polity. One of those values has been "altruistic democracy," a value that incorporates the sanctity of racial integration.

If what Broder and Gans both indicate is true, then reporters and editors would surely shy away from stories or potential stories that are dissonant with the values of altruistic democracy and racial integration. Injuries sustained by white males under affirmative action is precisely such a topic.

Lichter, Rothman, and Lichter have published a detailed study of a systematic sample of the 238 "men and women who put together the news at America's most important media outlets—the media elite" (1986: 21). The Lichters and Rothman found that 54 percent identified themselves as liberal, while only 17 percent were conservative. The predominantly white, college-educated males heavily favored liberal sources over business or conservative sources in obtaining data on controversial issues. Compared to a sample of businessmen given the same social science perception tests, the journalists were far more liberal.

With specific regard to the affirmative action issue, Lichter et al. offered little new data. They briefly compared the responses of their samples of journalists and businessmen to a report on the *Bakke* case. They found that the majority of both groups summarized the article in a straightfoward or neutral manner. But "among those remembering only a pro-affirmative action side, journalists outnumbered businessmen by 62 to 38 percent" (1986: 65). Lichter et al. cited another survey of 3,000 reporters and editors, in which 81 percent of the journalists voiced approval of affirmative action for minorities versus 57 percent of the public.

The findings of Lichter et al. with regard to coverage of busing by *Time*, *The New York Times*, the CBS evening news, and *The Washington Post* during 1970–79 suggest a positive portrayal of affirmative action. The authors found "a slight but consistent tilt in favor of pro-busing arguments. At all four media outlets, the majority of arguments coded presented busing in a favorable light" (1986: 233). Furthermore, "the anti-busing arguments were somewhat more likely to be criticized when they did appear" (1986: 234).

The liberal paraideology (to use Gan's term) of the press does not necessarily bias treatment of a given story or issue. More insidiously, the ideology and its taboos can deflect coverage and analysis of an issue or event altogether. As we shall see in the following chapter, when a spiral-of-silence situation is developing around an issue, neglect or censorship by the mass media can have enormous impact. Lack of a conservative counter-force in the media and considerable evidence of regional bias centered around New York (and *The New York Times* in particular) compound and reinforce such processes.[3]

Preview of the New McCarthyism

Joseph Sobran (1987) takes a darker, more critical view of contemporary journalism's liberal/progressive underpinnings. Sobran argues that this ideology has become deeply embedded in the thought, language and every-day etiquette of journalists and intellectual elites. A tiny violation of this ideology/protocol can be devastating, getting one labeled as racist, among other things. The elements of Sobran's analysis are intriguing:

The progressives' own value judgements don't have to be stated. They're built into the form of the stories themselves. The forces of the Past come equipped with a discernible set of traits: bigotry, greed, hate, selfishness, ignorance, zealotry, ex-tremism—terms that by now all have a "right-wing" whiff about them. Ever hear of a liberal or a left-wing bigot or hate-group?

By the same token, the forces of the Future can be discerned by their compassion, idealism, hope, intelligence, openness to new ideas. . . .

The mythology also generates an etiquette, a set of progressive proprieties, breach of which can mean embarrassment and even political ruin. . . . The media carefully observe the progressive etiquette, beginning with diction: "black," "gay," "spokesperson." One of liberalism's great coups has been to transmute ideology into etiquette: A code of behavior in minutiae is awkward to argue with. The wrong opinion, the wrong word, can be a headline-making "gaffe," a social blunder, disclosing lack of compassion, unraised consciousness, "insensitivity."

And "Racism." What's that?

It used to mean something definable: a belief in the superiority of one race. . . . The word now has no definition and would lose most of its utility if it did. It's a piece of liberal billingsgate, a name without a thing, though liberal social philosophers discuss it as if it were a real substance. . . . It's not up to anyone to decide whether he himself is a "racist." It's not a matter of squaring things with meanings anymore. We're in ideological wonderland now. If the relevant opinion cartel declares you "racist," you're racist. . . .

Think of all the energy expended nowadays *avoiding* being declared "racist" (or "sexist" or "homophobic"). The charges emanate from amorphous clouds of attitude and amount to cues to others of like attitude to look, note, smear, ostracize, boycott, denounce, deplore, or bomb, as time and means afford. An informal defamation league takes care of these matters. (1987: 33–34)

The implications of Sobran's analysis regarding the mass media's treatment of affirmative action are clear: speaking or writing incorrectly about the issue can get even the most well-meaning person labeled racist.

In his saga of busing in Boston, *Common Ground*, J. Anthony Lukas found that the press in Boston cooperated in a well-intentioned conspiracy, engaging in pro-busing, anti-Irish self-censorship to, in the words of an operations manager at the NBC outlet, "'use television to create an atmosphere of compliance with Judge Garrity's order'" (1985: 501). Lukas quoted a key reporter for the *Boston Globe* as stating, "'If they [white Boston Irish] don't like integration, we'll shove it down their throats'" (1985: 504).

Sobran's and Lukas's observations suggest more than the operation of a mere paraideology. Such descriptions suggest a more insidious form of censorship and thought control, which, in the next chapter, I shall describe as the New McCarthyism.

NOTES

1. Affirmative action–related articles were searched for under the *Reader's Guide* headings of "Discrimination," "Discrimination in Education," "Discrimination in Employment," and "U.S. Government, President's Commission on Equal Employment Opportunities" (the latter subsequently classified as a government agency). Articles dealing primarily with sexism or Title IX were excluded unless the article title included a direct reference to quotas or affirmative action. Beginning with the March 1975–February 1974 issue, a new category of "Minorities" (along with various subcategories) was included. The March 1979–February 1980 volume also included affirmative action articles under a newly added category, "Blacks."

2. On the other hand, the effect of affirmative action programs upon educational quality has sporadically surfaced with regard to athletics. In an article well in advance of its time, Roger Rappoport wrote in his *New Times* article on "The Illiterate Quarterback" (October 16, 1978: 32-38):

Dumb jocks have been a standing joke at American colleges for decades. . . . But in recent years, this amusing syndrome has taken a frightening turn as coaches exploit special admissions programs to recruit minority athletes who would ordinarily never qualify for college. Yesterday's dumb jock has become today's illiterate player, unable to even read the team playbook.

Widespread public debate over the relationship between athletics, minorities, and education awaited a 1982 proposal by the only black female on the governing board of the Los Angeles Unified School District. In that year, Rita Walters proposed, fought for, and won enactment of the "C" average requirement for student participation in extracurricular activities. Drawing upon the work of sociologist Harry Edwards, Walters argued that blacks who sacrificed their academic studies to the lure of lucrative careers in sports were "less likely to wind up like O.J. than with No J. (no job)." Walter's proposal immediately gained national attention and sparked a two-evening debate on ABC's *Nightline*. Similar rules have been enacted elsewhere, and arguments over minimum-standards proposals for athletes continue to spark debate in public school districts and in the National College Athletics Association (NCAA).

Perhaps this was simply an issue whose time had come. A movement for upgrading educational standards was clearly in the air, as evidenced by the government-sponsored report "A Nation at Risk," which was published the same year as Walter's proposal. However, some Los Angeles news commentators pointed out that such a minimum-standards proposal probably had to come from a black authority figure. It was assumed that any such rule requiring a C average would likely hurt black athletes more than any other group and that any white who proposed such a policy might have been called a racist.

There are many additional examples of avoidance of affirmative action in related contexts.

Critics might rightly complain that the evidence is anecdoctal. They would be correct, in part. Still, in combination with the other data in this article, I would argue that the examples cited in this note are broadly illustrative of a general pattern of inattention to or hypersensitivity about affirmative action in the mass media.

3. Conservative author and editor R. Emmett Tyrell, Jr., has bemoaned the lack of any conservative counter-culture in the press and media. He has complained that, even during the Reagan presidency, conservative writers and intellectuals remained insular and that their views have had little impact upon the press and media (Tyrell, 1987). On East Coast regionalism and the influence of *The New York Times* in agenda-setting in the press, see *Los Angeles Times* "East Coast Bias Colors the Media" (November 17, 1988) and "Read All About It—If It's In New York," (November 18, 1988).

Chapter 8

THE SPIRAL OF SILENCE
AND THE NEW McCARTHYISM

In the winter of 1982, a student whom I shall call "Bill" informed me after class that another faculty member, Professor X, was being called "racist" by a small clique of minority students. The charges had been voiced in a class taught by another faculty member and in various informal student gatherings.

"I respect Professor X," said Bill, "and I think what they're saying is bullshit. But I think he should know what's going on before it hits the fan. If he doesn't know, you should tell him."

A couple of days later, behind closed doors, I informed Professor X of the problem. He was stunned, saddened, and, not least of all, afraid. Professor X had received tenure the year before. But tenure was a thin shield against charges of racism and we both knew it. Initially, Professor X had absolutely no idea how such charges could have come his way. We were both aware of the irony of my informing him of such accusations, for I had voiced fears to him and to others that I might be called "racist" because of my research on affirmative action. (See "Doing Affirmative Action Research in California" at the end of Chapter 9.)

There was no formal complaint, no hearing before the dean or anything else. Just name-calling, which faded away. But the effects lingered on.

In 1988, I asked Professor X to re-assess the matter. He had no trouble recalling the event. He ascribed the incident to four minority students' misperceptions of his lectures on family structure and mobility. He had cited research in class which indicated that having large numbers of children at an early age—especially out of wedlock—was likely to inhibit upward social mobility. The four minority students, schooled in other classes against "blaming the victim," thought Professor X was doing just that and attacking their way of life. Not coincidentally, Professor X remarked, the accusing students had received low grades in previous courses they had taken from him.

This behind-the-scenes name-calling heightened Professor X's sensitivity. Already shy about mentioning matters of race to student audiences, he now rarely, if ever, mentions race as a variable in social research in his classroom. In spite of the fact that race and ethnicity often appear in the statistical data of his subject matter, Professor X prefers to "leave such matters to the text." When it comes to race, Professor X censors himself. Professor X is hardly alone. Most other social scientists and university faculty have felt the chill.

Self-censoring, "chilled" faculty reflect the power of ideological taboos that have dominated American intellectual discourse for nearly twenty years. Yet "chilled" and "taboos" are not quite sufficiently precise terms to understand how intellectual thought in America has been self-censored. The steamroller metaphor set forth in the first chapter comes somewhat closer to the process of what has happened. But there are more precise concepts to understand how people have perceived what they can and cannot discuss, regardless of public opinion.

Attempts to ignore or suppress Stanley Greenberg's research by politicians and the mass media suggest some degree of formal censorship. Far more powerful than formal censorship has been massive, informal censorship, which German sociologist Elisabeth Noelle-Neumann has aptly termed the "spiral of silence." The spiral of silence, in turn, must be linked with another reinforcing concept, cognitive dissonance. The operation of both of these processes has produced what is best described as a New McCarthyism.

THE SPIRAL OF SILENCE

Elisabeth Noelle-Neumann's spiral of silence theory attempts to explain how people may misperceive public opinion because one faction feels much freer than others to speak out in support of its views. The more vocal group's views, in fact, may not be the majority; nevertheless, they may become the majority, or considerably increase their numbers, because the populace perceives such openly expressed views as the majority and wishes to conform to the supposed majority view (1974; 1977; 1984).

Noelle-Neumann maintains that human beings are strongly attuned to the opinions of others. This sensitivity to public opinion is like a "social skin." Public opinion can be a potent source of social control in that most people find it more comfortable to conform to majority opinion. A long history of scholarship, coupled with more recent social psychological experiments, strongly suggests that people prefer to change their views rather than differ from majority opinion. Since we are social beings, humans fear isolation.

Noelle-Neumann acknowledged her indebtedness to Alexis de Toc-queville's concept of the "tyranny of the majority." But Noelle-Neumann wished to see how a majority opinion may arise out of a minority viewpoint. The process may build in a spiral, that is, the perceived majority group becomes even more emboldened to speak out while those not so perceived progressively go mute. Hence the spiral of silence.

Noelle-Neumann's initial interest in the spiral of silence occurred in the context of German elections in the late 1960s. Public opinion polls showed public support evenly divided between the Social Democrats and the Christian Democrats. Yet a student of Noelle-Neumann quickly removed a "Social Democrat" button from her coat because she had encountered too much hostility. The student had falsely perceived that she was being labeled as a proponent of an unpopular cause. Though she had the support of at least half the public, the student was made to feel quite otherwise. Those who supported the opposition were vociferous in their support and behaved as if public opinion were with them. In describing the political confrontation between the Social Democrats and the Christian Democrats in Germany at the end of the 1960s, Noelle-Neumann noted that originally there was an even split between the two parties.

Those who were convinced the new Ospolitik was right thought their beliefs eventually would be adopted by everyone. So these people expressed themselves openly, and self-confidently defended their views. Those who rejected the Ospolitik felt themselves left out; they withdrew, and fell silent.

This very restraint made the view that was receiving vocal support appear to be stronger than it really was and the other view weaker. Observations made in one context spread to another and encouraged people either to proclaim their views or to swallow them and keep quiet until, in a spiraling process, the one view dominated the public scene and the other disappeared from public awareness as its adherents became mute. This is the process that can be called a "spiral of silence." (1984: 5)

I shall not and cannot statistically test Noelle-Neumann's spiral of silence concept as it applies to public opinion on affirmative action. Nevertheless, the concept fits much of the data contained in this book and is a useful, sensitizing tool in understanding public opinion on affirmative action.[1]

Data on public opinion cited in Chapter 2 decisively demonstrate that the majority of Americans have been overwhelmingly opposed to affirmative action as quotas or preferential treatment. Yet interview data gathered here and elsewhere show that people perceive the pro-quota viewpoint as the majority viewpoint. Why? The spiral of silence suggests an answer.

It became obvious to the student interviewers and to me that we were cutting in on the spiral of silence simply by interviewing the thirty-two white males. It was sometimes even more obvious in background conversations with corporate officials or other corporate or government insiders. People were surprised to be asked about "the other side" of affirmative action.

The vast majority of views they had heard or read were either pro–affirmative action or held that it was a non-debatable issue, which had already been decided. As Noelle-Neumann had described, they had detected what they thought was the predominant opinion on the issue and acted accordingly. Thus, those interviewed for this study (and those quoted in secondary sources as well) were guarded and hesitant in stating anti-quota views even to friends and co-workers. They did not know that anti-quota views have been the majority.

Affirmative action proponents have been able to accelerate the spiral of silence because thay have been able to invoke collective guilt over past treatment of blacks in the United States. They have been able to target opponents as racists. The mass media were largely silent on affirmative action or took a pro–affirmative action stance. No wonder, then, most of those interviewed for this book felt their critical views of affirmative action were not held by a majority of Americans. Indeed, only two knew of public opinion polls on the issue at all, and only one of the two had an accurate idea of the results.

To compare a hypothetical contemporary situation with that which inspired Noelle-Neumann's interest in the spiral of silence: imagine an American college student wearing a button which stated "Get Rid of Affirmative Action Quotas"? The results would be at least as provocative as those encountered by the German student who wore the "wrong" political button.

The Role of Cognitive Dissonance

Cognitive dissonance has reinforced the spiral of silence on affirmative action. Cognitive dissonance occurs when two cognitive elements clash: two opposing attitudes, or an attitude and a contradictory situation, (Zajonic, 1968). In the case of affirmative action, cognitive dissonance can easily arise when the values of equality are juxtaposed with the history of unequal treatment of blacks. The ideal of equality and the legacy of slavery and discrimination contradict each other. This conflict generates tension, embarrassment, and guilt in the minds of most Americans.

People have a tendency to try to assuage guilt and resolve dissonance. Therefore, egalitarian or compensatory programs aimed at redressing past discrimination have a natural appeal in restoring cognitive balance: the imbalance and guilt caused by discrimination against blacks in the face of American commitments to equality can be eased by efforts to make up for past discrimination. Obviously, cognitive dissonance has been a powerful tool for proponents of affirmative action of all types. This is one reason affirmative action debates almost always focus upon blacks rather than the other minority groups (Hispanics, Filipinos, Pacific Islanders, Asian/Indians, and so forth) who have quietly been included in many race-conscious programs.

Cognitive dissonance over past treatment of blacks is woven into nearly every argument for and against affirmative action from settings of private discourse to the professional literature. Evidence of this same tension and guilt surfaced in varying degrees with nearly all interviews with white males conducted for this book. Manning Greene specifically used the term "cognitive dissonance" in explaining the awkward and embarrassed response of his friends. Other subjects mentioned past discrimination against blacks but protested that they were not responsible for this and that the current generation of white males should not suffer for the sins of the past. And, as mentioned in previous chapters, there were the obligatory neutralizations: "I'm not a racist, but. . . . "

This climate of intimidation and guilt cannot be overstated with regard to the expression of critical views on affirmative action. As was seen in the previous chapter, this social psychological setting was fostered by the neglect of affirmative action as an issue by the mass media.

Noelle-Neumann maintained that the role of the mass media in fostering a spiral of silence is complex and crucial. The previous chapter demonstrated that the mass media ignored and avoided affirmative action as an issue and avoided or sought to neutralize the policies' impact on white males. Public opinion polls on the issue were not well publicized. Instead, the media have highlighted the contradiction between past treatment of blacks and the ideal of equality.

THE OLD AND THE NEW McCATHYISM: PARALLELS

The post–World War Two phenomenon known as McCarthyism would seem to be a good illustration of the spiral of silence. Though Joseph McCarthy and anti-communist movements spawned by him never obtained the support of a majority of Americans, vocal anti-communist minorities nevertheless had enormous impact. Anti-McCarthyism opinion was chilled by individual fears of being labeled "communist."

The social forces suppressing criticism of affirmative action for the past twenty years have been strikingly similar to processes underpinning 1950s McCarthyism. First and foremost is the climate of fear and intimidation generated by both McCathyism and affirmative action. The steamroller methaphor fits both phenomena well. Name-calling and guilt-by-accusation were employed with deadly effects by both anti-communist groups in the 1950s and by pro–affirmative action people in the 1970s and 1980s. In the heyday of McCarthyism, people feared being labeled "communist" or "fellow-traveler." As we have seen in previous chapters, affirmative action critics have been fearful of being called racist for so much as raising questions about such policies.

As administrative social movements, policies spawned by both McCarthyism and affirmative action promoted behind-the-scenes screening of personnel in terms of, respectively, political affiliations or race/sex criteria. Blacklisting for suspected political activities is not unlike giving preference for race/ethnicity or gender or the exclusion of those with anti-quota views (see Chapter 9). The semi-secretive, legally ambiguous nature of both processes made it impossible to get straight answers from employers and government agencies. Possible divergence between real reasons and official reasons for personnel decisions—always a source of suspicion—was an even greater possibility under these screening processes.

Obviously, different groups supported McCarthyism and affirmative action; yet both of these mass movements can be seen as egalitarian and anti-elitist. McCarthyism has been portrayed as an "extremist" reaction in response to the "structural strains" in post–World War II America such as ethnic rivalries and America's new international role in the world. McCarthyism also has been seen as an attack on upper-class, white, Anglo-Saxon institutions such as Ivy League schools and the State Department. (See the articles by Richard Hofstadter, Seymour Lipset, Talcott Parsons, in Bell, 1964).

A similar system-stress interpretation can be advanced with regard to the rise of affirmative action. Sources of structural strain giving rise to affirmative action have been the civil rights movement, the revolution of rising expectations, black/white polarization (or fears of such) and collective urban violence of the 1960s. The movement of large numbers of women out of the home and into the job market can also be seen as another source of strain. Even more explicitly than McCarthyism, affirmative action can be seen as an attack upon elitist (and racist) Anglo-Saxon institutions and standards.

A conflict perspective on both affirmative action and McCarthyism is that both phenomena were manipulated by political and economic elites. Michael Rogin has argued that elites also capitalized upon McCarthyism (Rogin, 1967). Rogin contended that McCarthyism was not an irrational, agrarian, populist, anti-elitist movement produced by "structural strain." It was not a revolt against the elite, for some elites backed McCarthy. McCarthy did have "real support at the grass roots," with Catholic Democratic workers and southerners. But McCarthyism drew much of its power from conservative business elites and conservative Southern senators. McCarthy and his supporters were countenanced by moderate Republicans and even supported to some extent by liberal Democratic elites.

Fred Cook also concluded that elites either backed McCarthyism or simply withered in the face of it:

On the highest levels of intellect and leadership, the abdication of responsibility was all but complete. The Democratic-liberal establishment, which should have provided a rallying point, virtually disintegrated before the first onslaught and sought to camouflage itself by riding to the hounds with the foe. (Cook, 1971: 18)

The virulent fanaticisms of the past were truly fringe movements; they did not have behind them the power and prestige of the respectable and influential in American society. McCarthyism was different. It had the all-out support of ultra-conservative big business interests in rebellion against the twentieth century." (1971: 570)

If one substitutes "Republican-business establishment" for "liberal-Democratic establishment" in Cook's first paragraph, the paragraph aptly depicts the non-response to affirmative action. In the second paragraph, "affirmative action" can be substituted for "McCarthyism" and "ultra-liberal political, academic, and mass media interests" for "ultra-conservative big business interests." In chapter 10, it will be seen that a small number of institutional elites (notably in civil rights, the media, and government) promoted affirmative action, while other major elites acquiesced.

Whatever the role of elites in affirmative action and McCarthyism, the general parallels are strong. There is no denying the official bullying, the baiting and labeling, the manipulation of guilt and fear, the complicity of the media and institutional paralyses produced by both McCarthyism and affirmative action. Both were personnel screening practices designed with honorable intentions, though the means were less than honorable. Both processes could dissolve into crazes with lasting results: even today, employees of state universities in California must sign a "loyalty oath," a holdover from McCarthyist fervor. And both movements could run over victims who were too startled and disheartened to raise a protest while co-workers and friends looked the other way.

Affirmative Action as Craze

The term "craze" has been vaguely defined in the literature. The concept often has been applied to short-term outburst of widespread, irrational behavior which, depending on the definition, may be based upon fantasies of wish fulfillment. In this regard, economic booms are crazes as well as political bandwagons and more minor phenomenon such as hula-hoops. (On definition of crazes, see Smelser, 1962: 170-221; Turner and Killian, 1987: 146-148.) The term *craze* is often confused with the terms *fashion* and *fad*. There is also conceptual overlap between long-term, large-scale crazes and concepts such as "mass movement" or "norm-oriented movement" (Smelser, 1962; Turner and Killian, 1987).

The concept of craze has also been applied to deeper and longer-lived mass behavior such as the witchcraft crazes in Europe from the late Middle Ages through the seventeenth century. The McCarthy period in recent U.S. history has also been termed a "witch hunt" or craze or a manifestation of extremism. In both McCarthyism and the European witch hunts, unexamined beliefs and solutions became accepted, charges were made, action was taken. Heretics were punished. The population became cowed, if not terrorized. They simply went along with the craze, fearful of any other course of action and paralyzed by fear or guilt. (On the social origins of the witch crazes, see Nelson, 1970; Russell, 1972; Boyer and Nissenbaum, 1974). Much of this applies to affirmative action practices.

Forbes writer Bob Tamarkin clearly saw such parallels in his article, "Is Equal Opportunity Turning Into a Witch Hunt?" Writing in 1978, at the height of affirmative action efforts under the Carter administration, Tamarkin claimed that business was the most vulnerable target of government agencies and activist special interest groups who were "obsessively" pursuing corrective quotas.

On the other hand, it might be argued that colleges and universities have been more vulnerable than business to affirmative action pressures. As will be seen in the next chapter, academic institutions, long subject to "fashionable trends" in hiring (see Burstein, 1982: 11), have been ideologically susceptible to liberal or radical policies. Emotional responses to recent racial incidents on university campuses have undoubtedly contributed to emotional campaigns —if not outright crazes—to increase use of race-and-gender preferences (*Chronicles of Higher Education*, April 26, 1989).

Some of the accounts of affirmative action in Chapter 3, along with reports by individuals in Chapters 4 and 5, suggest that the drive for affirmative action has, at times, taken on the characteristics of a craze in certain organizational settings. That is, administrators appear to have gotten carried away with hiring by race and gender. Either with or without government threats, in an effort to make up for past discrimination, minorities and women have been hurriedly hired regardless of meritocratic criteria.

Examples from Chapter 3 and subsequent individual interviews would include: The quota craze in the California Department of Corrections; the attempt by the California Highway Patrol to recruit Mexican nationals to increase numbers of Hispanic patrolmen; Prudential Insurance's forced agreement with the Department of Labor that the company would locate inadequately trained people it rejected and offer those same persons remedial training and jobs; and the attempt to impose racial balance on Los Angeles High School academic decathlon teams, complete with "visual inspection." The case of California bureaucrat Robert Boggs, who was ordered to hire ten minority clerk-typists regardless of whether they could type, and the "only-whites-can-be-racists" memo circulated within the New York State Insurance Fund are two more examples. Bank administrator Bob Allen, describing affirmative action pressures in his environment, suggested irrational, craze-tinged behavior when he remarked that "everyone was accusing everyone else of being racist" and "we didn't know which statistics to use" in measuring policy compliance.

May and Houston reported on perceptions of craze-like behavior in their *Los Angeles Times* article:

Some affirmative action officers have been accused of overzealousness, of hiring "basket cases" solely in order to meet quotas. McCarthy, a white Boston police officer, charges that the force has actually hired criminals and illiterates in its efforts to boost minority numbers. "I think your professionalism and your standards are being dropped down." (1985:14)

The emotionally charged pursuit of unexamined goals with legally suspect strategies has been a hallmark of both the Old and the New McCarthyism. Dogmatism, a climate of fear and intimidation, and the threat or actual use of lethal labeling, generated self-censorship and a spiral of silence in both periods. The Old and the New McCarthyism also produced thousands—if not millions—of invisible victims.

In the previous chapter, we examined the mass media's role in promoting a spiral of silence and New McCarthyist taboos on discussion of affirmative action and related issues. The next chapter deals with an equally important source of such taboos and censorship: the university and, especially, the field of sociology.

NOTE

1. Carl Auerbach (1988) has also utilized the spiral-of-silence theory to explain data on attitudes toward affirmative action among faculty and students gathered by the Carnegie Commission on Higher Education during 1975. The Carnegie data indicate that large majorities of faculty and students opposed preferential forms of affirmative action. Auerbach suggests that the acutal majority is not perceived as such; hence faculty and students hesitate to criticize affirmative action. I shall discuss Auerbach's findings in somewhat greater detail in the next chapter.

Chapter 9

AFFIRMATIVE ACTION, THE UNIVERSITY, AND SOCIOLOGY

If we are to understand affirmative action fully, we must examine that policy's origins in its effects upon one of its primary sources: the academic community, especially the social sciences. How strongly did the spiral of silence and the New McCarthyism affect discussion and implementation of affirmative action in university settings? Did the universities practice what they preached on affirmative action? How actively did academicians, especially sociologists, study affirmative action, and what did they find?

It will be useful here to examine the university's links to the outside world, especially to politics. Of particular interest is the relationship between sociology and society. Sociology has been the flagship discipline of the welfare state and its philosophy. The fates of sociology, welfare-state liberalism, and affirmative action have been strongly interrelated.

THE UNIVERSITY AND WELFARE-STATE LIBERALISM

Although there has long been a general link between political liberalism and university life, the relationship became much stronger during the activist 1960s. Writing at the end of that decade, sociologist Alvin Gouldner observed that the politics of welfare-state liberalism had become the "official ideology" in wide sectors of the universities. This political establishment, he argued, has "reasons to lie" and is quite capable of functioning as an "intellectual mafia."

Political liberalism today instead verges on being an official ideology of wide sectors of the American university community as well as a broader strata of American life.

For many American academicians, liberalism is also an operating code that links academic life to the political machinery of the Democratic Party.

Far from being the conscientious code of isolated individuals, much of liberalism today is the well-financed ideology of a loosely organized but coherent Establishment. It is the dominant ideology of a powerful group that sprawls across the academic community; that is integrated with politics; that has its opinion leaders in various publications; that has its heroes whose myths are recited. Liberalism, then, is the mythos of one of the dominating American establishments; it is not simply the hard-won faith of a happy few. As the ideology of an establishment, such official liberalism has things to protect. It has reasons to lie. It has all the social mechanisms available to any establishment by which it can reward those who tell the right lies, and punish and suppress those who tell the wrong truths. In its meaner moments, it is an intellectual mafia.(1968: 112)

Sociologists Everett C. Ladd and Seymour Lipset argued that there was more political diversity within the university community than Gouldner suggested. Utilizing survey data, they found that liberalism was most deeply rooted in the social sciences, especially at the high-prestige research universities. Technical and applied professional teachers at community colleges, on the other hand, were quite conservative. The differences between the two groups "are of a magnitude rarely found in opinon research. The range of difference between the two groups runs from 40 to 60 percentage points on various questions" (1975: 234).

Though they did not confirm Gouldner's view of a coercive welfare-state liberalism, Ladd and Lipset nonetheless found the ideology had a powerful influence, especially at high-status institutions.[1]

In 1985, philosopher Nicholas Capaldi once again sounded Alvin Gouldner's theme of an orthodox and controlling liberal university establishment. Capaldi described the dominance of "doctrinaire liberalism" in the universities. He stressed that this ideology has been grounded in a taken-for-granted, metaphysical assumption: sociocultural determinism.

The central premise of sociocultural determinism holds that all human behavior is learned: people are a product of their social and cultural environment. Biological determinism, on the other hand, is anathema to this orthodoxy. The angry response to "sociobiology" in the 1970s was evidence of the clash in perspectives. "Racist," "sexist," and even "Nazi" have been some of the names hurled at sociobiologists.

THE PUBLIC REVOLT AGAINST
WELFARE-STATE LIBERALISM

The legitimacy and popularity of liberalism, the welfare state, and academically inspired social engineering schemes collapsed in the late 1970s. The passage of California's Proposition 13 heralded more tax revolts and the overwhelming victories of Ronald Reagan ushered in an era of "Reaganomics" and laissez-faire thought. By 1985, the bitter theme of the 1985 annual meetings for the Society for the Study of Social Problems was "Winding Down the Welfare State."

In addition to skepticism among the general public, the assumptions of welfare-state liberalism were subjected to increasing challenge from within the social sciences. Charles Murray (1984b) was one of the first sociologists to analyze extensively the failures and unanticipated consequences of the social-science–inspired social reforms of the past twenty years. Murray contended that policies regarding welfare, the family, crime, education, and jobs, actually made problems worse.

Initially, Murray's analyses met with a storm of criticism. But even Murray's most severe critics sometimes found broad points of agreement with him. Too much "folly and vice," Christopher Jencks concurred, has been "rewarded" by social engineering schemes (1985a).

Also by the 1980s, black scholars had begun to voice concern over increasing problems of black, inner-city families. Minority gangs and drug-related crime in the inner cities could no longer be ignored. The philosophy of rehabilitation in criminal justice became less viable as demands for certain and more punitive measures escalated.

The change in the political climate was reflected in the concerns of undergraduate students. The public sector had long been the haven for liberal arts graduates during the 1960s and 1970s (Littwin, 1986). But in the 1980s, the public sector was crippled by tax revolts and recessions. The liberal, change-oriented, public-spirited philosophy of the 1960s fell out of fashion. Occupational prospects for liberal arts students were considerably diminished. Therefore, the humanities and social sciences suffered spectacular enrollment declines as students stampeded toward majors they saw as more "marketable"—namely, business administration and engineering. Within the social sciences, economics and psychology suffered least, probably because those two fields remain more ideologically diverse and private-sector oriented than, for example, history or sociology.

Liberal reforms that proved problematic in society also turned troublesome in the university. Gross (1978), Capaldi (1985), and Bloom (1987) have described the havoc wrought within the universities when unqualified or unprepared minority students were admitted. Grade inflation took off; curriculum requirements were watered down. Also inflated were black and minority expectations, which were soon dashed by high drop-out rates or other kinds of disappointment, such as the high rate of failure by minority students on teacher competency tests and bar exams.

In spite of the bad news pouring in on enrollments, student attitudes, and the fate of social reform programs, university politics have remained relatively radical/liberal. Irving Kristol contended that college faculty are still "casting their votes for George McGovern" and that "These universities are living in a time warp, in a kind of self-imposed exile from

American realities. . . . For as the American people have edged rightward, our universities as institutions have moved rapidly and massively to the left" (1986).

These trends have been evident in the rapid acceptance by university officials of affirmative action/preferential treatment. In his analysis of academic perceptions of affirmative action, Paul Burstein argued that universities have always been susceptible to "fashionable trends" in employment (anti-Semitism, exclusion of blacks, women, etc.). Thus, "affirmative action and even reverse discrimination can enter the precincts of universities more easily than those of many other types of employers" (1982: 11).

Letters showing department chairs searching for "a black" or "a Chicano" to hire were published in the journal *Minerva* (1976: 14, pp. 97–117). (The article is reprinted in Appendix 6 of this book.) The article has rarely been quoted but obviously has much to say, especially about the back stage nature of affirmative action as fashionable trend. The letters, written before Allan Bakke's lawsuit in 1978, are refreshingly candid documents and demonstrate the early power of the affirmative action movement in academe. (Also in the pre-Bakke days, candidates were more frequently and explicitly told that they could not be considered because they were white males.)

Critics will charge that the letters in the *Minerva* article and accounts contained in Chapter 3 are merely anecdotal evidence. So be it. But how else would one otherwise obtain such candid information, especially in the wake of reverse discrimination lawsuits?

There is debate over the impact of affirmative action as registered in numbers of female/minority faculty who have been hired or promoted. But measurement of such data has been hampered by sampling problems and varying rates of survey questionnaire returns by various subgroups, especially minorities (Huber, 1985).

Howard Bowen and Jack Schuster (1986) found substantial progress for both women and minorities. They found that "given the substantial progress in the numbers of women in academic careers, and in their acceptance and promotion, one may reasonably expect that persisting discrimination in status and reward for women will be largely eliminated in the years ahead" (1986: 57). They found that the percentage of faculty positions held by women has risen from 20.9 percent in 1970–71 to 27.0 percent in 1981–82. Bowen and Schuster also found that the percentage of minority faculty has risen from 6.2 in 1973 to 9.1 in 1980, though they also maintain that non-Asian minorities are underrepresented (1986: 58–60).

The debates over hiring and promoting women and non-Asian minorities in university faculties almost always ignore a central dilemma. Few non-Asian minority students have gone on to graduate school in the fields that are in demand: the physical sciences, business, and engineering.

In 1986, no blacks earned Ph.D.'s in geometry, astronomy, astrophysics, accoustics, theoretical chemistry, geology, aerospace engineering, or computer engineering. All told, only 14 engineering and 25 physical science doctorates went to blacks out of more than 8,000 awarded—less than one-half of one percent. (Hirschorn, 1988: 26)

Non-Asian minorities who do obtain bachelor or master's degrees in the latter fields are lured by much higher salaries into the private sector.

Reports on academic affirmative action nearly always ignore imbalances of supply and demand in the academic marketplace. The result is that universities have been stampeded into the use of "set-aside" positions and "fast-track" hiring for minorities in the overcrowded and highly competitive humanities and social sciences (Hirschorn, 1988; also the items in the "Affirmative Action for College Faculty" section in Chapter 3). While blacks and non-Asian minority Ph.D.s are more plentiful in those areas, so are whites: applicant-to-position ratios about 300-to-1 are not at all uncommon in those fields (Jackson, 1986; Pierce, 1986).

AFFIRMATIVE ACTION AND DISSENT

Pressures to silence criticism of affirmative action in the universities commenced with the implementation of the policies. When he first voiced his objections to affirmative action quotas at a Harvard colloquium in the early 1970s, Norman Podhoretz remarked that "When I finished, the questions were so charged with hatred that I found myself wondering if a public reading of *Mein Kampf* could have elicited greater outrage. Almost everyone who took the anti-quota position in those days had similar tales to tell" (1979: 302).

One of the first sociologists to take an early stand against quotas was race relations expert Pierre van den Berghe. He published several articles attacking the concept of quotas, appeared as an opponent of quotas on television programs, engaged in professional debate forums, and resigned from his position on the Du Bois–Johnson–Frazier Award Committee of the American Sociological Association. Van den Berghe's comments were unique at the time in that his remarks were framed in a leftist (or "European Social Democratic") perspective (1971; 1972; 1984). But the opposition he encountered was so intense that van den Berghe withdrew because "it became obvious that race was beyond the domain of rational discourse in America" (1988).

In their 1975 book *The Divided Academy*, Ladd and Lipset observed that "few in academe openly resist the policy of judging the commitment of universities to equality for minorities and women in terms of willingness to use quotas" (1975: 306). As a minority graduate student at Berkeley during the early 1970s, Richard Rodriguez (1982) noticed the tendencies of the faculty there to keep criticisms of affirmative action to themselves, in spite of ongoing and obvious reverse discrimination against white male doctoral candidates.

After Lee Nisbet stated his objections to affirmative action in an article in *The Humanist*, his friends and colleagues immediately "expressed surprise and dismay over my new found 'conservatism'" (in B. Gross, 1978: 50–53). Sociologist Stephen D. Johnson published the results of his studies on the relationship between reverse discrimination and aggressive behavior in psychology journals (1980a; 1980b) because he felt strongly that he "would have had trouble getting these articles published in sociology journals due to the general liberal bias of many sociologists" (1982).

By 1978, psychologist Joseph Adelson observed that the university seemed unable to "resist the idea of its bigotry which is a major source of its current loss of dignity and self-respect. . . . Dissent [on quotas] is kept 'inside,' either inside the self, or inside the dialogue (as in the hinting and winking among 'insiders') or within the 'system'" (1978: 25). Adelson was counseled by a colleague not to release data that indicated the futility of affirmative action at the University of Michigan because "many of our colleagues become agitated when confronted with unpleasant facts about our quota system" (p. 25).

The most outspoken critics of affirmative action have had to possess tenure or other forms of job security. Nathan Glazer, a tenured faculty member in the School of Education at Harvard published the first book-length critique of affirmative action, *Affirmative Discrimination*. The review of Glazer's book by Jack Douglas (a tenured professor at the University of California, San Diego) was almost as iconoclastic and insightful as the book itself. Douglas spoke for many when he wrote:

The conflicts over racial and ethnic equality involve some of the great moral passions of the American people. . . . Little wonder that these conflicts so easily become melodramas of moralistic self-presentation and recriminatory denunciation that sweep aside the whisper of reason. . . .

In the social minefields of passionate conflict, the mines are red-hot political labels like "racist," "fascist," "sexist," "hippie," "nigger-lover," etc. The shrapnel consists of expressions of hatred and contempt, social isolation, job discrimination and sometime violence. In an era when such passions are unleashed most people, while feeling some of the passions themselves, become primarily concerned with avoiding the minefields and the bursts of sharpnel. They are anxious not to get involved and thus, not to have publicly visible beliefs. . . . What sociologist today has not sat through seemingly endless committee and departmental meetings in which the things everyong knew were the "really important things" could not be talked about because . . . well, you know. . . . What sociologist today has not felt the fear of being "mislabeled"? . . . Because of all the political passions that have embroiled our academic lives in recent years, we have unintentionally built up complex forms of community censorship and some cunning ways of talking around our collegial censors.

Nathan Glazer is one of the now endangered species of courageous (or foolhardy?) sociologists who insist on invading our American minefield of racial and ethic conflicts. . . . While many other sociologists are furiously fanning the passions with moralistic labels, he insists on *publishing* (not simply whispering) the things we all know, at least subconsciously, but hope we never have to face up to or, perish the thought, actually say in public. (1977: 539–540; original emphasis)

Tenure protected sociologists such as van den Berghe, Douglas, and Glazer. But tenure and a deanship did not, evidently, protect philosopher Theodore Gross. After he published a critique in *Saturday Review* (1978) of CCNY's open-admission policies, Gross lost his position as dean and moved to another university. Another CUNY professor has stated that he has received death threats for his views against racial quotas (Levin, 1985).

Nor did tenure and scholarly reputation protect University of Chicago sociologist James Coleman from the attempts by radical sociologists to brand him as a racist when he published data in the mid-1970s that busing led to white flight. Coleman recently reflected upon that period of controversy marked by "a tortured period of intellectual isolation," which resulted from his violation of "the strong consensus among social scientists that busing was an unalloyed benefit, and a policy not to be questioned" (1988: 6). The power of that consensus could be seen, Coleman argued, in that similar consensus-challenging research emerged only after senior and securely tenured scholars, such as Coleman, first published their data and took the heat. (Interestingly, Coleman never used the words "liberal" or "egalitarian" consensus; simply "consensus.")

More recently, Rosalind Rosenberg, associate professor of history at Barnard College, has been subjected to severe criticism by pro–affirmative action groups for testifying as an expert witness in defense of Sears Roebuck in that company's protracted battle with the Equal Employment Opportunity Commission. Rosenberg offered evidence in court that there were historical reasons why women might be less likely than men to be interested in or available for the corporation's commission sales jobs. EEOC's expert witnesses argued that the lack of proportional representation of women in commission sales jobs was a direct result of discrimination. Sears won. The judge in the case praised Rosenberg's testimony. But many feminists and academicians have offered anything but praise.

The American Historical Association's Coordinating Committee for Women in the Historical Profession passed an anti-Rosenberg resolution asserting that "as feminist scholars we have a responsibility not to allow our scholarship to be used against the interests of women struggling for equality in our society." ("Interviews with Rosalind Rosenberg," 1986: 21)

Carl Auerbach has pointed out the interesting finding that, though it often has been perceived that academicians are strongly in favor of preferential treatment for minorities and women, survey data gathered by the Carnegie Council on Higher Education in 1975 indicate that most faculty and students have opposed such policies. There were variations in response by discipline, with engineering and medical faculties most strongly opposed to policies of preference, while social work faculties were least opposed.

To explain the apparent paradox of perceived, widespread academic support for affirmative action with survey findings of large majorities opposed to policies of preference, Auerbach drew upon Elisabeth Noelle-Neumann's "spiral of silence" concept, the explanatory model utilized in the previous chapter. Seen with this concept, academics have tried to sense what the majority opinion has been on affirmative action before voicing their own. As with the general public, however, the majority opposed to affirmative action misperceived their own views as being in the minority—and thus, remained silent.

The Carnegie data cited by Auerbach found that a majority of faculty in only one discipline—social work—favored one or both hypothetical models of preferential affirmative action for minority student admissions proposed by the Carnegie researchers —one model with strict goals and timetables and one without. Only 29 percent of all social science faculty favored such programs as did 20 percent of law school faculty, 14 percent of business faculty, 9 percent of engineering faculty, and 19 percent of all faculty included in the surveys (1988: 1238). A similar response pattern was found for preferential treatment in faculty hiring. Sociologists were not differentiated from "social sciences" faculty, but it is reasonable to assume that sociologists were closer to social workers than, say, economists or psychologists.

Student Response to Affirmative Action

The Carnegie survey found that graduate student responses regarding preferential affirmative action for student admissions (with or without goals and timetables) followed a patterns similar to faculty approval of the same items: 47 percent of social work graduate students approved of such policies, 27 percent of social sciences students, 22 percent of all law school students, 13 percent of business students, and 8 percent of engineering students (Auerbach, 1988: 1238). Faculty and student opinions were also similar with regard to the same type of preferential affirmative action for faculty appointments.

For both faculty and students, the spiral of silence operated to keep dissent at a minimum. Though large silent majorities of both faculty and students opposed preferential affirmative action, the more vocal supporters created pressures for acceptance of such programs.

Allan Bloom was no doubt aware of the operation of a spiral of silence on college campuses when he wrote that white students have been "willing by and large to talk themselves into accepting affirmative action as a temporary measure on the way to equality." Still, there are so many contradictions involved in the policy that the final result is that "the tendency among white students is to suppress the whole question, act as though it were not there" (1987: 92).

In a similar vein *The New Republic* (June 27, 1989: 9) observed that affirmative action pressures on campus are such that "whites born after the Civil Rights Act . . . generally accept affirmative action measures that put them at a disadvantage to blacks in the closed economies of university admissions and hiring."

It is difficult to determine the extent to which white resentment over racial preferences and spiral-of-silence pressures have contributed to recent racial incidents on college campuses. But, in newspaper interviews subsequent to such incidents, white students complained of preferential treatment in admissions, use of dual standards, and racial favoritism by college administrators. Both blacks and whites complained that affirmative action quotas have led to stereotyping of non-Asian minority students as unqualified (*The Wall Street Journal*, April 3, 1987: A1; and especially, PBS *Frontline*, "Racism 101," May 10, 1988; see also the discussion of "Affirmative Action Stigma" in Chapter 12).

AFFIRMATIVE ACTION AND SOCIOLOGY

The period from the mid-1950s to the mid-1970s has been termed the "Age of Sociology." Student enrollments in sociology and the influence of the discipline both reached a zenith in the mid-1970s. Not coincidentally, it was also the high point of the popularity of welfare-state liberalism.

Welfare-state liberalism (Gouldner, 1968; 1970), or "doctrinaire liberalism" (Capaldi, 1985), has underpinned sociology even more than most other fields of the academic world as does liberalism's unquestioned faith in sociocultural determinism. Indeed, sociology's core premise has been that the "group is more than the sum of its parts." The policies of busing and affirmative action have been directly deduced from sociology's emphasis on groups and the power of change through alteration of the sociocultural environment.

Thus, the links between egalitarian social reforms and sociology have become exceedingly close: one is really speaking of product and producer. Affirmative action and busing have been sociology's most potent policy offspring. As public opposition to such programs mounted, sociologists became more defensive—recall the earlier discussion in this chapter concerning the attempt by some sociologists to have busing expert James Coleman branded as a racist when he published data critical of busing.

Yet it would be a mistake to portray sociology as a totally monolithic enterprise. The dominant ideological underpinnings of sociology are firmly moored to welfare-state liberalism. However, many sociologists have tried to free sociology from its public identification with liberalism/radicalism by cultivating a quantitative, "scientific" image for the discipline. Indeed, the spectre of the bearded ideologue has haunted and infuriated quantitative sociologists. They have led a five-decade drive to model sociology along the lines of the physical sciences. By and large, quantitative sociologists have been victorious. They are sociology's own "Establishment." They usually command the highest salaries, control the prestige journals in the field, and demand adherence to articles emphasizing the latest techniques in mathematical modeling and statistical measurement techniques.

This quantitative establishment nevertheless has had to co-exist in varying degrees of harmony with other types of sociologists, including those who take a more active ideological stance. As interest groups have proliferated in society, so have they multiplied in sociology. This was especially true in the wake of the activist 1960s. There are now many camps of Marxists, feminists, gays, blacks, Hispanics, and other groups active in the discipline. Some have their own forums and journals. Many of them have adopted a challenging, critical stance towards Establishment political institutions and Establishment sociology.

In *The Coming Crisis of Western Sociology* (1970), Alvin Gouldner had assumed that young sociologists coming of age in the 1960s would construct a new, restructured sociology and society. The younger sociologists would displace the older underpinnings of welfare-state liberalism. But the new, radical spirit surfaced in sociology just as society turned much more conservative. Instead of restructuring society, sociologists were forced to "market" their discipline to job-oriented students and job-hungry sociology Ph.D.s. Instead of changing the world, many young sociology Ph.D.s were forced to change careers and the discipline went into steep decline.

The upshot of these developments has been an ideologically induced blindness and defensiveness. Attitudes towards society and social reform have been shaped by defensiveness and demoralization wrought by the crash of the discipline. Sociologists have not been keen on looking at either the state of their discipline or the effects of pet social reforms such as affirmative action. Such tasks are depressing.

Sociologists at Bay

The end of the Age of Sociology was most evident in sharp enrollment declines. In the nineteen-campus California State University system, the number of majors in sociology fell by 90 percent (Schwieder and Cretser, 1986). Ironically, sociologists were amongst those in the 1970s who labored to abolish curriculum distribution requirements. They largely succeeded. It was assumed that students "liberated" from curriculum requirements would drink their fill of the sociology and liberal-arts courses. They did not. As noted above, students stampeded into business administration, engineering, and other practical majors.

James L. McCartney, the 1984 president of the Midwestern Sociological Association, admitted that the environment for sociology had deteriorated drastically. McCartney saw sociology beset by "multiple crises" and admitted that the discipline "shows signs of stagnation, decline, and demoralization" (1984: 439). McCartney glumly observed that membership in professional associations had declined, as had the number of submissions to journals. The Reagan administration had cut funding for sociologists. Academic prospects for younger Ph.D.s were terrible and sociologists had yet to establish their marketability outside the university.

Yet even McCartney could not cut to the core of the whole mess: that sociology continued to be viewed as a front for welfare-state liberalism/reformism. He could not face the fact that conservative-careerist students and other members of society had come to view sociology as irrelevant. This clash of world-views produced the enrollment crash and the related dilemma: sociology is not a marketable major, especially at the Ph.D. level. Sociologists, their philosophy, and their programs of social reform just were not wanted anymore.[2]

Yet officers of professional associations and major academic stars continued to deny or ignore the crisis of either sociology or its social policy offspring. Many simply refused to see what they didn't want to see either in their own profession or in society. Indeed, sociology's politics have continued to drift leftward in a perverse, "countercyclical" manner (Horowitz, 1987).

White Workers and Sociology: The Disdain of the Discipline

"It is an unlovely spectacle," columnist George Will has written.

White lawyers and editorial writers telling blue-collar whites that promotions or jobs or seniority systems must be sacrificed in the name of racial reparations. It calls to mind Artemus Ward's jest during the Civil War: "I have already given two cousins to the war, and I stand prepared to sacrifice my wife's brother rather than the rebellion be not crushed." (1985: 96)

Will might have added sociologists to the list of those instructing white males on the goodness of self-sacrifice on the altar of group equality. White males caught in the web of affirmative action are likely to receive scorn from sociologists and like-minded academicians.

Sociologists' antagonism towards the established middle classes comes somewhat naturally. In part, this antagonism toward the middle classes stems from the clash of collectivist assumptions of sociology with the individualist values of American society. But there are other inherent reasons as well. Peter Berger (1967) has pointed out that sociologists tend to be inherently distrustful; their studies may debunk respectable middle-class views of the world. Furthermore, sociologists value cultural relativism, a cosmopolitan view in which no culture is seen as inherently better than another. Since Berger's analysis, anti-capitalist and anti-bourgeois sentiments among sociologists have intensified.

In analyses of affirmative action, anti–middle-class biases slide easily into anti-white bias and rationalization of whites' individual injuries.

Sociologists are ill-disposed to see any genuine grievances among whites caused by affirmative action. Indeed, some sociologists have begun to posit a "new racism" amongst whites. With this newer, more sophisticated racism, white males excuse their economic and occupational failures by scapegoating blacks. Whites who express hostility to affirmative action quotas or minorities are dismissed as believers in antiquated individualism who do not understand the collective realities of stratification and the need for collective remedies.

James R. Kluegel proclaimed this view in the title of his article, "If There Isn't a Problem, You Don't Need a Solution: The Bases of Contemporary Affirmative Action Attitudes" (1985). Stanley Greenberg suggested the "new racism" explanation for white males' opposition to affirmative action in his comments for a *Los Angeles Times* article on "Racism Runs Deep" (March 8, 1987). Having described Greenberg's findings as showing that "dozens of white blue-collar workers around Detroit . . . blame their own hard times on blacks," the reporters quoted Greenberg as stating, "They [white males] feel the government that was supposed to protect them has instead given everything away to the blacks: Blacks get the jobs, blacks get the welfare; blacks get the loans. . . . They have no historical memory of racism, no tolerance for present efforts to offset it."

The reporters and Greenberg conveniently forgot to add: "present efforts" at whose expense?

Even Marxist-oriented, conflict theorists cannot see the class and age lines of cleavage inherent in affirmative action. They see no legitimacy in the complaints of white males toward such policies. (When I discussed the interviewing for this study, a Midwestern sociologist sniffed with disgust that the reverse discrimination reports of white males might have any merit: "Of course, you realize they'll probably be alibiing." And when a famous Marxist criminologist visited the campus where I taught, he asked about the nature of my current research. When I informed him about my studies of white males and affirmative action, he dismissed the results of the study in advance with a one-liner: "I'll bet your white males were angry." He then changed the subject.)

SOCIOLOGICAL RESEARCH ON AFFIRMATIVE ACTION

William Beer (1987a; 1987b) has recently analyzed English-language material under the topic "affirmative action" cited in *Sociological Abstracts* from 1977–86. According to Beer, "in the more than 20 years that have elapsed since the 1964 Civil Rights Act, there has been practically no attempt to find out what the societal consequences of affirmative action have been" (1987a: 1).

In his extensive review of the literature, Beer found studies which could be categorized under four topics: (1) legal and philosophical analyses, (2) polemical and persuasive arguments, (3) studies of manpower utilization and organizational effectiveness, and (4) empirial work that purports to look at various aspects of affirmative action's social consequences.

Beer found studies dealing with legal and philosophical aspects of affirmative action flawed for two major reasons. First, there was a tendency to confuse law and social policy with actual social behavior; the everyday effects of affirmative action policy were ignored. Second, such studies were quickly rendered obsolete by shifting court rulings and administrative rulings.

Beer found the philosophical analyses to be superficial and specious, based upon such questionable assumptions as "differences between groups are primarily caused by discrimination." Beer maintained that studies of affirmative action in organizations were too few and too small to yield significant results. As for empirical studies on the effects of affirmative action, Beer discussed four studies on attitudes towards affirmative action, all of which were plagued by problems with the meaning or number of items used to measure attitudes.

Beer made no mention of the important research by Johnson (1980a, 1980b), Leonard (1984a, 1984b), and Smith and Welch (1986). Yet his omissions are in themselves significant: the works of Leonard and that of Smith and Welch were by economists, not sociologists. Sociologist Johnson (as noted earlier in this chapter) surmised that his data on reverse discrimination and aggression would fare better in psychology journals. Therefore, Beer's thesis still stands. With the exception of Glazer's *Affirmative Discrimination* and Johnson's small study, not only have sociologists failed to devote significant attention and resources to the topic of affirmative action, but what major works there are, have been done by scholars based outside the field.

The current guardedness of sociologists regarding affirmative action is revealed in a 1988 book by the president of the American Sociological Association, Herbert Gans. In *Middle American Individualism*, Gans apparently had strategic reasons in mind when he chose to ignore affirmative action. Though largely concerned with examining the values of the American middle class, Gans also wished to reconcile such values to his proclaimed goal of an "egalitarian welfare state." Yet Gans was careful not to openly promote busing and affirmative action. Busing was not in the book's index but did receive two quick positive mentions. Affirmative action got two references in the index, but was rarely discussed explicitly, though it was clear where Gans's sympathies lay.

The more liberally orthodox sociologists would have cheered full endorsement of such policies. But Gans had read the public mood well and realized that Middle Americans have resisted such sweeping policies. He acknowledged as much when he complained that

redistributionist programs have to be structured in such a fashion that some present material or nonmaterial gaps between social and economic classes remain and people do not begin to fear having to compete with "lower" classes and status groups for significant amounts of prestige or resources. (1988: 150)

In other words: if Americans reject affirmative action and other egalitarian policies, the fault lies not in the policies but in the resentments of the citizenry.

The ASA president's neglect of affirmative action is emblematic of the entire profession. Affirmative action has not been a prominent topic at the annual professional meetings of the American Sociological Association. Participants in the most recent annual meetings of the American Sociological Association have displayed no great interest in the issue. Though the theme of the 1985 meetings was "Work and Occupations," there was no paper with "affirmative action" in the title.

The American Sociological Association has embraced affirmative action quota policies and there has been little debate. A minority fellowship program has pumped 100 minority Ph.D.s into the already saturated job market. In recent years, women and minorities have been very heavily represented in committee-picked nominations for the American Sociological Association. Nevertheless, in terms of ASA membership, the number of blacks and Hispanics has not increased appreciably—perhaps for the same reasons that overall sociology enrollments have dropped.[3]

Richard J. Hill has provided us with a case study of affirmative action in the University of Oregon's sociology department. In the academic year 1969–70, he noted that twenty-one professionals had some affiliation with the department of sociology; only one was a women and she was a part-time assistant professor. By 1981–82, there were nineteen persons affiliated with the department: six were women, four of whom had tenure; however, only one minority person had been hired, in spite of attempts to recruit more.

Among the factors cited by Hill in accounting for this slow-but-steady progress at Oregon were ideological pressures emanating from the federal government, the ASA ("pressure and education"), the central administration at Oregon, and an "articulate, action-oriented segment within the department" (1983a: 18). Indeed, Professor Hill informed me that there is a very strong consensus throughout the department on affirmative action (1983b). Evidently, the "articulate, action-oriented" faculty encountered no dissent or opposition on affirmative action. Nor were there perceptions or fears that "reverse discrimination is common," as Paul Burstein suggested (1982: 11). On the contrary, to judge from the tone of Professor Hill's article and his remarks to me, any problem with "reverse discrimination" was totally ignored.

The Revival of Dissent?

The liberal/welfare state/radical consensus in sociology is not without cracks or potential for change. There are signs of ideological fatigue. Coleman's remarks concerning his ostracism and isolation in the 1970s suggest that a period of sober reflection on past ideological excesses may be setting in (1988). Additional evidence of this was contained in Stanley Lieberson's 1988 presidential address to the Pacific Sociological Association.

Lieberson complained that there are ideological constraints which "leads us to ignore some research and all too quickly and unthinkingly embrace other studies of less merit." There are

a set of views about contemporary social and political issues that at least appear to be quite common to sociologists. In turn, results that clash with these views are treated differently than either those that are in harmony with them or deal with topics that have minimal relevance for contemporary policy debates. Our discipline has a set of illogical procedures and inappropriate ways of thinking about results that are implicitly defined as "unacceptable." (1988: 383)

DOING AFFIRMATIVE ACTION RESEARCH IN CALIFORNIA

Conducting research on individual and institutional responses to affirmative action during the 1970s and 1980s in southern California was very much like being in a play-within-a-play. In formulating the research and trying to discuss it with my colleagues, I was encountering many of the same responses that the white male interview subjects reported. Though I obtained some support from a small number of colleagues—usually behind closed doors—most others did not wish to discuss either my research or the underlying realities suggested by it. I was simultaneously encountering the spiral of silence in my own teaching-and-research milieux as I simultaneously gathered materials documenting that phenomenon and the New McCarthyism elsewhere.

My interests in affirmative action began to form in the early 1970s, though I did not begin to put any research into motion until the late 1970s. I mentioned the research only to a few colleagues, and I never brought up my research interests in the classroom until the mid-1980s. To raise the question was, ipso facto, to take a political stance, one not protected by academic freedom. I did not have tenure.

Freedom of inquiry on affirmative action has increased somewhat over the past decade. But there was a definite difference between the mid-to-late 1970s and the late 1980s. I encountered few direct threats in my immediate academic surroundings at an urban state university. Because I kept my research largely under wraps, I encountered no ugly incidents such as those described earlier.

On the other hand, there was considerable indirect and informal pressure to repress the research. Reading the incidents described above made me and my colleagues aware that there could be retribution for asking the wrong questions about affirmative action. The case of Professor X, described at the opening of Chapter 8, was a lesson well learned.

Until the mid-1980s, affirmative action was an unquestioned trend in academic life in California and in the public sector in general. Affirmative action advocates were quietly and relentlessly pursuing their goals. There were few openly critical voices anywhere, none that I knew of at my institution. Few people seemed to be asking "why," much less saying "no" to most affirmative action demands.

California obviously was in the forefront of affirmative action rhetoric and efforts. By the late 1970s, government officials were fond of predicting that the state would soon become a "Third World State" in terms of a "majority of minorities." Los Angeles was being termed by the national media as the "New Ellis Island." Governor Edmud G. Brown, Jr., proudly boasted of the large numbers of minority appointees he had made to state government, quotas were being imposed on local police and fire departments, and, as seen in Chapters 3 and 4, teachers were being transferred and assigned to schools on the basis of race while their students were bused for the same purpose. Through it all, the editorial page of the area's leading newspaper, *Los Angeles Times*, heartily endorsed any quota plan that made the news.

Faculty and a fledgling academic union picked up the change in rhetoric from "equality" to the more hard-line proportional term "equity." Every campus acquired affirmative action plans and officers. Special research grants and released teaching time were available to minority and female faculty. Fellowships for graduate study were available for "underrepresented" minorities, but not Asian males. (One of the first signals from students that it might be acceptable to mention my research in class was their laughter in response to my reading the list of preferred fellowship groups.)

There was one major defeat for the most aggressive proponents of affirmative action: a daring, behind-the-scenes attempt was made to delete most references to meritocratic criteria in the university affirmative action plan. This "reform" plan evidently died when it was exposed in the *Los Angeles Times* by former San Jose State University President John Bunzel. (This article is excerpted in Chapter 3.)

Most social-science colleagues were blissfully unaware of the affirmative action pressures all around them. As with other citizens, faculty were lulled by the media neglect of the issue. Closer to campus, lack of affirmative action awareness stemmed from the fact that there was little or no hiring in the humanities and social sciences during this period. The last full-time sociology faculty member had been hired in 1978. The next would not be hired until 1988. The number of sociology majors at our institution dropped from 1,075 in 1970 to 96 in 1985 (Schwieder and Cretser, 1986).

As was the case on many other campuses, there was an atmosphere of continuing crisis and despair from the late 1970s until about 1986. The administration repeatedly demanded drastic cutbacks in course offerings. Faculty who retired were not replaced. Plans were made, though not implemented, to lay off tenured faculty. Affirmative action, then, was not a major issue in their personal worlds. By the early 1980s, all had tenure. Affirmative action would not adversely affect them. Even the threat of layoffs affected only one or two less senior faculty. The only pressure with regard to affirmative action concerned one or two promotion cases and the composition of the part-time faculty. Again, it was not the best of times to be caught out in the open with controversial research.

Colleagues and friends agreed with my assessment of danger. In private, the few colleagues to whom I mentioned my research and to whom I showed professional papers and publications were highly supportive. "But don't show that to many people around here," urged a colleague during the late 1970s. Warnings came in from the East Coast as well. A department chair at one of the Seven Sisters colleges where I was to interview for a position said: "Look, I want you to get this job. Don't mention your research on affirmative action."

Max Weber has written of the tasks involved in exposing students to "inconvenient facts" (1946). The same was true with regard to faculty. Even the questions of my research were, in themselves, threatening to those who had quicky and uncritically assumed affirmative action was good. To study how white males had responded to affirmative action barriers suggested that white males had, indeed, been injured. To assess the mass media's role in helping or inhibiting discussion on affirmative action suggested that such programs were carried out covertly and implemented without the will of the people.

Two or three colleagues who were then—and remain—good friends, formed a sort of loyal opposition and did furnish input on the research. Yet they and others with whom I discussed my research or the issue in general were clearly disconcerted by the mounting evidence of affirmative action abuses and contradictions. Rapid responses to the dirty realities of affirmative action sometimes followed the "techniques of neutralization" patterns outlined by Matza and Sykes (1957): denial of the injury, denial of the victim, denial of responsibility, condemning the condemners, and appeals to higher loyalties. Disconcerting evidence was simply dismissed as false or as a plot by officials to sabotage good policies. White male victims were alibiing or lying, white males could not be victims anyway, or affirmative action programs really were not supposed to work that way. Finally, the appeal to higher loyalties: "someone has to get hurt" on the way to a newer, better society (i.e. "you can't make an omelet without breaking eggs").

Affirmative Action Comes Home

What was quietly going on in academe, of course, was slowly occurring in other societal sectors: increasing cognitive dissonance. Belief in the goodness of affirmative action was running up against incongruent evidence that the programs were ill-founded and being abused. Therefore, pressures mounted either to deny the evidence of reverse discrimination and other contradictions or let go of the belief in the purity of affirmative action. The latter became an increasingly difficult task.

As a trickle of hiring began in the humanities and in social sciences by the mid-1980s, faculty disillusionment with affirmative action on both the faculty and student levels was quietly clashing with the gathering administrative craze to boost the numbers of minority students and faculty.

Faculty who until five years ago seemed to know little of the realities of affirmative action are today directly told or simply "understand" that administrators are happiest when females or minorities are hired. This is especially true for junior-level positions where having a national reputation is not yet a factor. It is simply known that certain positions are "reserved." (Those who are insensitive may find themselves performing the same faculty or administrator searches two or three years in a row if they do not select the proper candidate.) Affirmative action appointment records are of increasing importance in evaluations of administrators and department chairs. There is always the threat of being labeled racist if one dissents.

A resolution passed by the California state legislature required that student enrollments at the University of California and the California State system mirror the ethnic proportions of graduating high school seniors by 1990. By the summer of 1987, this was not happening. Therefore, efforts to recruit minority students for higher education in California took on the trappings of a panicky military campaign. Some campuses sent student ambassadors to heavily minority high schools. Other campuses dispatched buses to bring students to orientation days on campus. Senior faculty have been asked to recruit high-school minority students using telephone lists.

Every California State campus acquired affirmative action officers. Rhetoric shifted from a more individualistic "equal opportunity" to a more group-based emphasis on "equity" and "diversity." By the end of the 1980s, a forgivable grant program was being put into place for (initially) two hundred minority and female students and lecturers to pursue Ph.D. studies elsewhere. (Though no future faculty positions in the California State system were explicitly promised to those who received the grants, pressures for such action have been assured with the provision that the loans would be forgiven if the grant recipient taught at a California State campus for five years.)

That the faculty were finally recognizing the realities behind the ideals of racial preference was a source of some comfort. More supportive was the increasing student receptiveness to my research, which I had begun to broach in my classes on law and society, taught in a new setting at a suburban public university.

The students who were most aware of and eager to talk about affirmative action were those who held jobs in the public sector or with corporations. None of the students knew the legal history of affirmative action. Most were totally unaware of the anti-quota provisions of Title VII of the 1964 Civil Rights Act. No one knew what the public-opinion poll data showed. Interestingly, women and minorities were among the most vocal critics of the policies. Several minority students began to voice the dilemma (mentioned earlier in this chapter) that, because of affirmative action, their student peers automatically regarded students of color as less than qualified. Some students made a point of stating to me after class that they "had never had a chance to discuss this topic."

The overall attitude of the students was fair-minded, pragmatic, but somewhat fatalistic. Nearly all opposed preferential treatment, watering down evaluation criteria, and dual standards of evaluation. However, as far as any sort of protest or opposition was concerned, they were acquiescent. They just did not think anything could be done about affirmative action; these things had simply been decided for them.

What we seem to have now in the university community is a grudging willingness to admit that preferential treatment is generating problems: rising racial tensions amongst students, problems with use of dual standards of admission and performance based on race/ethnicity and high rates of attrition among minority students. But there is an unwillingness to abandon such programs either for the university or for society.

NOTES

1. Lipset might also have taken into account another important variable affecting the relationship between sociology and liberalism: geography. Most of the high-prestige sociology departments (and their stars) are located in the most liberal areas of the nation: the "Bos-Wash" megalopolis, the Big Ten institutions (and the University of Chicago), and the large urban campuses of the University of California and the University of Washington on the West Coast.

2. According to 1985 data from the National Research Council on Higher Education, slightly over 50 percent of new sociology and anthropology Ph.D.s were still seeking academic positions when their degrees were conferred. Such data do not include the number of jobless Ph.D.s from prior years, about whom little is known. But past and present cohorts of Ph.D.s have formed a formidable surplus labor population. Applicant-to-position ratios for academic sociology positions may run upwards of 100 to 1 in desirable locations. In 1986, the University of California at Santa Cruz received 350 applications for one position. Even mediocre campuses, far from the surf and sand in California, may receive upwards of 100 applications for a

single slot. Darkly humorous papers quantitatively assessing patterns of letters of rejection have been presented at professional gatherings.

The American Sociological Association has issued reports that try to grapple with limited statistics on the situation, which ignore the horrendous job applicant/job opening ratios (D'Antonio, 1987). In a report on employment patterns in sociology, Bettina J. Huber estimated that there would be a surplus of *at least* 2,500 sociology Ph.D.s during the 1980s (1985: 18).

In the August, 1988, edition of sociology's in-house newsletter, *Footnotes*, William D. Antonio cited a figure which indicated the gravity of underemployment in sociology. More than one thousand of the twelve thousand member ASA identified themselves as earning under $15 thousand annually. D'Antonio admitted that this was probably due to the presence of a large number of people who could gain no better than part-time employment in their profession.

A more accurate description of the marketplace for sociologists was provided by a California department chairperson in 1987: "Insane."

3. Bettina Huber found that "women and minorities made relatively greater numerical gains than white men in both the academic and applied arenas between 1975 and 1981" (1985: 38). Also of significance: "The proportional increase in minority salaries was greater than for whites or women" (1985: 20). The latter finding reinforced the views of Howard Bowen and Jack Schuster (1986), who contended that universities have been actively seeking minority faculty—luring them with high salaries—but compete with one another in a limited pool of talent and with limited resources compared to what corporations and government can offer.

Most important of all is that hiring opportunities in sociology during the 1980s have been very limited because of the changing ideological and enrollment crash discussed above. One can hardly hire huge numbers of minorities and women when sociologists have been fighting to keep what academic slots they have. Sociology has also had to compete or cooperate by sharing positions with faculty in women's studies, Afro-American studies, etc.

The official position of the American Sociological Association has been strongly pro–affirmative action. Affirmative action proponents appear to have been busy and successful in getting women and minorities nominated for office in the ASA. In 1979, Mueller (1979) found that women and minority candidates were over-represented as officially selected candidates for ASA offices, compared to their numbers in the association. Mueller anticipated the possible unpopularity of his findings by adding, "Now I realize this little note may make me a few enemies (but, what the hell—I've got tenure!)" This trend has accelerated. In 1986, the ASA's Committee on Nominations selected only five white male candidates for thirty-six officer positions for the important Council Member-at-Large, Committee on Publications, Committee on Committees, and Committee on Nominations (below the rank of vice-president).

A report on the status of women and minorities in the ASA by Huber (1987), suggested that women have maintained representation on committees in proportion to their membership in the ASA, while "minority participation in several association activities has shown impressive improvement in the past few years" (1987: 21). Huber urged that efforts for greater female/minority representation be maintained or increased.

Yet the percentage of women and minorities in the ASA has not risen appreciably during the 1980s. What growth in minority membership there has been, is the result of increased numbers of Asian members. The lack of "progress" on substantially boosting female, black, and Hispanic proportions undoubtedly reflects the demand for black and Hispanics with undergraduate degrees coupled with the horrible job market for sociologists with advanced degrees. Lack of black and Hispanic advancement within the field of sociology is certainly not due to lack of effort and commitment.

How the rank-and-file members of the profession of sociology feel about affirmative action is difficult to discern. Most teaching sociologists are not members of the trend-setting American Sociological Association. (At at least one large state university in California, two-thirds of the sociology department faculty do not belong to the association.)

However, one indication of rather confused rank-and-file sentiments toward affirmative action might be gleaned from the Brown and Cook (1981) survey of ASA members' attitudes towards affirmative action. Forty-two percent of those in the sample did not return the survey form. Of those who did, 24 percent did not know about the Minority Fellowship Program at all. Of the remaining 34 percent (who did return the form and who did know of the program), 82 percent thought the fellowship program "useful." Fifty-eight percent of the respondents thought the program should be continued; 35 percent were not sure; and the remainder thought the program should be discontinued.

Chapter 10

ELITE ACCOMMODATION AND THE FLAWS OF AFFIRMATIVE ACTION

How did controversial social policy that lacked public support nonetheless become institutionalized? That has been a central question of this book. Chapter by chapter, a number of contributing factors have emerged: the individual and collective silence of the victims; the influence of sex-role behavior upon silence; the collective guilt and individual fear of being labeled racist; the elusive and capricious implementation of affirmative action policies; the ideological bias and self-censorship among the mass media and the social sciences; the spiral of silence; the New McMarthyism; and the craze-like behavior.

Affirmative action has evolved as a set of programs imposed from the top down, over and against public opinion. In this chapter, I wish to focus upon the question of how and why those in positions of power and influence—the elites—formulated or at least went along with affirmative action and other race-preference programs.

A standard starting point in examining the role of elites in American life is C. Wright Mills's classic study, *The Power Elite* (1956). Mills's framework, augmented by a recent attitude survey of elites by Verba and Orren (1985), provides a useful portrait of the role of elites in affirmative action policy.

In Mills's view, by the 1950s, a century of economic and political centralization produced three major institutional hierarchies in American society: the large corporations, the executive branch of government, and the military. By the term *power elite*, Mills meant "those political, economic, and military circles which as an intricate set of overlapping cliques share decisions having at least national consequences. In so far as national events are decided, the power elite are those who decide them" (1956: 18). Legislative bodies such as the Congress, Mills maintained, had been reduced to the "middle levels of power."

Mills made clear that he saw no well-organized, coherent, unified ruling class. His was a structural analysis of power, not conspiracy theory. What unity existed amongst the elite was due to two factors. First, the elite was "composed of men of similar origin and education. . . . There were psychological and social bases for their unity, resting upon the fact that they were of similar social type and leading to the fact of their easy intermingling" (1956: 19). Second, the corporate, government, and military sectors were brought together by similar economic and structural interests, most notably, "the development of a permanent war establishment by a privately incorporated economy inside a political vacuum" (1956: 19).

Mills's analysis is useful for this study in that Mills emphasized that: (1) elites are structurally interrelated, and (2) power lies in decision-making. Those who are in the top "command posts" of the major institutional hierarchies can make decisions of enormous consequence with few, if any, democratic checks on such powers. Mills was one of the first social scientists to discern the emergence of centralized, administrative power and rule in society.

Indeed, administrative law is the fastest-growing body of law in the land. The powers wielded by top corporate and government administrators have expanded greatly since Mills wrote *The Power Elite*. So vast are these powers that Allan Bloom has stated that an "administrative state" has replaced politics (1987: 85). Were he alive today, I suspect Mills would concur. (On the importance of administrative law, see Vago, 1988.)

Mills's emphasis on the giant administrative power wielded by the heads of major corporate and government institutions can be supplemented by a more recent study of elites by Verba and Orren (1985). Fortunately, for purposes of this study, Verba and Orren were specifically concerned with the attitudes of elites towards equality. They collected data on attitudes toward equality from 2,762 institutional leaders in nine elite sectors: business, organized labor, farming, civil rights organizations, feminist groups, political parties, intellectuals, the mass media, and a sample of college seniors at ten elite colleges (1985). Unfortunately, Verba and Orren ignored elites in the executive branch and military, two of Mills's three major organizational hierarchies. However, it can be reasonably assumed that the elites in the military have remained conservative. As for elites in the federal bureaucracy, it has already been seen that they have tended to be quite liberal and activist on matters of affirmative action.

On the other hand, Verba and Orren's addition of elites in the mass media and the intellectuals as well as the "challenging elites" in civil rights and feminist organizations is overdue. (Verba and Orren also included labor leaders in their survey of elites. Mills contended that the labor elites' powers were derived from legitimation and protection by elites in government. In the case of affirmative action, we shall see that unions usually went along with corporate or government administrators. Only rarely did unions take action on behalf of white males.)

Verba and Orren confirmed Mills's views on the social backgrounds of elites. The elites were mostly white, male, and college educated. Leaders of civil rights organizations, however, were nearly all black and the feminist elites were mostly female.[1] Yet homogeneity of background did not produce a unified outlook on equality or programs to remedy inequality. Verba and Orren found persistent polarities of attitudes between those elites aligned with the Democrats, on the one hand, and Republicans, on the other. Democrats saw poverty and racism as a result of "the system," while Republicans saw such inequalities in individual terms. Democrat-aligned elites favored more government intervention to assist the poor, but few wished to impose equality of results through the use of quotas. In choosing between more traditional equality of opportunity versus the newer and more radical equality of results, Verba and Orren found that the majority of leaders opted for the former:

American leaders on both the left and the right share the basic view that individuals may in fact deserve to be unequal in results, because of their own failures. The equality debate in America, therefore, is not over whether anyone really deserves to be at the bottom or whether the losers are always worthy of help from the government, but over whether those currently at the bottom are the ones who deserve to be there, and thus whether the government should assist them. (1985: 83)

Quotas for blacks and women in jobs and education were overwhelmingly rejected by all elites except those of civil rights organizations and feminists. Three out of four black leaders and a majority of feminist leaders supported the use of quotas for blacks in jobs and education. On quotas for women, blacks approved, but feminist leaders split down the middle. As for other liberal groups: "Democrats, youth, labor, and intellectuals, who blame the system for black poverty almost as much as black and feminist leaders do, nevertheless deplore the use of quotas" (1985: 84).[2]

In addition, Verba and Orren found that the elites ranked national priorities differently, and most put race and gender equality towards the bottom of the list.

American leaders give different priorities to equality as a national goal, particularly to equality for women and for blacks. . . . Gender equality appears at or near the bottom of the ratings more often than any other goal. Half of the groups place it last, and everyone but feminist leaders, who rank it first, and youth place it among the three lowest categories. Equality for blacks does not fare much better. . . . Only blacks rate it near the top. (1985: 120)

ATTITUDES VERSUS BEHAVIOR ON AFFIRMATIVE ACTION

Based upon Verba and Orren's work, affirmative action quotas can hardly be seen as the product of a consensus agreed upon by national leaders. On the contrary, most elite members opposed quotas, and the elites were split on a variety of related issues.

Yet there is no question of the imposed-from-above nature of affirmative action. Capaldi (1985) even likens the process to fascist-imposed "reform." What, then, was the role of elites in the affirmative action revolution?

Verba and Orren's study contains a major flaw common to attitude studies: the gap between attitudes and actual behavior.

Did elites behave in a manner consistent with anti-quota attitudes? The data presented in Chapter 3 strongly suggest that they did not. Especially in the years since Verba and Orren's survey (1976-77), corporate and political elites appear to have yielded with minimal resistance to quotas imposed by judges or federal agencies. More than that: corporations and government agencies have initiated their own affirmative action quota procedures. Representatives of the corporate and business communities have been filing friends-of-the-court briefs exclusively on the side of pro-affirmative action forces in the Supreme Court.

Why?

A Convergence of Organizational Interests on Affirmative Action

A fusion of economic and bureaucratic interests can be seen in the contemporary acceptance of affirmative action procedures.

The desire to "do something" about the minority poor gained initial impetus in the wake of searing urban disturbances—Watts, Detroit, Newark —in the 1960s. There was a sense of crisis and fears of economic and racial polarization (Jencks, 1985b). Hiring more blacks at General Motors and in government agencies in Detroit, for example, could clearly be seen by elites as a tactic for cooling urban unrest and bringing members of the underclass into the system.

Once affirmative action rules were formulated, organizations subject to equal opportunity regulations expediently accepted such plans and procedures as routine overhead expenses. Simply in terms of risk management, it has been easier to put up with affirmative action paperwork than to risk harrassment by government agencies, lawsuits, and bad press. A given number of affirmative action hires, who do not perform on a par with non-affirmative action hires, can be tolerated (Jencks, 1985b; Murray, 1984a).

A case that illustrates all of this was Sears, Roebuck and Co.'s victory in a protracted struggle with the Equal Employment Opportunity Commission. Sears prevailed largely because the corporation had implemented its own vigorous quota plan in the 1970s. (See also the description of the Sears case in Chapter 3.)

Business and government entities have learned to live with, even embrace, affirmative action. The U.S. Chamber of Commerce, whose 1,800,000 members include thousands of small businesses typically hostile to government regulation, took no position in the Santa Clara case. Many business organizations filed amicus curiae briefs supporting the program and praised the Supreme Court ruling.

The reason for the business support is simple: a tough affirmative action program now can stave off expensive discrimination suits later. Sears, Roebuck and Co. has spent 15 years fighting charges by the Equal Employment Opportunity Commission, first in administrative proceedings, then in court. The trial alone lasted 10 months in 1984–85. The 806-store retailer refuses even to reveal how much it spent on lawyers, though it gives a hint. Expenses, including hiring statisticians, sociologists and other expert witnesses, came to $6.8 million and one can guess fees to attorneys were probably at least twice that much.

Sears finally won at trial—the judgement is on appeal—against a charge that its female employees tend to be concentrated in lower-paying sales jobs than men because of discrimination. The company's chief litigator in the case . . . specifically credits the court victory to a race-and-sex-conscious hiring program Sears started in 1968 for its work force, now at 300,000. "They have the best," declares Morgan. "Out of every two job openings at Sears they filled one with a black or a woman."

Governments, especially in large cities, similarly view affirmative action plans as a small price to pay for political harmony. (*Insight*, April 27, 1987: 9)

Yet Sears's victory was a long and costly one: twelve years and $20 million. "The transcript of the 10-month trial in the last case alone is 15 feet high. At one point, Sears employed 250 people full time to compile information, some of it dating back to 1960, to meet EEOC investigatory demands" (Weiner, 1986).

Many other corporations simply capitulated to EEOC rather than drag out negotiations and court contests. When EEOC won a landmark 1973 discrimination settlement with American Telephone and Telegraph,

EEOC tried to run up the score with charges against General Electric Co., Ford Motor Co., General Motors Corp. and the United Auto Workers. GE settled in 1978 for $32 million for training programs, payments to employees and other steps. Ford's 1980 settlement cost $23 million, and GM's pact in 1983, with the UAW as co-signatory, is about $42.5 million. (Weiner, 1986)

Therefore, it makes economic sense to maintain in-house quota programs, even if a corporation must tolerate a number of unqualified or incompetent workers.[3]

In 1985, the National Association of Manufacturers voted a fresh endorsement of affirmative action. Monsanto and DuPont also have strong affirmative action plans in place and like it that way. Personnel executive

David Buchanan of the Ford Motor Company has stated, "Business decided that affirmative action is the right thing to do. It has become a way of life" (*U.S. News and World Report*, June 17, 1985: 67).

The use of race-and-gender quotas to ward off legal action by government agencies or lawsuits by members of minority groups had a catch until 1987: the counter-threats of reverse-discrimination lawsuits by white employees. However, in 1987, by a 6–3 decision in *Johnson v. Transportation Agency of Santa Clara*, the Supreme Court upheld preferential treatment for women based upon numerical under-representation. That decision seemingly released employers from the threat of reverse discrimination lawsuits. But the court's most recent decision in *Richmond v. Croson* (1989), again opened the door to legal redress by whites. In its *Richmond* decision, the 6–3 majority held that even the use of "benign quotas" likely violates the rights of white males. The court also cast doubt upon the use of any preferences where there was no evidence of intentional, past discrimination against specific minorities.

Nevertheless, as emphasized in the opening chapter of this book, white males very rarely win reverse discrimination lawsuits; the *Bakke* and *Johnson* cases have been the exceptions, not the rule. Reports in this study and in press reports suggest that the EEOC takes a skeptical view of reverse discrimination claims. Employers and educational institutions have undoubtedly become aware of this. It will take several more decisions similar to *Richmond* before the legal odds change. In the meantime, elites and their institutions clearly have the upper hand. And they know it.

Elites, the Steamroller, and the Spiral of Silence

Though most of those interviewed in the Verba and Orren survey rejected quotas and equality of results, there was a split in views on whether the system or the individual was to blame for poverty situations. Verba and Orren found that a "system-is-to-blame" belief concerning black and female inequality was shared by majorities of Democrat-inclined elites and amongst smaller factions in other elites.

Verba and Orren's finding of a split in the system-is-to-blame philosophy only partially confirms Charles Murray's more sweeping description of a transformation of elite wisdom in the 1960s. Murray argued that the shift moved elite thinking from blaming the victim to blaming the system (1984b). Verba and Orren's findings indicate that a blaming-the-system outlook gained a sufficient number of vocal, elite adherents who intimidated opponents of race-conscious remedies and inhibited organized opposition: the spiral of silence.

To draw a parallel between the behavior of elites and white males interviewed for this study: it is probable that elites have been ignorant of—or have misperceived—the consensus in public opion opposing the use of quotas. This is especially likely since, according to Verba and Orren, most of the elites ranked equality for blacks and women as a low-priority issue. Issues of low importance typically do not merit much attention and analysis. Since elites did not devote much attention to equality issues, it is reasonable to posit that, when they did, they assumed the vociferous minority and women's groups—through a quietly sympathetic mass media —were articulating popular views. Thus, it is likely that Elisabeth Noelle-Neuman's concept of the "spiral of silence" applies equally well to attitudes amongst elites as to attitudes amongst the public at large.

The twin forces of the spiral of silence and the New McCarthyism would have much greater impact among the elites more than among rank-and-file citizens. A major corporate or government leader obviously has a great deal to lose from being tagged as a "racist." Not only might the stigma become attached to the person, but also to the corporation. (One personnel officer interviewed as a background source for this study admitted that he did not discuss affirmative action outside the corporation because he feared that a slip might get not only him but his corporation in trouble.)

In his discussion of Congress's behavior toward affirmative action, sociologist Nathan Glazer implied a spiral-of-silence situation. "In Congress a point of view that may well reflect the opinions of a minority holds sway. The protection of affirmative action is in the hands of Congressmen who care, reflecting the views of civil rights organizations; most others stay away from the issue" (1988: 107).

To be exposed to charges of "racism" is terrible public relations for a corporation or government agency. There is little doubt that corporate and government elites remain wary of such labels and judge that going along with affirmative action, whatever the attendant costs, is less costly in terms of the public's goodwill than being labeled racist or sexist.[4]

Elite accommodation to affirmative action preferences, then, can be explained in terms of good public relations, coupled with a desire for stability and "industrial peace" with government agencies and minority/women's groups.[5] Elites are also aware that the odds for legal action by individual white males are small and that the chances for a white male winning a reverse discrimination lawsuit are even smaller. There has been no organized recognition of white males' grievances by major political groups. Following affirmative action preferences directives, then, has been the line of least resistance.

Omitted from this equation was the damage done to white workers and the continued oversight of serious legal and sociological flaws in affirmative action. These flaws, however, have begun to surface as problems in policy management and pose even more dilemmas in the future.

THREE LOGICAL/SOCIOLOGICAL FLAWS IN AFFIRMATIVE ACTION

As mentioned in the opening chapter of the book, the restructuring of American society through the use of race-and-gender preferences has many flaws. This two-factor strategy ignores the many other variables that affect human behavior ranging from personality traits to cultural values to social class.

Even within the boundaries of sociological analysis, however, there are three sizable flaws in the logic of affirmative action. Amazingly, these gaps in sociological reasoning are usually ignored, even by those opposed to policies of preferential affirmative action.

The three sociological flaws of affirmative action are the immigration-with-preference paradox, the assumption that inequality equals discrimination, and the clash of group preferences with the norm of distributive justice.

IMMIGRATION-WITH-PREFERENCE PARADOX

Most affirmative action debate has been centered on the black/white dimension, far less often on the male/female dimension. The increasing list of preferred non-black minorities also has been ignored by the social sciences and the print and television media. A strategic reason for focus upon blacks has been the obvious history of discrimination and deep sense of national guilt. The black/white issue is thus the strongest possible case for affirmative action advocates. Even affirmative action critics wind up fighting proponents on this emotionally charged turf (see, for example, Glazer, 1975; Murray, 1984a, 1984b; Capaldi, 1985; Bloom, 1987). High-visibility debate concerning affirmative action for non-black minorities is next to nonexistent.

Contrary to Nathan Glazer's recent reappraisal of affirmative action (Glazer, 1988), many non-black minorities have been, and continue to be, included in affirmative action programs: the numerous Hispanic groups (Mexicans, Cubans, Puerto Ricans, Central Americans, and so forth), Pacific Islanders, American Indians, Asian/Indians, Filipinos, Vietnamese, Cambodians, and homosexuals.

Why have so few people asked directly: on what basis do these groups ground their claims for redress through quotas, preferential treatment, or proportional representation? On what basis do we include some groups and exclude others? Especially when many, if not most, of these groups have only recently arrived in significant numbers in the United States?

The omission of non-black minorities from discussion of affirmative action becomes even more extraordinary in view of recent immigration history: by including non-black minorities, one obtains a curious immigration-with-preference paradox.

Most of the government-preferred non-black minorities were present in the United States only in relatively small numbers before 1970. Historical measurement of the Hispanic population is plagued with definitional problems in census procedures, especially prior to 1970. But the numbers of

Hispanics in this nation have been relatively small until the recent large-scale and sustained immigration from Mexico and other Hispanic nations (Moore and Pachon, 1985: 24). A quick historical and sociological portrait is given by Gann and Duignan:

During the first decade of this century, the Hispanic population of the United States was of small account in statistical terms, numbering less than a quarter of a million—less than the total number of Swiss immigrants in the United States. Seventy years later, in 1980, counted Hispanics in this country—excluding uncounted illegal immigrants—numbered 14.6 million. They constituted 6.4 percent of the U.S. population (compared with a known percentage of 4.5 percent in 1970). Of the Hispanics, 60 percent were Mexican, 14 percent Puerto Rican, 6 percent Cuban, and the remaining 20 percent from Central America and South America with a small percentage from Spain. (1986: 315)

In 1960, the Hispanic population in the U.S. was approximately 6 million, in 1970 was approximately 9.1 million. By 1980, it had grown to 14.6 million (census data cited in Cafferty and McCready, 1985: 15). By 1986, the estimate was 18 million (*Los Angeles Times*, July 27, 1987, p. 8). In other words, in sixteen years, the Hispanic population in this nation has doubled. Sixty percent are Mexican immigrants. Officially counted Hispanics now approach 7 percent of the total population.

Aside from those of Chinese and Japanese ancestry, most Asians in this nation are foreign-born: of the 2,539,800 persons living in the United States who were born in Asia, 47 percent immigrated here in the period from 1975 to 1980; 22.4 percent from 1970 to 1974; 12.0 percent from 1965 to 1969, and 6 percent from 1960 to 1964. The remaining 12.5 percent immigrated here before 1960.

Another example: for U.S. citizens born in India, 43.7 percent migrated here during 1975 to 1980, and another 33.1 percent from 1970 to 1974.

The point of all this is obvious: why should recent immigrants be given preference over native-born American citizens? What does the United States owe these newly arrived immigrants?

This curious immigration-with-preference paradox, in fact, becomes more astonishing when one realizes that the situation can operate—and probably has operated—on a same-day basis: a non-citizen, either legally or with forged credentials, can cross the border and immediately become eligible for affirmative action preference. Incredibly, the immigration-with-preference paradox rarely, if ever, surfaced in the public debates surrounding recent immigration reforms.

Employers have recently discovered that the new immigration act has placed them in something of a dual dilemma: they may be fined for hiring illegal aliens but sued for discrimination if they refuse to hire a worker with dark skin. On the other hand, especially when immigrants may work for lower pay than citizens, affirmative action might provide a useful device to give preference to legal or illegal immigrants and, thereby, fulfill affirmative action quotas at the expense of citizens. Only rarely has this phenomenon been examined.

Brief discussion of the immigration-with-preference paradox came in the wake of the huge Cuban boat-lift migration in the late 1970s. Black spokespersons in Miami accused hotels and other employers of unskilled labor of hiring the newly arrived Cuban immigrants rather than blacks to fill affirmative action quotas. The same accusations have surfaced from time to time with Asian employees, leading to the on-again, off-again preferential status of various Asian groups.

Gann and Duignan pointed out that the new ethnic system of classification worked out by egalitarian elites has had many problems:

Assuming that entire ethnic groups have rights over and above those of individuals, how exactly are these groups to be defined? . . .

In attempting to define "disadvantaged" groups, American civil servants labored mightily to fit Mexicans, Puerto Ricans, Cubans, Dominicans, and Argentinians—a heterogeneous collection of the most varied ethnic backgrounds—into the American racial mold by constructing a new category known as "Hispanic." Puerto Ricans or Mexican Americans had not originally defined themselves as Hispanics; their leaders had not agitated for the establishment of such a category; Congress had not legislated the new ethnic definition; it came only by administrative fiat. The new category, in turn, became a working tool for demographers and statisticians. Its creation and use in public policy reflected a wider concern on the part of egalitarian reformers in the courts, the media and the civil service with the real or supposed unfairness of competition in American society . . .

Under this new dispensation, Chileans, Puerto Ricans, Cubans, Dominicans, and Mexicans all became "Hispanics," and all were part of a vast and heterogeneous collection of the disinherited—as distinct from "whites." (1986: 259–260)

Gann and Duignan also described the tasteless complexities faced by civil servants in racially classifying their employees "correctly." Dark-skinned Algerians are classified as "white," but blonde Castilians and red-haired Uruguayans are "Hispanics" according to government procedures. Agencies have also tried to cope with an employee's refusal to state his ancestry or—worse—to do so erroneously. Gann and Duignan suggest that continued non-cooperation could conceivably lead to a South African or Soviet-style system of officially documented racial classification (1986: 261).

This emperor-has-no-clothes quality regarding group preferences for non-black ethnics leads one to wonder just how social scientists have avoided the issue. Gann and Duignan (1986), White (1982), Glazer (1985), and Lynch (1985b) are among the few others who have raised this important aspect of affirmative action. Most social scientists and policy makers have ignored the multiplication of "protected groups" in the United States.

Thomas Sowell has wryly observed that the number of "protected groups" in the United States has multiplied to the extent that 70 percent of the population is covered by some form of affirmative action (1985: 14).

None of the white males interviewed for this study nor any of the personnel or affirmative action officers with whom I conducted background discussions had even thought of the immigration-with-preference dilemma. No one knew quite what to say when I raised the issue.

Nevertheless, the vexing problem of non-black minority preferences that has been surfacing, as in that dispute, is also the violation of the norm of distributive justice, another fundamental flaw in affirmative action theory and practice.

INEQUALITY EQUALS DISCRIMINATION

Another flawed assumption underpinning affirmative action's proportional representation has been exposed by social scientists, most notably economist Thomas Sowell (1981; 1984). The civil rights vision underpinning affirmative action, writes Sowell, is that "statistical disparities in incomes, occupations, education, etc., represent moral inequities and are caused by 'society'," that is, by discrimination and oppression (1984: 15). Discrimination against a group, it is assumed, results in collective poverty, which requires government action to remedy the situation. Group inequalities are, ipso facto, the result of discrimination.

Discussion of inequalities, notes Sowell, has been infected by a dangerous polarity: "The civil rights vision tends to dichotomize the spectrum of possible reasons for group differences into (1) discrimination and (2) innate inferiority. Rejecting the latter, they are left with the former. Morever, others who reject the former are regarded as believing the latter" (1984: 21). Thus, anyone who does not believe group differences are due to social and economic discrimination can be labeled "racist" (see Chapter 9).

Critics of Sowell have accused him of building a false polarization, a straw construction that he can easily knock down (see Harrington, 1984). But the polarization is not false. It has surfaced again and again in both popular and professional discussions.

Both Sowell and Glazer have steadily maintained that group differences may be due to myriad factors. For example, age structures of minority groups differ markedly. On average, "Blacks are a decade younger than the Japanese. Jews are a quarter of a century older than Puerto Ricans. Polish Americans are twice as old as American Indians." Likewise, most Latino groups are seven years younger than the white population as a whole. Cultural differences, principally age at marriage and number of children, have much to do with this. "Half of all Mexican American wives were married in their teens, while only 10 per cent of Japanese American wives married that young" (1984: 43). Sowell makes the common-sense observation that those who marry young and have several children may handicap future mobility.

Aptitudes and abilities may vary by culture and ethnicity. In the case of mathematics, "a study of high school students in northern California showed that four-fifths of Asian youngsters were enrolled in the sequence of mathematics courses that culminate in calculus, while only one-fifth of black youngsters were enrolled in such courses" (Sowell, 1984: 43–44). In looking at nationwide results on the Scholastic Aptitude Test, ethnicity/culture can override even socioeconomic background: "Black, Mexican American and American Indian youngsters from families with incomes of $50,000 and up score lower than Asians from families whose incomes are just $6,000 and under"(1984: 44–45). In obtaining higher eduation degrees, "More than half of all black doctorates are in the field of education, a notoriously undemanding and less remunerative field" (1984: 45).

In dealing with ethnic inequality, then, Sowell demonstrates that one must take into account age structure, fertility, and culture, including reverence for education, frugality, and the work ethic. Most of the successful groups, Sowell pointed out, restricted their fertility, worked hard, and saved in order to give their children educational advantages. Ethnic group attributes, even IQ scores, have changed over time, usually with acculturation to U.S. society (Sowell, 1981; 1984).

Mobility chances for Hispanics are clearly limited when less than half are high school graduates and more than half are functionally illiterate in English (*U.S. News and World Report*, August 10, 1987). Yet these problems are not evenly distributed within the Latino community: Cubans fare better than Mexicans and Puerto Ricans on most indices.

This diversity of subgroups within official ethnic categories presents another logical problem for affirmative action practitioners. Mention was just made of Hispanic diversity, but even within the black community there are diverse lifestyles and, more troubling, increasing economic and cultural polarization. Critics, such as Sowell and Walter Williams (1982), charge that affirmative action helps blacks already prepared for upward mobility while leaving untouched those mired in the culture and poverty of the ghetto (see also Jencks, 1985b; 1988).

AFFIRMATIVE ACTION VERSUS DISTRIBUTIVE JUSTICE

Affirmative action-as-quotas runs directly counter to one of the elementary rules of social behavior delineated by George Homans. In his behaviorist theory of human behavior, Homans posited a principle which he termed *distributive justice* (1958; 1974). Briefly put, the principle of distributive justice holds that people think that their costs (time, energy, work, etc.) should be proportional to rewards. The process is comparative:

people judge their own rewards by looking at others'. Does Joe receive as much money as Sam for the same amount of work? In addition to costs, Homans brought in the idea of investments: attributes such as experience, seniority, and level of education. Therefore, both investments and costs should be proportional to rewards.

In his earlier writings, Homans thought that persons who felt they had not obtained distributive justice would find aggressive behavior rewarding; such persons would be frustrated by not "getting what they deserved" and would find aggressive behavior an automatic reward to let off steam (Homans, 1958). Later, Homans slightly modified his views. He may have had the fate of white males under affirmative action in mind when he wrote:

A person who does not get the reward he needs feels dissatisfied but not necessarily angry: though he needs more, he may have no reason to expect to get it. But a person who does not get what he expected—and what he expected is always becoming what he deserves—is apt, by the frustration-aggression proposition, to find the results of aggressive behavior toward the source or beneficiary of his frustration rewarding. His frustration brings in a new and highly important value, which may change the terms under which he will take part in social exchange. He may be willing to forgo other rewards in order to get back at his tormentors. (1974: 241)

As previously discussed in Chapter 4, Stephen Johnson tested the theory of distributive justice and reverse discrimination in a social psychological experiment. The subjects were told that their responses would be judged against those of a competitor, who was actually non-existent. Half of the subjects were told they had lost to the competitor because the latter's solution of the puzzle was better; half were told that the competitor had been assigned a bonus score based upon the other's economic deprivation. Half of the subjects were told the competitor was black; the other half were told their competition was white.

Attitude measurements taken before and after the experiment indicated that, of the subjects who were told they had lost because of the "economic deprivation" factor, there was more aggression and perceived injustice towards black competitors than toward whites. On the other hand, "when the S's loss resulted from the other's superior performance . . . the white S's were less aggressive toward the black other than toward the white other" (1980: 15). In other words, the subjects perceived reverse discrimination when told they had lost in competition to a black due to an arbitrary criteria, economic deprivation, assigned by the experimenter. No such reaction occurred when they were told they had lost to the competitor's superior performance.

A RECIPE FOR CONFLICT

Anyone with elementary training in social science should have been able to identify the above flaws as a recipe for resentment, tension, confusion, and conflict, but most experts have avoided public acknowledgement of these contradictions.

Materials already presented in this book illustrate the problems caused by these logical holes. In the next two chapters, I will to examine the conflict and other latent consequences of affirmative action problems in greater detail.

NOTES

1. A 1987 survey of business executives by *The Wall Street Journal* (March 20, 1987: 21D) yielded similar results: most were white, male, college-educated.

2. An apparent anomaly here would be Verba and Orren's discovery of an anti-quota majority among the intellectual and media elites in the mid-1970s. By way of explanation, Verba and Orren suggest some members of these elites may see their current positions or future promotions at risk (1985: 84–85). They ignore the obvious fact that if people are already in an "elite" they are not likely to be easily threatened by quotas usually aimed at new-hires and middle-level managers.

Data presented in this book and in studies of the media of Gans (1980) and by Lichter et al. (1986) strongly suggest that either Verba and Orren's finding are incorrect or that attitudes have changed. If attitudes have changed, the spiral of silence and the New McCarthyism surely are factors. Clearly, reporters and commercial television writers do not like to deal with affirmative action, especially as reverse discrimination. When such matters are discussed, there is the "progressive" language and etiquette of the media described by Sobran (1987).

3. Tamarkin noted that 100,000 employee grievances per year were pouring into the EEOC and that "American industry has shelled out more than $1 billion in back pay, promotions and training for minorities and women" (1978: 29).

It is ironic that private business bears the brunt of the onslaught by bureaucrats and activists for business has made more progress in equal employment opportunity than any other sector of society, including federal and state government, educational institutions and unions. . . .

The federal government, nevertheless, is committed—almost obsessively—to correcting "patterns and practices" of discrimination against entire classes of employees, mainly women and blacks. . . .

The present atmosphere is one in which the government and activist groups—often acting together—serve as prosecuting attorney and often treat business as if it were guilty unless proven innocent. (1978: 29–30)

4. In addition to the overt costs, "there's no way to calculate the cost to Sears's image, but the retailer worried about it constantly after feminists led a smear campaign. The National Organization for Women, for instance, created a Sears Action Task Force, and local NOW chapters, sometimes claiming in surveys of Sears employees to be partners in the EEOC investigation, launched their own probes of the company's alleged sexism. . . . T-shirts displayed at the group's 1975 convention showed the Sears Tower and the demand, '$100 Million and Nothing Less,' Sears court filings show" (Weiner, 1986:1).

5. An additional benefit of affirmative action is that it can be used as a technique to threaten or replace older, expensive, or "troublesome" white male employees. There were indications of such mischief in both the press accounts cited in Chapter 2 and in the individual interviews in Chapters 4 and 5.

Chapter 11

MANIFEST CONSEQUENCES OF AFFIRMATIVE ACTION

In 1985 and 1988, sociologist Nathan Glazer reappraised the status of affirmative action. The author of *Affirmative Discrimination* (1975), the first major sociological analysis of the issue, found that a stalemate currently prevails on affirmative action. These controversial policies have neither expanded nor contracted. Proponents and opponents have settled into a form of protracted "trench warfare." Only the Supreme Court could break the deadlock.

As was discussed in detail in the previous chapter, Glazer found that affirmative action has become institutionalized in business and government. The majority of congressmembers avoid the issue, while a committed few continue to try to protect race-conscious policies.

Glazer acknowledged the triumph of affirmative action quotas over public opinion: "The strength must give one pause: it seems to make nonsense of polls showing that three-quarters of Americans oppose quotas" (1988: 108). By way of explanation, Glazer returned to his 1975 argument that affirmative action quotas drew their legitimating power from white guilt over the plight of blacks. He was, however, closer to the truth when he also admitted that critics of quotas have been attacked for opposing any form of affirmative action. (Glazer did not mention the hate-label "racist.")

Glazer was relieved that the number of groups covered by affirmative action quotas has not expanded, but he recommended gradually removing Asians and Hispanics from the affirmative action preference categories. Glazer contended that "we have seen a substantial reduction of the gap in earnings between blacks and whites, but we have seen other key measures of black well being decline" (1988: 109). Glazer noted that teen pregnancies, family breakup, drugs, and declining participation in the work force have not been amenable to affirmative action remedies.

Much of what Glazer had to say has been corroborated by materials already presented in this book, but there has been a great deal left unstated in Glazer's articles. His description of a bloodless "stalemate" masked the dangerous continuing conflicts and human costs promoted by these policies. (Glazer did not cite Greenberg's findings of whites' intense feelings of anger and betrayal toward government-imposed quotas.)

Glazer's analysis dealt mostly with what Robert Merton (1968) termed the "manifest" or intended and obvious consequences of affirmative action. But the primary interests of this chapter are the unintended and non-obvious consequences of these policies, which are at least as important as the intended purposes. Some of these semi-hidden effects are actually quite obvious, such as the exacerbated problems with race relations. Others, such as the impact of affirmative action quotas upon corporate planning and the anti-government, anti-tax mood, require deeper investigation and interpretation.

First, however, I wish to pay brief attention to the level of analysis addressed by Glazer regarding manifest consequences of affirmative action. The question "has it worked?" usually refers to whether or not the policies have brought women and blacks into educational and occupational structures, thus narrowing earning gaps between these groups and white males.

Briefly, let us see how matters stand.

MANIFEST FUNCTIONS OF AFFIRMATIVE ACTION

To fully examine all the possible changes in educational and occupational structures would take—and has taken—entirely separate book-length reports. What I wish to do here is to provide a brief overview of others' data as to whether or not affirmative action has increased chances for minority/female advancement in education and occupational structures.

There have been changes in the occupational structure. With regard to full-time employment in professional managerial occupations, there have been changes in the ratios of minority males and both white and minority females compared to white males (see Table 6).

Black or minority males, then, have achieved the greatest gains in professional and managerial professions in comparison to white males. Minority women have achieved gains almost as great. The rate of change for white females has not been as great, but their status compared much less favorably to white males in 1964.

Both Richard Freeman (1984) and James Smith and Finis Welch (1986) agreed that, for blacks, gains have been greatest for young, educated black males and for those in the South. Smith and Welch studied income patterns

Table 6
Changes in Ratio of White/Non-White Employment by Gender in
Managerial-Professional Occupations, 1964–1982

	1964	1982	Change
White men	1.00	1.00	
Black or non-white men	.32	.62	.30
White women	.68	.80	.12
Black or non-white women	.35	.60	.25

Source: Freeman, 1984, 24

for the past forty years among various segments of the black community. They discovered an "emergence of a black middle class, whose income gains have been real and substantial. The growth in the size of the black middle class has been so spectacular that as a group it outnumbers the black poor" (1986: 12). Also:

Nowhere are those changes more dramatic than when we focus on the contemporary economic elite. For the first time in American history, a sizable number of black men are economically better off than white middle-class America. During the last twenty years alone, the odds of a black man penetrating the ranks of the economic elite increased tenfold. (1986: 13)

There also has been a progressively sharp divergence in black male and black family incomes. Black family income was 41 percent of that of white families in the 1940s. By 1970, it was 61.2 percent, but barely rose after 1970 to only 62.5 percent in 1980. On the other hand, black males income rose steadily from 1940 through 1980. By 1980, black male income was 73 percent of white incomes. Intact black families (husband and wife) earned 82 percent of what intact white families earned. Young, college-educated, black intact families have incomes at or above parity with similar white families. Like other analysts, Smith and Welch attribute the polarization in income and occupational attainment within the black community as a function of the steep rise of female-headed low-income families.

Women have also made substantial progress. In 1973, only 5.8 percent of lawyers were women, compared with 15.3 percent in 1983; in 1973, only 1.3 percent of engineers were female, compared to 5.8 percent in 1983; in 1973, 18.4 percent of managers were female, compared to 32.4 percent in 1983.

Women in bank management have made some especially dramatic gains. For example, 64 pecent of BankAmerica's management jobs are held by women; 58 percent of management jobs at Wells Fargo are held by women (*The Wall Street Journal Special Report,* "The Corporate Woman," March 24, 1986: 7D). A 1986 survey for the Equal Employment Opportunity Commission found that from 1980 to 1985 black women became corporate managers and officials faster than any other group (*Los Angeles Times,* February 28, 1988:IV, 3). Yet some affirmative action advocates still complain that most women managers are at the middle ranks and that, for example, only 20 percent of BankAmerica's 3,500 executives are female; at American Telephone and Telegraph, only 15 percent of district managers are female, and only 3 percent of the top 880 executives.

With regard to women, the much-cited figure that female workers make fifty-nine cents for every dollar made by males also is considerably narrowed when one controls for age and marital status.

A look at the distribution of women and blacks in occupational categories may be instructive. (See Table 7). Women and blacks are still heavily represented in such low-paying and traditionally segregated jobs as "cleaning jobs," "postal cleark," and—for women—"elementary school teachers." On the other hand, as indicated in the studies cited earlier, there have been gains for young blacks in the professions, and the percentage of women in the professions has jumped markedly.

But there is a vexing question: to what extent were such changes caused by affirmative action? For example, the number of women students in business administration has been steadily rising without any affirmative action

Table 7
Percentage of Blacks and Women in Selected Occupations, 1987

	Percent Who Are	
	Women	Black
Corporate executives	36.8	5.2
Doctors	17.6	3.3
Nurses	94.3	6.7
Lawyers	18.0	2.9
Elementary school teachers	85.2	10.8
Sales supervisors	30.5	4.0
Postal clerks	43.5	29.8
Firefighters	1.9	7.8
Police and detectives	10.9	14.6
Cleaning jobs	41.5	23.8
Construction supervisors	1.6	3.8
Construction workers	2.8	15.0
Truck drivers	2.1	13.8
Total Work Force:	44.4	9.9

Source: *Time*, April 6, 1987, p. 20

pressures. Changing social and individual attitudes simply made the choice of a business career more acceptable to women (Glazer, 1985).

In studying employment trends, Freeman (1984) suggests that affirmative action has been a factor in helping women and minorities achieve occupational gains:

In short, for workers with jobs, there is considerable evidence that in the period of intense affirmative action and EEO activity protected groups gained in earnings and occupational position. . . . In spite of the controversy, the evidence from virtually all rigorous research studies shows that affirmative action or EEO activities are, indeed, operating to accomplish the purpose of shifting demand for labor to minorities or women. (1984: 25)

For blacks, Freeman adds, the greatest gains have been for younger and better-educated black men and for those in the South.

Freeman cites the work of Jonathan Leonard (1984a; 1984b), who found that federal contractor employers (covered by affirmative action guidelines) produced greater gains for "protected groups" than did non-federal contract employers.

On the other hand, Smith and Welch concluded that the greatest gains by blacks occurred prior to the enforcement of affirmative action policies, especially during the 1940s. They also cite Leonard's studies as showing that affirmative action resulted in a radical reshuffling of black jobs in the labor force. It shifted black male employment towards

EEOC covered firms and industries, and particularly into firms with federal contracts. Reshuffling is the right term, because the mirror image is that black employment in the non-covered sector plummeted. Affirmative action also increased the representation of black male workers in the managerial and professional jobs in covered firms. (1986: xxi)

Smith and Welch concluded that affirmative action had no significant long-run impact upon the male racial wage gap. Affirmative action did have a significant, though short-term, positive effect on wages of younger black workers. A study by the U.S. Civil Rights Commission, "The Economic Progress of Black Men in America" (1986), drew the same conclusions as Smith and Welch.

With regard to income and economic data, gross figures for black/white and male/female differences indicate that gaps have narrowed, though not as much as many would prefer. But use of statistical controls reveals many subpopulations among both blacks and women. For example, black college-educated males and females outside the South earn as much as, or more than, their white counterparts. A major problem with closing black/white gaps has been the recently recognized polarization within the black community, between the middle class and the growing population of black, lower-class families (Murray, 1984b; Smith and Welch, 1986).

Education

Education statistics show a closing of the black/white gap in levels of schooling during the 1970s. Smith and Welch observe that

Education levels of each new generation of workers increased over the last forty years. While this trend exists for men of both races they [the increases] were much sharper for black men. Educational differences still persist between the races, but they are far less today than at any time in our history. In 1980, a typical black man had a year-and-a-half less schooling than the average white male worker. (1986: 27)

Enrollment of blacks in colleges and universities rose in the 1970s, but has leveled off or dropped slightly in the 1980s. Charles Murray, however, cautions that these gains might not be as dramatic as they appear since the quality of education—measured by standardized tests—appears to have dropped significantly in inner-city black schools (1984b: 100–106).

Women now constitute a majority of college students. Their enrollments in law school have risen from 5 percent in 1964-65 to about 33 percent in 1983-84; in medicine, the corresponding figures are 5 percent and 27 percent; in dentistry, the figures are 1 percent and 20 percent; in veterinary medicine, 11 percent and 42 percent (*USA Today* survey, July 22, 1987; see also *U.S. News and World Report*, August 6, 1984). All or most of these gains have occurred without affirmative action pressures.

Other Manifest Functions of Affirmative Action

At least three other major functions or purposes have been advanced on behalf of affirmative action. It has been argued that such policies would: increase the number of role models for women and minorities, compensate victims of past discrimination, and promote sociocultural diversity.

The increasing numbers of women and minorities in the professions have, no doubt, provided role models. However, insofar as some may have been marginally qualified "tokens," their value as exemplars is dubious. Also, the importance of same sex or same ethnicity role models can be questioned. For example, Sowell (1985) points out that most immigrant groups to this nation have been taught by members of previously arrived groups. Jews and Asians who had Anglo, German, or Irish teachers have done very well indeed.

Affirmative action was also designed to compensate victims of past discrimination. This is a highly complex matter. An individual who has evidence that an employer discriminated against him or her undoubtedly has been helped by the presence of such programs. The individual is no match against an organization in a court of law. Affirmative action regulations provide less expensive and intimidating measures of redress, an extra measure of due process, an extra measure, it should be noted, not accorded white males.

On the other hand, affirmative action proponents often take a collectivist tack, arguing that compensation for past discrimination need not be awarded on an individual basis but can simply be accorded to any member of an oppressed group. Whatever the logical and ethical problems involved with this position, data would indicate that advocates of "group justice" have had some success: though parents who suffered discrimination have not been directly redressed, younger minorities—especially educated blacks—are achieving more than their parents. Younger women, too, are more successfully pursuing careers. But to what extent affirmative action is responsible for the gains of young women and young blacks is open to question.

As for sociocultural diversity, that goal may have been undermined by intergroup conflict between whites and minorities and among minority groups competing for preferential status. Murray (1984b) and Bloom (1987), for example, cite black student separatism rising on college campuses. Rodriguez (1987) complains of the burdens of the separatist "minority student" label imposed by both outsiders and members of the minority community. He, too, notes that "romantic" aspirations towards integration on the campuses have been replaced by intergroup tension and hostility.

As an example of the affirmative action revolution "in motion," let us look at race-based admission policies and student politics in the University of California. The stuggles in that institution of higher education illustrate both the manifest or intended functions and the latent or unintended functions of these policies.

Racial Spoils in the University of California System

Struggles to set standards and allocate resources and positions according to race-based criteria have troubled the University of California system for several years. In admissions, the primary conflict has involved access to the campuses at Berkeley and Los Angeles, the two most prestigious campuses in the nine-campus UC system.

It was probably inevitable that every problem and pressure associated with affirmative action preferences would converge in crowded, multicultural California. With applications soaring and budgets stagnating, university officials have had to cope with an angry babble of group claims and counterclaims of discrimination and preference, of "biased standards," of hidden quotas, and furious alumni whose children have been rejected. Complicating this cacophony of interest groups has been a 1974 legislative resolution which ordered the UC campuses to make the racial compositions of their student bodies match the racial compositions of each year's high school graduating class by 1990.

Despite a decade's efforts,

blacks and Latinos remain underrepresented in the UC system. Both Berkeley and UCLA had set aside a growing number of places in their freshmen classes for these minority groups; that means that, under affirmative action programs, both campuses accept minority students who do not meet ordinary eligibility standards. Berkeley enrolled 728 blacks and Latinos in its 1986 freshman class; at UCLA, 25 percent of the freshman class was black and Hispanic. (Mathews, 1987: 28)

The corresponding effects of affirmative action upon whites have been dramatic: the proportion of whites in Berkeley's student population has fallen from 68.1 percent in 1975 to 45 percent in 1986; at UCLA, the proportion of whites fell from 69 percent to 46 percent.

"The reason for this drop in white enrollment," Berkeley's [director of admissions] Bailey said, is that "affirmative action is working. All the special efforts . . . we have made to get more minority students into the system are clearly paying off. . . .

"There is no question who is taking the brunt of this affirmative action effort," Siporin [UCLA director of admissions] said, "it's the white student.

"It's a simple matter of mathematics," she said. "If you've got a pie and you don't change the size of the pie and you give somebody a bigger piece—which we as a state and society have decided to do—then someone is going to get a smaller piece. To a certain extent, Asians may be feeling the new cuts. But it is clearly Caucasian students who are experiencing most of it." (*Los Angeles Times*, November 26, 1986: 3, 39)

In an effort to cope with competitive pressures and to boost black and Hispanic enrollments still further, in 1986 both campuses de-emphasized strictly academic criteria such as grades and test scores. Only 40 percent of Berkeley's 1987 freshman class were admitted strictly by an academic index. Berkeley Chancellor Ira Heyman wrote that the 1988 admissions-by-merit figure was somewhat higher at 58 percent (*Los Angeles Times*, February 7, 1989: II, 5). Nevertheless, a *Newsweek* article (February 6, 1989; 63) indicated that whites continued to be excluded from Berkeley, with the proportion of the white enrollment in Berkeley's 1988 freshman class falling still further to 37 percent.

According to Mathews (1987), UCLA abandoned sole reliance on grades and test scores altogether. Every applicant is reviewed and evaluated on "subjective criteria" as well as grades and test scores. These subjective criteria include quality and content of students' courses, overall difficulty of their high school programs, and their extracurricular activities. According to a director of admissions, "we also give extra points to the kids who open up computer software businesses in their garages, or have to work after school in their parents' grocery stores, or those who lost their parents and live with their grandparents. We see all those attributes as advantages, adding to the diversity of the class" (p. 26).

The lead editorial in the December 10, 1986, edition of the *Los Angeles Times* hailed the plan as a "model policy." The editorial writers never once mentioned race or ethnicity, but that was a semi-hidden factor in the plan. An earlier report made it clear that whites and Asians would have to compete on grades and test scores and other meritocratic criteria, while members of underrepresented groups would merely have to meet the minimal requirements (*Los Angeles Times*, November 23, 1986).

By 1988, press reports openly admitted that the primary subjective criteria in the UC admissions scheme was race and that, in the competition for admission to the freshman class of 1988, more than 2,000 students (white and Asian) with perfect 4.0 grade point averages had been rejected at UC Berkeley and UCLA (*Los Angeles Times*, December 1, 1988).

The major news organizations have silently shrugged off the white enrollment decline. But outcries from the Asian community over possible restrictions resulting from the plan have received more attention. Rather than to frontally attack preferences for blacks and Hispanics, Asian spokespersons have charged that the new criteria are designed to maintain the level of white enrollments. In view of the drastic declines cited above, this was not an unreasonable argument.

UCLA Law School professor Reginald Alleyne summed up the absurdity of the situation in the title of a *Los Angeles Time* Op Ed essay, "Everyone Needs Affirmative Action." Alleyne cut to the core of the problem: "The problem for the university is that anything it does to admit students affects the admissions interests of some racial or ethnic group" (1987: V: 5).

The spirit of ethnic struggle in the wider society has molded campus politics at UCLA. According to a *Los Angeles Times* account, contests for campus positions are "no longer simply popularity contests among fraternity brothers; student elections are now rife with sophisticated ethnic-coalition politics."

But the recent elections are not necessarily a sign of growing tolerance. Indeed, the process of choosing student governments today is one of racial tensions and strange new alliances among ethnic, social and religious groups on campus.

"It's also the new un-American politics," said UCLA's Chancellor Charles E. Young, a political scientist by training. "During the last 15 or 20 years we've moved away from the melting pot, the idea of assimilation. We've got the opposite now, the idea of separatism, even nationalism."

Compounding this diversity, Orbach (provost of the College of Letters and Sciences] noted, is that the stakes are higher in UCLA campus government than at most other universities. Elected student officials and their appointees are given sole discretion of the allocation of about $200,000 a year. This means that organizations and clubs, such as the Iranian Student Group, the Asian Coalition, or the Gay and Lesbian Association, must lobby the president and the 18-member undergraduate student council for money just to operate. (November 16, 1987)

The 1986 student elections at UCLA were "a war between the races."

Before the campaign was over, Florez found himself in a clear-cut "race" race. His opponent, a white male, had the support of fraternities and various predominantly white groups. . . . Florez had the support of virtually all the minority organizations except the Jewish student union. Quickly, the rhetoric on both sides—not from the candidates themselves but from some of their anonymous supporters—became mean-spirited and clearly racist. . . .

By the time [Florez] took office, he discovered what some of his predecessors had already learned: that the war of the races was just beginning. But it was not just dark-skinned students against light-skinned. It was Latinos against Anglos, blacks against Jews, Jews against Palestinians. In other words, the situation generally mirrored what was happening in the world outside the university. . . .

While the scramble for power and money may be foremost in most student leaders' minds, there is at least one *issue* dividing the various ethnic and racial groups on campus. That is affirmative action. . . .

The intensity of ethnic feelings even affects operation of the student newspaper. Just last month, for example, the editor-in-chief and art director of the Daily Bruin were suspended briefly by a student-run communications board for publishing a cartoon strip parodying affirmative action. (March 16, 1987)

Violence finally flared during student elections on the campus in May 1988. A Latino candidate for student body president was disqualified because of poor grades. Groups of minority students then marched into the balloting areas and fist fights broke out. In the weeks before and after the election, some candidates reported death and rape threats. The elections were postponed and rescheduled two weeks later with security police at the ready.

What has happened in the University of California is an affirmative action meltdown, a quickening proliferation of claims and counterclaims on the state made purely on ascribed bases. This system of government-sponsored racial preferences has increased conflict, not decreased it. This is true not only for the University of California, but also for the wider society. But social scientists and political analysts have been slow to acknowledge this and other unintended consequences of what has become a racial spoils system.

Chapter 12

RESTRUCTURING SOCIETY BY RACE AND GENDER: LATENT FUNCTIONS OF AFFIRMATIVE ACTION

Proponents of affirmative action have attempted to restructure American society using race-and-gender preferences. Their aim has been to establish race-and-gender equity based upon proportional representation. Advocates of preference policies have focused exclusively on two factors, race/ethnicity and gender. They have ignored the long list of other major factors that influence human life including culture, family, social class, personality characteristics (motivation, need-achievement, and intelligence), size of generational cohort, migrations, and technological change.

In attempting to transform American society, proponents of preferential affirmative action have caused many unintended, unanticipated changes and conflicts. The scope and aggressiveness of affirmative action goals, in combination with these "latent functions," have combined to produce an atmosphere of crisis and doubt concerning these policies.

In this chapter, I will examine some of these unanticipated, "latent functions" of affirmative action policies (Merton, 1968). A valuable outline of many of the latent consequences of race-conscious policies has been provided by Christopher Jencks (1985b: 756):

1. Affirmative action policies have "often" led to discrimination against white males, especially those who were beginning their careers in the 1960s and 1970s (i.e., the Baby Boomers).

2. Dual standards were commonly used for screening blacks and whites for jobs and for promotions.

3. Affirmative action has led to severe feelings of self-doubt among blacks.

4. At the same time, the policies reinforce racial hostility and stereotypes among whites.

5. These policies and problems make up a situation that "once looked to liberal whites like a temporary, transitional problem [but] now looks like a permanent condition.

Many of these problems were illustrated in the previous chapter's description of the racial spoils system evolving in the University of California. And they are magnified in the larger society, especially in the growing racial polarization in American political life.

RECOGNITION OF RACIAL POLARIZATION

Journalists and social scientists have usually assumed that whites, especially the much-sought-after "Reagan Democrats," have not been concerned with busing and affirmative action quotas. *Los Angeles Times* reporter David Lauter contended that the Reagan administration's "record on civil rights [is] not central to the concerns of working-class white Democrats who voted for Reagan in 1980 and 1984" (*Los Angeles Times*, August 2, 1988). But Lauter and like-minded observers are wrong. As Greenberg's studies of white, working-class voters suggest, affirmative action is a potent, divisive political issue. The issue lies just beneath the growing black/white political polarization that has become inceasingly obvious to many journalists and political scientists.

The title of the *The New Republic* article by John Judis, "Black Donkey, White Elephant," bluntly phrased the ominous problem. "Over the last four decades," Judis wrote, "the American political system has become increasingly polarized along racial lines." (1988: 25) Initially, Judis acknowledged Greenberg's findings that Walter Mondale's 1984 pleas for "fairness" were interpreted by whites as calls for favoritism for blacks. But Judis dismissed Greenberg's findings of whites' disapproval of quotas by stating that Democrats gave up support of quotas long ago; therefore, quotas are no longer an issue. (This, of course, is not true.)

Political commentator Hodding Carter (1988) also complained about the effects of racial polarization between the political parties. Carter accused the Republicans of pandering to white racism, while Democrats were taking their monopoly on minority political support too much for granted. Though Carter contemptuously referred to Ronald Reagan's opposition to "every civil rights proposal," he did not mention affirmative action quotas as a possible source of racial polarization.

In the summer of 1988, political scientist William Schneider provided the most detailed analysis of racial polarization between Republicans and Democrats. "The big story of the past twenty-five years has been the Democratic party's loss of the white middle class vote" (1988a: 56). But Schneider, too, omitted any mention of affirmative action.

Schneider's long analysis, "An Insider's View of the Election" (1988a), was a fascinating example of professional avoidance of the seen-but-not-noticed issue of affirmative action. Schneider and those he interviewed repeatedly hinted at battles stemming from affirmative action/race-preference systems, but no one would use those words per se. Quotas and affirmative action went unmentioned in Schneider's long discussion of racial politics in Chicago. Nor was affirmative action mentioned as Schneider discussed the crucial political role of the white ethnics in the north and the white southerners. One of Schneider's interview subjects explained that "Politically, that's what the Republicans are living off, those tensions within the Democratic Party" (1988a: 37). Schneider did not yet ask: What tensions? Generated by what policies?

Nowhere in Schneider's analysis was there a reference to Stanley Greenberg's research. Nevertheless, Greenberg's findings were implicit. Schneider maintained that the Democratic party had become "a top-down coalition of elite professionals and the dependent poor. In the 1988 presidential primaries, the Democratic party seemed to be reduced to two core constituencies—blacks and white liberals" (1988a: 56). Schneider might have asked: does this coalition of liberal elites and blacks push affirmative action quotas? (Answer: Of course.) And what would be the effect upon white working-class individuals injured by those policies? Could such injuries be a factor in leading them to abandon the Democratic coalition? Might government-sponsored racial preference lead to "a generalized resentment of elites and establishments" (1988a: 56)?

Schneider answered some of his own implicit questions later that same year in an analysis titled "Anti-Government Mood Fuels Politics of Race" (1988b). Schneider acknowledged that large numbers of the white middle class no longer viewed big (liberal) government as friendly to their interests. Government was identified with blacks and other minorities who, Schneider maintained, still saw government in highly positive terms.

But Schneider could not bring himself to admit that whites had any legitimate, rational basis for opposing reformist or redistributive government. Instead, he characterized such motives as founded on (irrational) fear and resentment. Schneider could not see that working and middle-class whites paid for such redistributive schemes.

After the 1988 presidential election, former Democratic Secretary of Health, Education, and Welfare, Joseph Califano, had no trouble spotting Democrats' support of affirmative action quotas and busing as alienating white voters and inflaming racial tensions. Echoing Schneider, Califano observed that, with the exception of Lyndon Johnson, Democrats had not won a majority of white voters since the election of Harry Truman in 1948. Unlike Schneider, Califano was understanding, if not sympathetic, regarding whites' anger toward affirmative action and busing.

We should take the race issue out of the closet and debate it with less cant and more candor.

There continues to be widespread support for job training, education, health care, housing and other programs to help provide the poor, who are disproportionately black, an opportunity to share in our economic wealth. In my view, what bothers many white, middle-class voters is the Democrats' refusal to discuss frankly the serious shortcomings of many programs aimed at disadvantaged blacks. They see that refusal as evidence of an open-ended commitment to blacks as *blacks*, regardless of economic status, and they resent it as unfair pandering to black constituents. They view such a perpetual commitment as founded not on need or social justice but on a guilt they refuse to accept.

For Democrats, the white hot racial button is affirmative action, the preference of blacks over whites for slots in colleges, jobs, and promotion. . . .

Over the years, as the economy softened and Democrats seemed to promote affirmative action as a permanent part of the legal landscape, a new generation of whites viewed preferences for blacks as "quotas" that helped blacks enter college ahead of whites with better grades and win promotion ahead of "better qualified" white colleagues. These Americans saw continuing such preferences as an unjust insistence by Democrats that they do penance for an era of slavery and discrimination they had nothing to do with.

We Democrats should be proud of the courageous stands we have taken on civil rights . . . but we must also be willing to re-examine policies that have failed. The simple truth is that Democrats' continued support of programs that are not achieving their goals may aggravate rather than ease racial tension (1989:29; original italics).

In other words, Califano had discovered that affirmative action violated the norm of distributive justice (see Chapter 10). In so doing, such policies contributed to the powerful, anti-government, anti-tax mood of the 1980s.

Racial Politics and the Anti-Government Mood

If William Schneider had reversed the title of his October 1988 essay to read "Politics of Race Fuels the Anti-Government Mood," the title might have been closer to the truth. It appears that government-sponsored race preferences may have alienated whites not only from the Democratic party but from government and public spiritedness as well.

Greenberg found that Michigan whites saw government and tax moneys as primarily serving inner-city minorities and their problems. Whites saw few government benefits for themselves. "These Democratic defectors have not turned away from government; in an important sense, they believe the government has turned away from them," wrote Greenberg (1985: 19). The government was also seen as actively getting in the way.

It will be difficult to confront the problem of Democratic defection without facing up to the intense racial feelings of these voters. . . . These Democratic defectors believe the government has personally intervened to block their opportunities. Appeals to fairness, opportunity, etc. are now defined in racial terms and have been stripped of any progressive content. (1985: 56)

Sociologist Johnson's small group experiments, the interviews for this study, Greenberg's pulse-taking of Michigan voters, and the dozens of other accounts contained in this book clearly demonstrate that race-and-gender preferences generate alienation and anger. This anger, as noted in the last chapter, is a natural response to a violation of the norm of distributive justice. Race-preference programs also violate the assumption held by 70 percent of whites that "blacks have the same opportunity to live a middle-class life as whites" (Orfield, 1988; see also Kluegel, 1985). Therefore, it is not surprising that a poll commissioned by the *Los Angeles Times* found that

blacks and Reagan Democrats are poles apart in their notions of how much help minorities are entitled to from the federal government. . . . Three-fourths of blacks said Washington "pays too little attention to blacks and other minorities." But three-fourths of the Reagan Democrats said the government pays either "too much" or "the right amount" of attention. (July 17, 1988)

If reactions by whites towards affirmative action quotas have fueled an anti-government mood, then such unstudied undercurrents also likely contributed to the most famous anti-government event in decades: California's Proposition 13 tax revolt and the era of Reaganomics, which followed on the national level.

There are, no doubt, many cultural forces animating California's decade-old tax revolt and anti-government mood: rampant materialism, "yuppies" and the "me generation," and the postponement or abandonment of child-bearing by the white middle classes. According to many analysts, the white middle classes in California, many of them childless, have decided that they do not use and do not care to fund public services such as schools, public health facilities, parks and recreation facilities, social service programs, and prisons. All the white middle classes need are fire and police protection for their largely privatized work and leisure activities (see Whitehurst, 1983; Stahl, 1987; Garamendi, 1988).

If this line of analysis is correct, then most of the middle classes probably realize which groups do use such facilities: the poor and minorities. Therefore, why fund programs for them? This self-interest is doubled for working- or middle-class whites who perceive themselves or their children quotaed out of jobs or promotions in the public sector.

According to California State Senator John Garamendi, "A recent report issued by the California Economic Development Commission concluded that nothing less than a pact involving all major segments of society would be necessary to address the challenges before us and maintain the quality of life we have come to expect" (1988: V, 5). But trying to build a spirit of public cooperation in California (or the rest of the nation) while distributing access to education and careers on the basis of racial and ethnic preference is to pursue incompatible, contradictory policies. If tax money and public services are perceived as rigged against those who are paying the taxes—well, what would a conflict theorist predict?

The legally sanctioned use of race-and-gender preferences has given the seal of government sponsorship to the most primordial divisions among humans: those based on the ascribed blood ties, of tribe and kinship. During the 1960s, these were just the sorts of ties that social scientists had hoped and assumed would fade in developing nations. More secular, civil ties would supplant tribal, religious hostilities. Achieved criteria, it was assumed, replaced ascribed criteria as civilizations advanced. Instead, affirmative action advocates have revived such forms of government-sponsored tribalism in the "postmodern" United States.

Paradoxically, then, those who most favor an active, cooperative role for government in society have sabotaged such goals with the group preference policies of affirmative action.

The Affirmative Action Stigma

One of the latent effects of affirmative action, which Christopher Jencks noted, was an increase of self-doubt among blacks and an increase of racial stereotyping by whites. As in so many aspects of affirmative action, there has been little systematic study of this problem. However, reports following anti-minority incidents on campuses suggest that one latent consequence of affirmative action has been that non-Asian minority students are often regarded as "less qualified" or "unqualified" compared to white and Asian students. Minority separatism on campus has heightened such feelings of "differentness" (see Bloom, 1987; Rodriguez, 1987; *The Wall Street Journal*, April 3, 1987; and, again, PBS *Frontline*, "Racism, 101," May 10, 1988).

A long report on minorities' problems on college campuses in the *Los Angeles Times* illustrated the affirmative action stigma:

"Nearly all Chicano students have a story about a first-year English composition professor who doubts they have written the paper they turned in," said Alfred Ramierez. . . .

"Often what you get is that the majority of the faculty and other majority students expect all minorities are there on waivers of standards. They expect [minorities] are all 'affirmative action' admissions and do not expect them to do well. There is the Pygmalian effect of prophecy fulfillment," said Sarah Mendez of the American Council on Education. (January 6, 1988: 16)

Aspiring screen-writer Migdia Chinea-Varela perceived a sense of segregation and stigma in affirmative action "access programs" offered by some major Hollywood production companies. When asked to apply for such programs she responded in a *Newsweek* "My Turn" column:

Why not take advantage of every opportunity that comes my way? The answer is: I've been in this situation before and I don't like the way it makes me feel. There's something almost insulting about these well-meaning affirmative action searches. . . .

I've asked myself the obvious questions. Am I being picked for my writing ability, or to fulfill a quota? Have I been selected because I'm a "twofer"—a female Hispanic, or because they were enthralled with my deftly drawn characters and strong, original story line? My writing career, it appears, has taken a particularly tortuous course. I've gone from being a dedicated writer to dedicated *minority* writer. . . .

In my view, there can be no affirmative action without segregation—nor any end to the segregation if our names must be kept on separate lists. (December 26, 1988: 10)

In the same year that Chinea-Varela voiced her criticisms of access programs in the competitive screen-writing profession, the feelings of doubt implied by affirmative action appeared in the highest realms of fiction writing. Black novelist Toni Morrison was ultimately convinced she had won the 1988 Pulitzer Prize on merit. Yet Morrison admitted that lobbying for the Pulitzer on her behalf by forty-eight prominent black writers was a source of stress. "It was too upsetting to have my work considered as an affirmative action award" (*Los Angeles Times*, April 1, 1989).

This stigma is a regrettable, but hardly unexpected, development if universities and other organizations are forced to use dual standards based on race/ethnicity to "get the numbers up" (Jencks, 1985b). Indeed, the affirmative action stigma has become so pronounced that some minorities are refusing jobs or promotions when such offers are tainted by preference policies (*Wall Street Journal*, June 27, 1989: A1, A7).

Avoiding the Overhead Costs of Quotas

The effects of affirmative action quotas upon ethnic antagonism, racial stereotyping, and minority self-doubt are not difficult to discern if one asks about such consequences in the first place. It is more difficult to assess the desire by corporate officials and the general public to avoid the monetary costs and personnel conflicts that accompany affirmative action programs. With these topics, one must engage in deeper, sociological interpretation beneath superficial charges made by some critics of "racism" in corporate policy and the anti-tax, anti-government political movements.

No one has calculated the total bill paid by corporations and government agencies for affirmative action quotas in terms of drawing up and maintaining plans (including the expenses of researching labor-pool data and gathering information on the ethnic/gender composition of the current workforce), the costs entailed in hiring and promoting less-qualified or unqualified persons, and coping with the alienation and hostility from non-preferred groups (see Chapter 10). Litigation and administrative hassles can be expensive, as was discussed in the case of Sears, Roebuck in the previous chapter.

It would be foolish to think that corporate executives have not given some thought as to how to minimize such overhead expenses. Some news reports suggest that they have.

Critics have leveled charges of racism against Japanese and American manufacturers who have built new plants in rural areas far from concentrations of racial minorities. It is difficult to disentangle "real" racism, anti-unionism, and the desire to avoid affirmative action hassles, not to mention potent tax incentives and other rewards offered by job-hungry states. Nevertheless, the Equal Opportunity Employment Commission was successful in obtaining a settlement with Honda for the Japanese-based corporation's discriminatory practices in its new Ohio plant.

It's a pattern cropping up all across industrial America. Optimists talk of "rein-dustrialization" by pointing to the spate of new plants, mainly Japanese, popping up in Rust Belt states such as Michigan, Ohio, Indiana and Illinois. But the new factories, unlike those they are supplanting, are mostly in small towns. So, rural whites are hitting the jobs jackpot, while urban minorities are hitting the streets.

Many blame that change on simple geography—and an effort to move away from unions. But some critics also accuse the Japanese companies of deliberately avoiding blacks. Honda and the U.S. Equal Employment Opportunity Commission settled a big racial-discrimination case last month. (*The Wall Street Journal*, April 12, 1988:A1)

The rural locations for these new plants might have been chosen even if there were no government-backed pressures to hire minorities in urban areas. But the probable lack of affirmative action pressures in such areas may have added considerably to their allure.

Another matter related to the overhead costs of affirmative action is the sheer expense and the diversion of resources from other organizational needs. For large organizations, the costs to implement an aggressive affirmative action program can be sizable. A recent example of what aggressive affirmative action commitments can entail can be seen in the state appropriations for the California community colleges system where the second and fifth largest budget items are for affirmative action. (See further discussion below.)

Competition for funding—as well as hiring and promotion authority—between affirmative action personnel and other organizational officers deserves further study. Conflicts over organizational resources and authority may weaken affirmative action, but such competition will not end it.

AFFIRMATIVE ACTION FOREVER?

Affirmative action has been an administrative revolution imposed by judges and bureaucrats. The drive to reshape American society by race-and-gender preferences has rolled ahead of long-delayed Supreme Court decisions. A major lesson to be learned from the study of affirmative action has been that the letter of the law and actual, everyday enactment of social policy need not be congruent. If social policy is framed within a loose or vague legal framework, then those who implement the policy may exercise an amazing degree of discretion. That is precisely what has happened with affirmative action.

During the past twenty years, affirmative action has moved steadily "leftward" toward open emphasis on race-and-gender criteria to achieve proportional group representation. The progressively radical drift in this revolution-from-above calls to mind historian Crane Brinton's (1938) study of revolution. In studying four major social revolutions, Brinton detected a "right-center-left" ideological progression. That is, the drive for more drastic change became stronger after the initial, mild "reform" stages of a revolution. Brinton used the metaphor of a fever increasing in intensity, followed by a sudden break and a convalescent period.

The direction of the affirmative action revolution has clearly followed Brinton's cycle. The original intent of affirmative action was clearly a moderate, even conservative, enhancement of equality of opportunity for individuals. The policies were intended to open up competitive selection processes. As we have seen in this book, however, the aims of the policy have moved from a "conservative" emphasis on non-discrimination to a more "radical" policy aimed at achieving ethnic/gender equity through the means of affirmative action quotas.

This revolution-from-above likely entered its most radical stage in the mid-1970s under President Jimmy Carter. During that era, affirmative action administrators increased their powers, their numbers, and their institutional bases. The Supreme Court's *Bakke* decision in 1978 was a partial victory for this expanding policy network. While the *Bakke* decision ruled out explicit use of quotas, the use of race as one of several criteria was declared legally permissible. This partial victory was made more complete by the *Weber* decision, which permitted employers, even those not found guilty of past discrimination, to set up their own affirmative action programs. Meanwhile, the New McCarthyism quelled protest.

The rise of a cadre of ideologically commited bureaucrats made it possible to wage a largely successful, protracted resistance against the anti-preference aims of the Reagan administration in the 1980s. Despite eight years of a conservative presidency—or perhaps because of this continuous confrontation—the course of affirmative action continued moving leftward toward a more collectivist vision of state-enforced proportional representation.

The majority opinion by Supreme Court Justice William Brennan in *Johnson v. Transportation Agency* (1987) may have been the high-water mark for the radical era of affirmative action. In *Johnson*, Brennan held that preferential treatment may be used to remedy "manifest imbalances" in the workforce as long as the rights of white males were "not undully trammeled." Brennan circumvented the anti-preferential treatment provisions of Title VII of the Civil Rights Act or, to use the words of dissenting Justice Scalia, "inverted" Title VII altogether, converting that section of law into what Scalia acidly termed an "engine of racism and sexism."

For all practical purposes, Brennan's decision in the *Johnson* case legalized all but the most obvious and egregious acts of reverse discrimination against white males. Even before *Johnson,* white males could successfully sue on charges of discrimination only if government or corporate officials were especially blatant or clumsy in admitting discriminatory intent. And, even if institutional spokespersons were careless enough to admit discriminatory intent or of set-asides procedures, the resolution of the case could take. many years—as has been seen in interviews for this book.

Armed with Brennan's opinion in the 1987 *Johnson* decision, and after years of trench warfare with the Reagan administration, preferential treatment proponents appear to have redoubled their efforts in the late 1980s. Especially in academic settings, there has been renewed, open emphasis upon hiring faculty and staff primarily on the basis of "diversity."

One of the more open and aggressive attempts to impose ethnic/gender equity in the workforce is embodied in the new state plan for the California Community Colleges system. Under the new legislation contained in Assembly Bill AB 1725, the Board of Governors is developing a new system-wide plan for a stepped-up affirmitive action plan, currently being drafted in a document entitled *Toward a New Diversity.*

In an analysis of AB 1725 prepared by the Board of Govenors of the California Community Colleges, it was stated that:

Concerns about affirmative action and staff diversity are thus woven into the very fabric of AB 1725 . . . . Numerical and percentage goals for the system as a whole are stated, an unprecedented step. (1989: 19)

AB 1725 creates the Faculty and Staff Diversity Fund, administered by the Board of Governors, to pursue two goals (as opposed to quotas or mandates) for the *system*: (1) by 2005, the cumulative workforce of the colleges should proportionately reflect the adult population of the state; and (2) by 1992–93, 30 percent of all new hires in the system should be ethnic minorities. (1989: 21)[1]

These directives have been backed up with financial priorities. The second and fifth largest budget items in the initial appropriations for AB 1725 were for "faculty and staff diversity fund" ($1,000,000) and "affirmative action" (major service function to assist districts in locating and recruiting ethnic minorities—$300,000). Financial penalties and rewards have been provided to encourage districts to achieve diversity goals. These state allocations supplement funds for affirmative action already established by the individual community college districts.

Insofar as California continues to be a bellwether state in leading national changes, variations of this plan will likely spread to many other community college systems around the nation—as will the radical's preferred terminology of "equity" and "access."

Triumph of Radical Terminology: "Diversity" and "Equity"

The terms "diversity" and "access" are being heavily promoted as goals by affirmative action bureaucrats and powerful ideological allies in foundations, universities, and the mass media.[2] There are progressively fewer references to terms from the earlier conservative or moderate policy stages such as "equality" or "equality of opportunity."

Thus, in the universities, mandatory courses on "cultural and gender diversity" are in place or are being readied. "Diversity Day" is celebrated at the University of Michigan. For those outside the universities, a parallel trend is taking place with mandatory "affirmative action seminars" for employees of several large corporations and government agencies.

As Allan Bloom (1987) clearly saw, what we have here is not only the climax of the radical agenda for preferential affirmative action but the triumph of cultural relativism. The drumbeat of diversity is yet another way of establishing the use of multiple standards of evaluation for different groups. It is an attack on universalistic, equal-treatment-for-all criteria such as grades and test scores.

The ability to override equal treatment in pursuit of diversity has had some degree of legal standing ever since Justice Powell held in the *Bakke* decision that diversity could be a goal in college admissions. It was given its strongest backing in Justice Brennan's controlling opinion in the 1987 *Johnson* decision.

I think we can expect future legal arguments to embody even more strongly the position that it is fully legal and desirable that employers and educational institutions select persons on the basis of race and gender in order to achieve diversity. The issue of equality will be down-played or ignored entirely.

The Bush administration has shown signs favoring a revival of affirmative action pressures. Bush himself discounted the *Richmond* decision by the Supreme Court, which suggested that whites must receive equal treatment. Corporations appear to be taking note of a possible change. More than two months after the *Johnson* decision, *The Wall Street Journal* (March 3, 1989: A1) noted that "minority recruiting quickens on perception that Bush really cares."

Sociologist Charles Murray has suggested that preferential treatment by race may become even more open and aggressive. Murray contends that political liberals will not easily give up the present system of race-and-gender preferences. Even as these policies' legitimacy and effectiveness are called into question, Murray suggests that liberals will nonetheless doggedly adhere to such programs in order to cover ideological lapses on other issues.

> The next decade will witness a dangerous combination: a continuing belief, no longer even questioned, that it is legitimate for government to treat people as members of groups, but without the moral passion which undergirded that belief twenty years ago and even without any faith that the original goals are capable of achievement. In short, liberalism is becoming unmoored . . . . In the name of doing good, they will in a few years be ready to undertake race-based measures of a nature that once would have appalled them. (1988: 32)

Racial Preference Conflicts in the Twenty-First Century?

Officially-sponsored race-and-gender preferences have already exacerbated generational tensions in this century. Should demands for race-and-gender equity continue into the twenty-first century, the conflict could dramatically intensify.

A latent function of affirmative action quotas in the twentieth century has been to strain relations between older citizens and the competitive Baby Boom generation. Older members of white elites have compelled younger, middle and working class, white males to redress historical inequalities through quotas applied to new-hires and lower-level promotions. In conjunction with other social policies, notably the tax revolts, affirmative action has limited the social fortunes of the white, male Baby Boomers. This has exacerbated a widening economic and opportunity gap based upon *age* —a major social division still ignored by many social scientists. Those who obtained good jobs and homes before the mid-1970s have been on one side of a great economic divide; many of those who did not achieve then are members of an oft-noted Baby Boom generation of "declining expectations," a generation in which many, if not most, do not expect to live as well as their parents (Littwin, 1986). Until the late 1980s, it was the Baby Bommers, especially the younger members of this cohort, who had to shoulder the burdens of affirmative action.

Now, in the late 1980s, yet another generation is becoming entangled in affirmative action: the children of the Baby Boomers have begun to encounter race-and-gender barriers in higher education and the workforce. While affirmative action machinery may have become semi-permanent, white children of the Boomers seem less ready to accept such mandated inequities. Affirmative action disputes, never fully vented, may intensify.

The fusion of generational divisions with demands for ethnic equity could have even more explosive potential in the next century. By approximately 2030, the nation will likely harbor an older, smaller population of whites and a younger population with a much higher proportion of blacks, Hispanics and Asians. In some states, such as California, white males (and females) will be members of a shrinking, but prosperous, white minority.

Generational cleavages could combine with ethnic equity tensions as larger numbers of non-whites chafe at paying taxes and social security to service older whites. Thus, the author of a Brookings Institution report on this looming conflict warned that

young black and Hispanic workers may well question the equity of paying income and payroll taxes to support older people, particularly the dominant group of white retired workers, when they already have lower average incomes, higher poverty rates, and lower expectations that they eventually will receive equal program benefits. (*The Wall Street Journal*, June 14, 1988: A1)

It would be ironic—and doubly unfair—if the Baby Boomers, already subjected to racial preferences in the formative years of their careers, were to face renewed or continuing demands for reparations in their retirement years. Such a scenario may sound far-fetched. But twenty years ago, when the 1964 Civil Rights Act was passed, a system of government racial preferences also sounded preposterous—as Hubert Humphrey and other liberals insisted when they nonetheless went along with the anti-preference language of Title VII.

THE CRISIS OF AFFIRMATIVE ACTION

"What can we do?" sighed a nervous Midwestern Democratic party official when questioned about Stanley Greenberg's findings of anit-quota feelings among whites. "White males between the ages of twenty-eight and forty seem to think they're locked out. What are we going to do?"

Such remarks capture the emerging crisis of affirmative action. Powerful ideological and organizational forces are committed to maintaining or expanding the system of race-and-gender preferences. This drive to reshape American society is colliding with the serious tensions produced by affirmative action. Even more serious conflicts may lie ahead. Increasing recognition of these policy-produced problems has increased the salience of this crisis, but cannot solve it. The policies of race-and-gender preference need to be re-examined totally in terms of both philosophical and sociological justification as well as the actual, everyday impact of these programs.

Even though the Supreme Court has begun to restrict the use and duration of race-and-gender preferences, it will be at least a decade before practices are actually abandoned. During two decades of legal limbo, ideologically commited elites have been able to generate pro-affirmative action rhetoric and bureaucracies which sustain such policies. Neither ideology nor bureaucracy change quickly. Quota culture and policies have become institutionalized in private and public sectors.

As Allan Bloom (1987) has remarked, Americans live in what is basically an administrative state. The nation is run by giant bureaucracies managed by elites. Affirmative action has been useful for many elites in many ways. Affirmative action is now seen as a viable defense against discrimination lawsuits and good public relations. Pro-affirmative action rhetoric has also served to manipulate employees, setting whites against minorities and intimidating older white workers fearful of replacement. The victim-generating potential of affirmative action is perhaps as useful to employers as is the victim-compensating rhetoric.

Bureaucratic inertia, ideological entrenchment, elite accommodation, and the New McCarthyism atmosphere of self-censorship will continue to collide with massive alienation and anger among white victims, conflict among non-whites for preferred-minority status, and dismay and confusion among an increasing number of high-level officials. The increasingly fragile consensus of norms and values in American life will continue to be strained. Can anything be done?

The solution to this question is both simple and difficult: talk about the issues. As has been demonstrated in this book, affirmative action has never been subjected to widespread public scrutiny and debate. If citizens could vote on such policies, race-and-gender quotas would be defeated overwhelmingly among whites and women and probably by a majority in most other groups. These divisive policies have simply been imposed by adminstrators and judges—and avoided by politicians, journalists, and social scientists. Increased public debate, still rare on affirmative action, may lead to heightened recognition of many of the contradictions and injustices discussed in this book. Silence under the New McCarthyism has been the ally of affirmative action radicals. Widespread talk can be a potent instrument of change (Gouldner, 1976).

There is much more talk today about affirmative action than there was even five years ago. Ten years ago, the subject was just seeping into mass media and public awareness after a decade of outright neglect and censorship among the news media and social scientists.

As mentioned at the outset of this book, cracks have begun to develop in the left-radical, New McCarthyism. Too many social problems once deemed unacceptable for public debate have percolated into public consciousness. With specific regard to affirmative action, the Supreme Court's 1989 decisions may loosen New McCarthyist taboos against criticism of preferential treatment and encourage more open endorsement of color-blind, gender-neutral policies of non-discrimination. The emperor-wears-no-clothes question concerning which groups deserve preference and why should be continually raised. In so doing the immigration-with-preference paradox should surface and, thereby, destroy the case for most currently preferred groups. The huge variations in income, education, and family styles among blacks should be kept in mind. These variations contradict the simplistic all-blacks-are-poor and inequality-equals-discrimination assumptions and raise questions of any categorical race preferences. And the fate of white males under affirmative action—still an awkward topic—must be raised with greater vigor.

The explosion of controversy concerning the proposal of a "mommy track" for women executives who wish to better balance career and family roles is another indicator of the crisis of affirmative action and also suggests the weakening of New McCarthyist taboos. Richard Lewis, chairman of *Corporate Annual Reports*, noted that the career-family issue could only have been broached by a noted female consultant, Felice N. Schwartz. Males in the corporate world had avoided the problem. Like the related issue of affirmative action, the career-family conflict had not been publicly acknowledged. Said Lewis:

I think it is a landmark subject and it has not been talked about publicly before. I think the reason is that on the one hand the feminist point of view had been that women and men essentially are equal and there should be no discussion of differentiation. In big business, there is a great concern over being labeled anti-feminist. Men just don't want to do that, they'd rather just duck the issue. Consequently, it really took a prominent woman with impeccable credentials to bring the subject to the table. (*Los Angeles Times*, March 19, 1989: IV,3)

Whatever the worth of such proposals, they are symtoms of the problems involved in trying to achieve full gender equality in the workplace. While sexism no doubt remains a force in American life, a growing amount of evidence indicates that sexual inequality in the workplace is largely the result of male/female gaps in education, skills, and experience (Smith and Ward, 1984). Male/female differences in experience, in part, reflect interruptions in career paths with regard to child-bearing. Thus, in many professional categories, single women under thirty-five earn nearly 95 percent of comparable males' salaries. Such data point to the highly complex cultural and psychological choices made by women with regard to marriage and child-rearing lifestyles. As emphasized in this book, intergroup inequalities have not been the sole product of prejudice and discrimination.

In moving toward a resolution of the crisis wrought by affirmative action preferences, sociologists and analysts in the mass media ought to re-emphasize and discuss with greater vigor the diverse sources of individual and group variations. Race and gender are potent forces in shaping social life. But a host of other powerful factors influence human behavior including culture, family structure and background, social class, peer group, generational cohort, and personality characteristics. The feasibility and legality of trying to arrange educational and occupational outcomes with policies based soley upon two factors out of many deserves re-examination.

Though the New McCarthyism may be on the wane and though there is growing discussion and awareness concerning the problems with affirmative action policies, additional focus upon the issue will not come easily. Talk seems to remain centered upon basic grumbling. Collective protest still seems distant —though it is emerging in voting patterns. Individual action against preference policies remains difficult, time-consuming, distant, and uncertain.

In addition to formidable institutional forces, there are other, deeper barriers to overcome.

TALK, TABOOS, AND SELF-CENTERED WORLDS

One of the most depressing lessons I have learned in fifteen years of sociological research is this one: people shape their perceptions of the wider world by what happens in their own back yards. Most people, certainly most Americans, have always been self-centered folk. The "Me Decade" of the 1970s and the 1980s' "Age of Reaganomics" have done little to dampen such an outlook.

To a remarkable degree, human beings, even those in the media and social sciences, live in their own little worlds. They are often incapable of understanding events that do not directly affect them. In addition, through the powers of individual or collective denial, people can refuse to see ongoing events and processes. Individual biases can block perceptions to a remarkable degree as will collectively generated taboos.

Nor are people willing to confront uncomfortable realities if such events have not directly affected them. It is a very old story in human cognition: if it doesn't happen to me, it does not matter. In combination with the taboos against seeing whites and men as victims, and the mass media silence on the problems of affirmative action, the self-centered "it-hasn't-happened-to-me" basis of human perception has been a major block in studying and understanding affirmative action and its abuses. This is especially true for white males over age forty, most of whom obtained positions before affirmative action quotas took hold. It is also true for many white males in engineering and scientific fields where there are, as yet, few non-Asian minorities.

Even white males who have directly encountered reverse discrimination have experienced doubt and confusion in perceiving themselves as victims of policies of racial preference. They did not complain among themselves, and there have been few organizations that would hear, much less champion, their grievances. White males who have encountered reverse discrimination have remained invisible victims as the media, social scientists, corporations, and politicians refused to openly discuss affirmative action, much less acknowledge that a new class of victims was being wrought by well-intentioned social policy. Indeed, more recently, verbal "male-bashing" and hostility toward white males seems to have become acceptable, even seen as "overdue," in some media and academic circles (Farrell, 1988).

The role of the mass media in reinforcing or breaking cultural taboos is more crucial than ever before. The nightly newscasts, commercial television programming, and major motion pictures can open up or close down issues and perspectives on those issues. Media elites can choose to reinforce a party line and try to impose their version of reality on the lives of individuals.

Yet it should be noted that even journalists and social scientists are constrained by less specific and more general cultural prescriptions. Race, religion, and politics have ever been the bane of polite conversation in middle-class society. To some extent perhaps this is as it should be. Yet conversational taboos on such topics have sustained any number of harsh, social realities. Racial segregation, sexism, religious bigotry, and other unlovely phenomena were sustained by polite niceties. Alcoholism, child and spouse abuse, homosexuality, and drug addiction were dilemmas shielded from discussion and, hence, awareness and possible positive action.

As always, the young are less restrained by tradition and convention. They are all too willing to see abuses that their elders do not wish to acknowledge. And it has been the young who appear most eager to talk about the injustices of race-and-gender preferences. As Jospeh Califano observed, they are less burdened by collective guilt. They are less willing to become a new generation of invisible victims.

Unfortunately, some anger against affirmative action may have surfaced in the form of ugly expressions of racism. There is racism among the young just as there is among their elders. But sociologists and journalists should not be so quick to label all objections to affirmative action as racist—when voiced by the young or anyone else. As I have pointed out in this analysis, there are many rational, legally sound arguments against policies that seek to restructure society according to general and ill-defined categories of race and gender.

The history of affirmative action is a sobering lesson in American civics. Bob Allen, the politically liberal bank administrator interviewed for this study, summed up very well a key aspect of the crisis of affirmative action:

We have institutionalized a counter-white-male bias. We've created a new group who are being discriminated against. . . . You've got no access to legal recourse or power. We have institutionalized discrimination against one group. *When does it end?*

NOTES

1. The program for faculty and staff diversity supposedly will take into account "availability data which will determine the percentages of underrepresented group members who have the requisite education and experience to work in the various community college occupations" (*Comprehensive Analysis, 1989*: 21). And "ethnic minorities" is supposed to include women, the disabled, and Vietnam veterans.

Whether such distinctions will be retained in actual practice—or whether some district officers will rely on overall population data as a basis for hiring—should be a subject for future study.

2. Brochures from two of the giant foundations, Ford and Carnegie, are full of the new equity/diversity rhetoric coupled with priority program goals that support the implementation of this philosophy—especially in education. See the Ford Foundation's *Current Interests 1988 and 1989* and the Carnegie Corporation's *List of Grants and Appropriations, 1987.*

Appendix 1

REVERSE DISCRIMINATION ACCOUNTS

G. Gordon
Pressured to engage in reverse discrimination in hiring and treatment of subordinates while a middle-level California correctional officer in the mid-1970s. Saw super ordinates subjected to reverse discrimination. Gave up on promotions. Obtained disability pension when injured in prison disturbance.

P. Elton
Also pressured to engage in reverse discrimination in hiring and treatment of subordinates as an upper-level officer in the California correctional system during the mid-to-late 1970s. Lost one major promotion to less-experienced female from outside the system. Promised promotion could not be obtained because person Elton was to replace was unable to be moved due to affirmative action needs.

J. Smith
Joined California correctional system as part-timer in 1976. Repeatedly frustrated in obtaining full-time status when minorities with lower test scores were moved by him. Moved to a rural prison unit, unattractive to minorities, in order to obtain full-time status. As was the case with G. Gordon, he took a disability pension after being injured in a prison disturbance.

F. Sanders
Research psychologist with a large government agency who has been unable to obtain promotion in 14 years. Feels he has been bypassed by at least one less-qualified female. Was told point blank a woman was easier to promote. Filed grievance to no avail. Sanders remained with agency because of lack of external opportunity and because he likes his work.

B. Allen
Department manager of a large financial institution who reported being bypassed on promotions three times—twice by less qualified females—one of whom he had hired the year before. He remained because he felt he would eventually be promoted and because of lack of opportunities elsewhere.

B. Watson
Administrative analyst for a major corporation, was bypassed in favor of less experienced minorities. Transferred to undesirable location when he complained. He was later returned to a worse job than he left. Watson was told jobs above him were reserved for minorities. Watson quit when he qualified for minimal pension benefits.

S. Huddleston
White-collar worker for large division of state of California. Had troubles getting promotions in late 1970s, when females or minorities with lower examination scores were promoted over him. Finally won promotion himself.   ·

S. Clark
White-collar worker for large division of state of California who also had trouble in the late 1970s in obtaining promotions, which were explicitly stated as being "reserved for protected groups." Finally got promotion when black manager fought division's equal-opportunity section to get Clark promoted.

S. Mulligan
White-collar worker with a large division of the state of California (same as previous cases), who lost promotional opportunities when females or minorities with lower scores were promoted. Eventually won promotion in early 1980s.

T. O'Neil
Also a low-to-middle level white-collar worker for the state of California, who watched women and minorities obtaining special training, scheduling, and other preferences and then saw them obtain promotion with lower test scores during mid-to-late 1970s. Finally obtained promotion himself in 1980s.

A. McWhirter
Repeatedly screened out of firefighter jobs when minorities with lower test scores were hired during the late 1970s and early 1980s. Read about quotas in the local papers and was informed of pressures by hiring agents.

R. Oakes
After being laid off as a permanent staff cameraman from a local television station in the early 1970s, film cameraman Robert Oakes nevertheless hoped to regain a similar position. While working in a city-wide pool of cameramen used by various television stations, Oakes and others were asked to train minority apprentices, who subsequently got any available staff cameraman positions with the stations. Meanwhile, Oakes and other white males in the camera pool received a dwindling number of assignments. Oakes now is a free-lance cameraman.

G. Mann

Shared similar situation with R. Oakes, though he has not been hurt as badly financially or psychologically. Mann has just been hired by a major corporation.

G. White

Had difficulty obtaining firefighter position in mid-1970s. Repeatedly applied and took exams and was finally hired in 1978. White claimed he was handicapped by both his non-minority and non-veteran status. Discovered Hispanic friends with lower scores were hired while he was not.

N. Garfano

Had been a driver for a bakery for some years and claimed to have been promised a supervisory position when such a slot opened up. When this occurred, however, a less experienced Hispanic was hired instead. Garfano left to go into his own trucking business.

E. Coles

Had been hired to temporarily replace a faculty member at a small California college. Though he applied to fill the same job on a more permanent, tenure-track basis, he was not even formally considered, and a black male with fewer qualifications was hired in his place. After one low-status, non-academic job, Coles found a series of part-time academic positions and finally obtained a tenure-track job at a midwestern college.

D. Loftis

On two occasions during the mid-to-late 1970s, Loftis applied for tenure-track positions in departments in which he held temporary positions. In both situations, he was told that the goal was to hire a woman or minority. According to Loftis, his chairman stated, "If you were a black or a woman, I could get you a job in a minute." In the first instance a woman was hired; in the second, a male with social-science mathematical skills was hired after a female finalist who listed quantitative skills on her résumé presented herself in an incompetent manner when she was interviewed for the position. Loftis left the academic world for a position in government.

D. Elliot

Applied for an instructor position in 1977 at a California community college where he had taught part time for two years while working on his Ph.D. The job went instead to a black male from a small Midwestern school who had only an M.A. degree and, as was discovered on his arrival, lacked qualifications to teach in one of the areas for which he was hired. Elliot left the academic world for a position in government.

E. Mathis

Applied for a part-time job at a bookstore chain as means of support while going to graduate school. Manager interviewed him and told him the job was all but his; then called the next day and said she had to hire someone else: a black female. Upon obtaining his graduate degree, Mathis claimed to have also encountered reverse discrimination incidents in the television/communications industry.

H. Overton

Was appointed to fill as acting administrator at a large public university well known in the area for its aggressive affirmative action policies, regulations under which Overton had hired his own subordinates. He applied to fill the position on a permanent basis and was one of three finalists interviewed. A less qualified female from a private school obtained the job.

G. Miller

Administrator at a large public university who applied for a promotion in the same division. After much delay and paperwork, Miller was selected as one of three finalists. After giving Miller a perfunctory interview, a less-qualified, less experienced black female from another campus was given the job. After vigorously protesting the decision, Miller began searching for a new position.

S. Gray

Community-college instructor who applied to be a dean. Gray was ranked first through most of the screening process until he was interviewed by the minority chancellor of the district, who appointed another minority to the position. Gray sued and has received near-unanimous support from his colleagues. Gray's case was heard in federal court in 1988 and resulted in a hung jury. Gray and his lawyer intend to get the case retried.

L. McCall

Was repeatedly bypassed for a tenure-line position in a community-college mathematics department. McCall had already moved from part-time to full-time status. After losing out to a white female and then an Asian female candidate, McCall tried for a third position. After interviewing for that position, he claims to have been a co-finalist. When the other co-finalist took a position at another campus, McCall assumed he would get the position, but the campus president put pressure on the chair to hire a Filipino female not even on the finalist list. McCall took a position at another campus.

D. Hathaway

Elementary school teacher who entered volunteer teacher-transfer program designed to achieve racial and ethnic balance in the Los Angeles Unified School District. He did this in order to ensure being permanently returned to his home school after three years of teaching in a predominantly minority area.

F. Goldberg

Randomly selected by district-wide lottery to participate in L.A. school district's teacher-transfer program for racial and ethnic balance. Managed to return to another suburban school after three years.

D. Brown

High-school art teacher who was caught in the L.A. school district's reshuffling of teachers due to race/ethnic balance needs and budget cutbacks in 1980. Minorities with less seniority were allowed to stay, and at least one minority teacher was brought in within weeks of his layoff. After being transferred twice, he quit and started his own business.

M. Greene
Another high-school art teacher caught up in the Los Angeles school district's teacher transfer program in 1984. Minority teachers with less seniority were allowed to stay on. After being put in substitute teacher pool for several weeks, Greene, through friends, managed to locate a new position at another high school.

S. Schwartz
After teaching eighteen years at one high school, in 1980 Schwartz was laid off, then transferred in the L.A. school district's racial balancing program. He managed to be transferred back to a suburban school after two years.

T. Tuperman
Also caught in teacher transfer program in 1980. Tuperman fought and beat the system and won reinstatement in his original job.

S. Faulkner
Admitted to county sheriff's academy in 1975, but chose to pursue a career as a professional boxer for a few months. When he reapplied, he did well once again on the written exams but did not do as well on the oral. When he obtained the results of his oral exam, he discovered that minority and female members of the committee had made inaccurate and negative comments. Faulkner protested but to no avail. He tested and was immediately hired by sheriff's department in neighboring county.

F. Nunn
Had an administrative position in a metropolitan government agency not covered by the municipal civil service. When the agency was brought under civil service in 1977, Nunn and others took the required exams, and Nunn was ranked first. Nunn claimed that he was fired and removed from the list in order to move two minorities up high enough in the rankings to retain their positions in the agency being reclassified. Though the Civil Service Board ruled unanimously in his favor, and though Nunn received another job, he nonetheless filed a reverse-discrimination suit against the city. He lost his suit in federal district court in 1986.

M. Grant
Had not had a promotion in his state bureaucracy since the late 1960s. Grant claimed to have seen less qualified minorities hired and promoted by him for nearly fifteen years. In 1983, he was invited to apply for a high-level position. Other positions like it were occupied mostly by minorities, so Grant and others felt there would be no affirmative action problems. Grant claims he was given the job, accepted, and began to train for the new position. His appointment was formally announced in some small gatherings, but three weeks after he began training in his new position, he was summarily told by his superior that he "was the wrong color." A Hispanic person was hired in his place, and Grant returned to his old position. He eventually resigned and filed a lawsuit. I was unable to locate Grant for a reinterview after 1987.

Appendix 2

SOCIAL CHARACTERISTICS
OF RESPONDENTS

	Age[1]	Indiv. Inc.[2]	J/inc.[2]	ED.[3]	Resp. Occ.[4]	Wife Occ.	Fath. Occ.	Moth. Occ.	Rel.
G. Gordon (R)[5]	47	$20	$37	13	Collect. agy/worker	Nurse	Crop Hvstr	Crop Hvstr	Prot.
P. Elton (R)	50	$24	$40	16	R. Est. contrtor	Teach.	Const. contrtor	Nurse	Prot.
J. Smith (R)	36	$21	—	15	Salesman	—	Police Chief	Store mgr	Prot.
F. Sanders (D)	45	$45	$50	19	Research Psychol.	Teach.	Teacher	H.W.	Prot.*
B. Allen (D)	40	$20	$25	16	Personnel Mgr	P/T Teach.	Farmer	H.W.	Prot.
B. Watson (R)	33	$20	$40	16	Flight Ins. (P/T)	Cler.	Doctor	H.W.	Cath.
S. Huddleston (I)	42	$26	—	16	Md/mgr St. of Cal	—	Fact. Labor	H.W.	Prot.
S. Clark (R)	38	$27	$57	14	Md/mgr St. of Cal	Nurse	Aircft Engr	Sec.	None
S. Mulligan (D)	44	$23	—	16	Md/mgr St. of Cal	—	Adv. Exec.	H.W.	Cath*.
T. O'Neil (R)	36	$25	$50	16	Md/mgr St. of Cal.	Md/mgr St. of Cal.	S. Empl. Bus.	H.W.	Prot.
A. McWhirter (R)	27	$25	—	13	Cameraman	—	Mechan.	Sec.	Cath.*
R. Oakes (R)	56	$25	$50	13	Cameraman	R. Est. sales	S. Empl. Bus.	H.W.	Mix
G. Mann (R)	46	$50	$50	12	Cinematog.	H.W.	Refrig. Eng.	H.W.	Prot.
G. White (R)	30	$42	$42	13	Law Enfc.	H.W.	Ware-housem.	Sec.	Cath.
N. Garfano (R)	31	$32	—	12	Truck Driver	—	Truck Driver	Dry/Cl Worker	Cath.*
E. Coles (R)	34	$22	—	20	Assoc. Prof	—	Elec. Engr	Probation Worker	Cath.

Name	Age	Income	Joint Income	Educ.					Religion
D. Loftis (R)	34	$18	$36	19	P/T Lect. and cons. wkr	Teacher	Const. Contrtor	Teach.	Prot.
D. Elliot (R)	30	$30	—	19	P/T Lect.	—	S. Empl.	Sec.	Prot.
E. Mathis (R)	36	$13	$25	19	P/T Lect.	Teacher	Mgr of Drugstore	H.W.	Prot.
H. Overton (D)	39	$46	—	19	Univ. adm.	—	Ministr	H.W.	Prot.
G. Miller (D)	29	$25	—	16	Univ. adm.	—	Salesm.	Clerical	Jewish
S. Gray (D)	49	$40	$58	18	College Inst.	Sec.	Barber	H.W.	Cath.
L. McCall (D)	30	$20	—	18	College Inst.	—	Auto Dealer	H.W.	Prot.
D. Hathaway (D)	58	$33	$58	16	Teacher	Teacher	Time & Motion Eng.	H.W.	Cath.
F. Goldberg (D)	57	$30	$50	16	Teacher	Teacher	Dentist	Lawyer	Jewish
D. Brown (D)	49	$40	$40	16	S. Empl. Bus.	Work w/ Husband	Barber	H.W.	Prot.
M. Greene (D)	57	$35	$70	19	Teacher	Teacher	Salesm. Store Mgr	Salesw.	Prot.
S. Schwartz (D)	47	$35	$72	18	Teacher	Teacher		H.W.	Jewish
T. Tuperman (D)	45	$35	—	17	Teacher	—	S. Empl. Bus.	Sec.	Jewish
S. Falkner (R)	34	$35	—	16	S. Empl. Bus.	—	Truck Driver	Sec.	Prot.
F. Nunn (R)	46	$20	—	18	Law Stud.	—	Printer	Teach.	Jewish
M. Grant (R)	52	$20	$35	15	S. Empl.	R. Est.	Leather worker	H.W.	Prot.

¹Age at time of interview. Not, necessarily, age at time of alleged discrimination incident.

²Income and Joint Income figures in thousands.

³All persons with 16 years of education had bachelor's degrees; all but one of those with 19 or 20 years of education had Ph.D's.

⁴Occupation at time of interview (not necessarily occupation in which alleged discrimination occurred).

⁵Indicates official registration as Democrat, Republican, or Independent.

*Indicates currently active in religious organization.

Appendix 3

RESPONSES TO AFFIRMATIVE ACTION SETBACKS AND THE NATURE OF SOCIAL SUPPORT

	Job/Prom[1]	Initial Response[2]	Protest[3]	Outcome	Social Support			
					Wife	Co-Wrk	Rel.	Friends
G. Gordon	P	Demoralized	No	Quit	S	S	S	S*
P. Elton	P	Angry at system	No	Quit	S	S	ND	S*
J. Smith	P	"Let it ride"	Yes	Injured/Quit	—	S	S	ND
F. Sanders	P	Acquiesced	Yes	Remained No altern.	S	MS	ND	ND
B. Allen	P	Acquiesced	No	Remained	S	S	ND	ND
B. Watson	P	Angry	Mildly	Was trans. Later quit	N	MS	ND	S
S. Huddleston	P	"Unfair"	Yes	Eventually promoted	—	S	S	S
S. Clark	P	"Impropriety and exclusion"	Yes	Eventually promoted	MS	MS	ND	ND
S. Mulligan	P	Anger; Frustration	Yes	Eventually promoted	—	S	S	S
T. O'Neil	P	Angry and upset	Yes	Eventually promoted	MS	S/NS	S	ND
A. McWhirter	J	Depressed	No	Got job elsewhere		MS	S	MS*
R. Oakes	J[5]	Some rage; saw it coming too late	No	Set up own business	S	S	ND	S
G. Mann	J[5]	"Thought talent would win out"	No	Set up own business	—	S	ND	S
G. White	J	Frustrated, angry	No	Got job elsewhere	—	ND	ND	ND
N. Garfano	J	"Cheated," helpless	No	Got job elsewhere	—	ND	ND	S
E. Coles	J	"Real defeat"	No	Got job elsewhere	—[4]	MS	S	MS

Name	Type	Response	Left	Action				
D. Loftis	J	Hurt; angry	No	Changed careers	S	ND	S	ND
D. Elliot	J	Acquiesced	No	Changed careers	—	ND	S	S
E. Mathis	J	"Mad as hell"	No	Changed careers	S	NS	S	ND
H. Overton	P	"Totally devastated"	Yes	Got job elsewhere	—	S	S	S
G. Miller	P	Angry	Yes	Looking	—	S	S	S
L. McCall	J	Angry	No	Got job	—	S	S	S
S. Grey	P	"Mad as hell"	Yes	In court	S	S	S	S
D. Hathaway	T⁶	"Like a form of rape"	Yes	Transferred; Returned	S	S	S	S
F. Goldberg	T	"One step short of violence"	Yes	Transferred Returned to suburbs	S	S/NS	NS	NS
D. Brown	T	Initial depression; then glad to get out	Yes	Changed careers	S	S/NS	ND	ND
M. Greene	T	Discovered I was dispensable; then glad for change	No	Got job elsewhere	S	ND	ND	ND
S. Schwartz	T	Felt dispensible	No	Transferred Returned to suburbs	S	MS	S	MS*
T. Tuperman	T	Fought and reinstated	Yes	Reinstated	—	S	ND	S*
S. Falkner	J	"Totally unfair"; embarrassed; hostile"	Yes	Got job elsewhere	—	S	S	S*

| | Job/Prom[1] | Initial Response[2] | Protest[3] | Outcome | Social Support | | | |
					Wife	Co-Wrk	Rel.	Friends
F. Nunn	J	"Turned other cheek and got the shit slapped out of me"	Yes	Quit; Sued	MS[4]	NS	NA	NS
M. Grant	P	Shocked, angry, embarrassed	Yes	Quit; Lawsuit	S	NS	S	ND

[1]Loss of "Job" or "Promotion" due to alleged discrimination.
[2]Initial emotional response.
[3]Protested discrimination incident (either written or through strong oral protest).
[4]Loss of job due to discrimination scutled pending marriage.
[5]Job not renewed due to technical reclassification combined with affirmative action quota pressures; far less experienced minorities hired in his place.
[6]"T" indicates "transferred" under one of the ethnic balancing plans of the Los Angeles Unified School District.
*Most friends are also co-workers.
S = Support.
MS = Mixed or moderate support.
ND = Not discussed.
NA = Not applicable—person not married at the time or had no relatives with whom to discuss the matter.
NS = No support.

Appendix 4

OTHER REACTIONS TO
AFFIRMATIVE ACTION SETBACKS

	Damage to Self-Concept[1]	Changed views on Soc./Soc. Inst.[1]	Need for any form of A.A.[1]
G. Gordon	"Probably. I didn't apply for promotions."	A.a. added to jaundiced view of society.	Merit alone.
P. Elton	"Oh, sure . . . general pressures."	Lost faith in system.	Merit alone.
J. Smith	"Yeah. Lost self-esteem. Others didn't understand."	System more corrupt; more suspicious.	Equal opp., no preference.
F. Sanders	Job immobility hurt self-esteem.	Disappointed the "experiment" failed.	Merit, but allow for redress.
B. Allen	"No, not at all."	"No; courts might be too activist."	No.
B. Watson	"Somewhat."	Reinforced previous views.	"Get rid of it."
S. Huddleston	No.	Lost faith in gov.	May be needed in priv. sector.
S. Clark	"Less motivated."	No difference.	No quotas; some a.a.
S. Mulligan	"Yes, for a few years."	Lost faith in admin. and judiciary.	No.
T. O'Neil	"More withdrawn and prejudiced."	Lost faith in judic. Has taken too long to get rid of a.a.	No!
A. McWhirter	"A little. Got tired of chasing & losing jobs."	"All politically biased."	No.
R. Oakes	"No. Lost faith in the system, the nation."	Lost faith in govt.	No.
G. Mann	"No, but did lose some drive."	Lost faith in nation.	"Only way minorities can advance."

G. White	"Lost confidence until I finally got promotion."	No change.	Merit.
N. Garfano	"Some damage to self esteem; slowed me down."	"More cynical."	No quotas; a.a. o.k. in some instances.
E. Coles	Heavy impact. Depression, some drinking.	More anti-govt. than before	No.
D. Loftis	Hurt his pride.	Reinforced views.	No.
D. Elliot	No.	Reinforced views.	Nec. in early 1960s; not now.
E. Mathis	Absolutely; giving up on academic career.	Lost faith in Congress, courts.	Nec. years ago; not now.
H. Overton	Very much so; nearly didn't go through with new job interview.	Critical of courts, but took it out mainly on himself.	No.
G. Miller	Depressed for a time; angry.	Not political.	Merit alone.
L. McCall	Initial reaction of self-doubt.	"Made me think a lot about quotas."	Merit alone.
S. Gray	No.	"The courts are a crap shoot. The legal system grinds you down."	Needed "watch-dog" years ago.
D. Hathaway	Had to cope with new situation.	Lost faith in school district; already distrusted govt.	Merit alone.
F. Goldberg	"Just something that happened." Anguish and hardship.	Lost faith in govt. and social engineering.	No.

	Damage to Self-Concept[1]	Changed views on Soc./Soc. Inst.[1]	Need for any form of A.A.[1]
D. Brown	Depressed and confused.	No faith in unions.	Merit dominant but should help people.
M. Greene	"About a month in the doldrums . . . a real blow."	Lost faith in liberalism.	Yes; but not sure how to implement it.
S. Schwartz	Shock; depression; self-doubt.	Learned a lot about how poor live.	Hate quotas; but support remediation.
T. Tuperman	No.	No.	Should implement a.a differently.
S. Falkner	Saw it as another obstacle to overcome.	No.	Might be needed in some places.
F. Nunn	Severe depression; Constant fight.	More cynical about lib. politicians.	Not sure.
M. Grant	Ambiguity and doubt.	Confused over sympathy for minor., but angry over his own situation.	Not fair to create more victims; give minorities remedial training.

[1]When direct quotes are not used, wording is as close to subjects' phrasing as space permits.

Appendix 5

INTERVIEW SCHEDULE

Name: _____ Age_____

Address: _____ Place of birth: _____

____Married (1,2,3)   ____Divorced   ____Single

   Children: ____Boys (Ages:)

                ____Girls (Ages:)

How long at current address?

How long in California?

Father (and/or stepfather)
   Age____
   Occupations _____
   Educational attainments_____

Mother (and/or stepmother)
   Age____
   Occupations _____
   Educational attainments_____

Brothers and Sisters (Ages, occupations, education, residence):

Subject's education:
   Did you finish high school?
   What about college.

Graduate or professional school?
Other training?

In what religion were you raised?

Do you currently belong to any religious organization?

What is your current occupation?

What did you do before that?

Would you mind telling me your current annual income (from your job alone—not wife's)?

Are you a member of any civic or social organizations? Which ones?

What magazines or newspapers do you suscribe to?

What about television? What do you like to watch on the tube? (Probe for entertainment and news viewing habits)

What job were you in when you first detected discrimination against you because of your race or sex?

Do you think it was your race or your sex which was held against you—or both?

Was your awareness sharpened by a specific event or was it more of a cumulative pattern of happenings?

Do you remember the approximate date when you became aware of this?

What, exactly, were the circumstances involved?

How did you respond to this situation? What were your feelings?

Did you "speak out" about this? (If subject did not, ask why.)

What happened when you (or others) did speak out?

Did others at your work setting share your perceptions?

Were any other white males being (hired or promoted) at that time? How do you account for the ones who were? How did they account for it?

One thing which is sometimes mentioned in regard to these cases is that "other factors" were involved—such as the employee's personality, his real or suspected sexual or drinking habits, his politics, etc. Could any of these "other factors" have had a bearing on your case, do you think?

How did your wife respond to your situation? (First and second wives if applicable.)

What about your parents and your in-laws? How did they respond?

Did you mention this to brothers, sisters or other relatives?

What about your friends? What did they say?

How do you think the majority of people in this country feel about preferential treatment for women and minorities—that is, about quotas? (Probe for any knowledge of public opinion polls.)

Are you currently registered with any political party?

How would you classify yourself politically and philosophically? Would you say you are conservative, liberal, moderate, or what? (Probe here on atitudes towards E.R.A., women's liberation, gay rights, Prop. 13, defense spending, welfare, etc.)

For whom did you vote in the last Presidential election? Why? What about this year's elections? (For California respondents ask about gubernatorial race in 1982.)

How has your experience with reverse discrimination set with your political and philosophical views? Have you had any change of mind or heart because of this?

It has generally been assumed in this country that each individual is responsible for his or her own success or failure. Do you think this ever has been or is now true, generally speaking?

Would you say that your experience with affirmative action has made you lose confidence in yourself, that it has damaged your self-esteem?

What about your views on society? Has your experience made you "lose faith" in society overall or in any of its key institutions (such as business, Congress, the courts, government bureaucracies, the military, the police, etc.)?

Do you believe that race and sex quotas—or any other type of affirmative action programs—might be necessary in some form in various areas of our society?

Appendix 6

FROM
"THE CRITERIA OF ACADEMIC APPOINTMENT IN AMERICAN COLLEGES AND UNIVERSITIES: SOME DOCUMENTS OF AFFIRMATIVE ACTION AT WORK"

This remarkable article (from Minerva, *September 1976) is rarely referred to in most of the literature on affirmative action. I have omitted* Minerva *editor Edward Shills' brief inroduction. He does not state how the journal obtained the letters, only that specific names of individuals and institutions have been deleted.*
The letters speak for themselves.

LETTERS FROM A LEADING PRIVATE UNIVERSITY
ON THE WEST COAST

3 December, 1971

Chairman
Department of Political Science
University of . . . .
Dear Sir,—I am writing you to inform you of an opening at Y . . . in American politics, and to ask you for assistance. The position is at the assistant professor level with a salary in the $11,000-12,500 range, depending on experience. Our primary need lies in the area of urban politics, but want to emphasize that we are looking for the strongest possible candidate, regardless of field specialization.

Y . . . University is deeply interested in increasing the number of minority members and women on its faculty. Toward this end, the University has recently announced an affirmative action program to assist individual departments in recruiting such candidates. If you know of anyone who might be interested in this position, would you please have them send their credentials and letters of recommendation to me?

Thank you for your assistance in this matter and I look forward to hearing from you.

Sincerely yours,
N . . . . M . . . .
Chairman, Search Committee

10 August, 1971

Professor P . . . . Q . . . .
Chairman
University of . . . .
Dear Professor Q . . . . ,—The Provost of Y . . . has asked our department to make a special effort to assemble a roster of Chicanos who have recently been awarded the Ph.D. or who are expected to receive the Ph.D. in the next year or two. I am, therefore, writing to ask whether Chicanos have been among your recent graduates or are expected to be. If that is the case, I should be very grateful if you would send me their names and, if they are available, their curricula vitae.

Sincerely yours,
R . . . . S . . . .
Chairman

LETTERS BETWEEN A MAJOR STATE UNIVERSITY AND A STATE COLLEGE

3 December, 1971

Professor A . . . . B . . . .
Department of Economics
University of . . . .
Dear Professor B . . . . ,—All of the . . . state colleges have been requested to implement a program of active recruitment of qualified faculty of minority background, especially Negro and Mexican-American.

Since I am unable to determine this type of information from the resumes you have sent me, I should very much appreciate it if you could indicate which of your 1972 candidates are either Negro or Mexican-American.

Sincerely yours,
N . . . . M . . . .
Chairman
Department of Economics

8 December, 1971

Professor N . . . . M . . . .
Department of Economics
. . . . State College
Dear Professor M . . . . ,—I was most distressed by your request that I classify our 1972 employment candidates by race. It is one thing, and highly creditable, for an institution like yours to make sure that no qualified candidates are overlooked for reasons associated with race. It is quite another aim, as on reflection I hope you will agree, to discriminate on grounds of race within a group of qualified candidates.

The list of candidates we sent you contained the names of fine young men and women, a number of whom would be (I feel) well qualified to teach at . . . . While these young people have a striking variety of ethnic origins, we do not classify them by race nor do we recommend them on any basis other than their individual professional merit. As an institution financed by citizens of all races and origins, I do not see how we can do otherwise.

I am, of course, quite aware of the pressure on all academic institutions these days to engage in "benevolent" racism in their employment decisions. However, you might be interested to know that among the dozens of inquiries I've received about our candidates, yours was one of the very few indicating that race was to be a major criterion for hiring. I sincerely hope, for both your sake and ours, that you will find yourself ultimately able to give due consideration to all our candidates without regard to race.

Sincerely,

A . . . . B . . . .

Placement Chairman

Department of Economics

22 December, 1971

Professor A . . . . B . . . .

Department of Economics

University of . . . .

Dear Professor B . . . . ,—I feel compelled to respond to your letter of 8 December.

I did not intend to suggest, nor did I indicate in any way, "that race was to be a major criterion for hiring." When I go to New Orleans[1], I shall be seeking the very best people I can find. I have always done this and I don't intend to change. However, we are faced with a peculiar situation, not unknown in bureaucratic organizations such as ours. The powers-that-be are holding back faculty positions that become available only to those departments that happen to come up with qualified minority candidates. Since I have two positions allocated to economics when I really need four, I have adopted the strategy of filling the two positions with the best qualified people. If I can also find qualified minority candidates, the college doubly gains and my department gains as well. The department and the college gain by obtaining an extra economist. The college additionally gains by our using one of the held-back positions instead of its going to the Department of Sociology.

It turns out that as a result of my letter I obtained from Y . . . . University a curriculum vitae that for some reason had not been included in the original batch. Thus, I shall be able to consider someone (in this case a Negro) of whom I would have been completely ignorant otherwise.

I agree with your comments about racism. For this reason, and others, I have already submitted my resignation as chairman of the department.

Sincerely yours,

N . . . . M . . . .

Department of Economics

3 January, 1972

Professor N . . . . M . . . .

Department of Economics

. . . . State College

Dear Professor M . . . . ,—I was gratified to recieve your fine letter of December 22nd. The situation you mention concerning the discriminatory allocations of positions to your department is of course not exceptional, but almost "normal" in colleges and universities today. At [my university] also, the administration has indicated that almost any candidate who can meet barely minimum qualification standards will be a most welcome appointment—even in the absence of an open budgetary "line"—if he or she falls into the currently preferred "minority" groupings. For all others, of course, the highest academic standards are supposed to prevail.

On this, perhaps one or two comments may be in order. First, I feel that faced with such pressure it is incumbant upon all of us to resist. For, there is no natural stopping-point to the evil of this process. I have just learned, for example, that in New York City Italian-Americans have now been assigned to the category of preferred "minorities!" Eventually, someone will be making demands for ideological quotas, too. Second, administration problems being what they are, the added budgetary line you receive for this purpose today is all too likely to be taken away tomorrow. So any departmental "profit" is likely to be short-lived.

As to our specific candidates, I do not know if you met any in New Orleans. However, if you'd like further word on them please let me know.

Sincerely,

A . . . . B . . . .

Department of Economics

LETTERS BETWEEN A LESSER STATE UNIVERSITY AND A LESSER PRIVATE UNIVERSITY

23 February, 1972

D . . . . E . . . .
Department of Sociology
 . . . . University
Dear Mr. E . . . . ,—We have received a letter from Professor F . . . . G . . . . sent to Professor H . . . . I . . . . concerning your possible interest in joining our department. At the present time it does not appear likely that our department can act on this inquiry.

Here are the facts. The whole university is on a zero growth basis. Sociology was not held to this basis because of the great demand among students for courses in sociology. We thus had good reason to believe that we could undertake strong efforts in recruitment. We have now learned that recruiting throughout the university is almost completely limited to certain categories of persons whose employment would enable the university to meet certain equal opportunity requirements.

I am extremely sorry that we have not been able to respond more definitely to your inquiry. I want to thank you for your interest in our university and our department. There may be a chance later that we can get in touch with you on this matter.

Sincerely yours,

M . . . . N . . . .

Chairman

Recruitment Committee

Department of Sociology

16 March, 1972

Professor M . . . . N . . . .
Chairman, Recruitment Committee
Department of Sociology
University of . . . .
Dear Professor N . . . . ,—Attached is a copy of a letter to the *American Sociologist* concerning "reverse discrimination" in hiring. It refers to the letter which you sent to my student, D . . . . E . . . . , although not mentioning you or your department by name.

As the letter indicates, I am very disturbed at the policy which you indicate in your letter. It sounds like this is university rather than department policy, but I would urge you and other department members to make whatever efforts you can to change this policy.

I would appreciate your reactions to my letter.

Sincerely,
F . . . . G . . . .
Associate Professor of Sociology

24 March, 1972

Professor F . . . . G . . . .
Dept. of Sociology and Anthropology
. . . . University
Dear F . . . . G . . . . ,—Of course I am sorry to have to send a letter to D . . . . E . . . . informing him of the constraints in our recruitment. I trust that you will show this letter to him. Perhaps I can describe in some greater detail those restraints at our University this year.

(1) The chief restraint is on recruiting generally; our University has entered upon a policy of limitation in the size of the student body. The vast majority of the departments have had no opportunity to undertake recruiting and at the present time our department is equally held back: only one opening is now available in our department—a replacement for a special teaching assignment. Now I am not even sure that that is a policy because we are hoping that before the semester is out we may be able to compete for a highly limited number of openings in the College of Arts and Sciences.

(2) At the time I wrote the letter, although I had no official document I had the strong impression the University was trying to fill certain teaching positions to be coordinated with special educational opportunity programs for Blacks, Chicanos, Indians and other designated minorities. The students in these programs have made very strong requests that those teaching positions related to their programs be filled by persons from their respective ethnic backgrounds. It is true that the federal government has also strongly encouraged the hiring of teachers drawn from particular ethnic groups, "thus encouraging the University to meet certain equal opportunity requirements." I hope that you can read this last quote phrase from a previous letter of mine to mean that at least two sorts of pressures are involved: the government encouragement to hire teachers from particular ethnic groups and the strong requests on the part of the students for teachers hired from those groups.

Now all of this has not been set forth as University policy. I would join with you in any protest against any continuing and commanding policy that would not mean exactly equal opportunity for all persons, especially over any extended period of time. I do know that there is tremendous need for improving the special education programs. As the recruitment chairman I am working very hard to bring candidates from the minorites to the University who are concerned with and able to work within these programs. Thus my interest has been functional.

(3) I cannot see that there is a continuing and comprehensive University policy on this matter. The department itself has requested the hiring of a teacher to handle special sorts of topics within the department. Persons from a wide range of backgrounds have been considered for this particular position. The chief candidate with whom we are now negotiating happens to be an Anglo.

At our University there has certainly been serious consideration given to the ethnic backgrounds of persons. Up to now I should say this consideration has been directed honestly towards the need for special teaching requirements. And I shall be surprised if more than three persons in the University are hired as a result of this consideration.

Please extend to Mr. E . . . . my regret that I sent a letter that could have troublesome interpretations.

Sincerely yours,
M . . . . N . . . .
Department of Sociology

LETTER FROM A PROFESSOR OF RELIGIOUS STUDIES AT AN "IVY LEAGUE" UNIVERSITY

23 December, 1971

Dear Professor J . . . . ,— . . . in the June encounter of chairman with the HEW "team" (three people!), the chairman explained that we did not get many applications for our program in Biblical Studies because at the graduate level knowledge of Greek and Hebrew is required. The HEW response is that we should discontinue such old-fashioned programs, in which minority groups could not participate, and instead establish programs without language requirements, which they could do—e.g., a Ph.D. in black theology or whatever. Since our department receives no government support at all, we did not feel we had to give serious consideration to the discontinuance of language-requirements at the doctoral level. But I think we would discontinue our programs before we would lower their requirements to meet the demand of HEW. At any rate all this is documented.

Sincerely,
K . . . . L . . . .
Professor of Religious Studies

LETTERS FROM SOUTHERN STATE UNIVERSITIES

19 January, 1973

Chairman
Department of Politics
. . . . University
Dear Sir,—The enclosed notice calls your attention to a new position in this department, beginning in August, 1973.

This is a permanent position within the department. We expect to fill it at the assistant professor level.

For this particular vacancy, the department desires to appoint a woman staff-member.

You will notice that we are interested in candidates in the general field of International Politics, who also have an area specialty (Asia or Africa). We are prepared to be quite flexible in working out the exact teaching responsibilities of the new staff-member.

The department also specifies that candidates for this position have the Ph.D. degree "in hand," or plan to receive the degree by June, 1973. (The department will not consider candidates who will be "ABD" after June, 1973).

If you know of suitable candidates among your present graduate students or recent Ph.D. recipients, I would appreciate your calling our position to their attention or letting me know their names and addresses.

Cordially yours,

T . . . . U . . . .

Chairman

Department of Political Science

24 March, 1972

Chairman

Department of Politics

. . . . University

Dear Sir—This department is very interested in the possibility of adding a Black, female faculty member to its staff.

Departmental staff needs lie primarily in the field of: international relations; international organization; area studies (Asian and African studies); and the "developing nations."

The department is willing to consider any qualified candidates who might be appointed at a rank and salary level appropriate for their training and experience.

I would very much appreciate your assistance in suggesting possible candidates for our consideration in this matter.

Sincerely,

T . . . . U . . . .

Chairman

Department of Political Science

2 February, 1972

Professor V . . . . W . . . .

Dear Professor W . . . . ,—Since I last corresponded with you regarding the possibility of a position in this department, decisions have been made by the top administration of the University that have created some awkwardness in our recruiting efforts.

The decision I refer to is that all unfilled positions in the University must be filled by Blacks or females. Since I have no information regarding your racial identification it will only be possible to consider you for a position in the event that you are black.

I might add that we have received letters from your references and have been enthusiastic about your candidacy.

Sincerely,

X . . . . Y . . . .

Department of Sociology

28 March, 1972

Professor AA . . . . BB . . . .
Department of Sociology
. . . . State College

Dear AA . . . . ,—Here's the situation—all our energies are going into hiring a senior person and a methodologist and apparently you do not fit into either one of these categories. If you were Black or a woman, we might also be able to give you some encouragment. So that's the situation. However, please do not hesitate to write to me in a few weeks just in case the situation has changed.

Sincerely yours,

CC . . . . DD . . . .

Professor and Chairman

Department of Sociology

27 May, 1971

Professor EE . . . . FF . . . .
Placement Officer
Department of Economics
University of . . . .

Dear Professor FF . . . . ,—Your prompt response to my letter of 12 May with four candidates, all of whom seem qualified for our vacancy, is greatly appreciated. Since there is no indication that any of them belongs to one of the minority groups listed, I will be unable to contact them at present. My instructions are to exhaust every opportunity for recruiting a qualified person from among a minority group, including women. If this attempt is fully documented, I will then be given permission to seek the best qualfied person regardless of race, color, or creed, which has always been our practice in the past. If I get this "green light," I would certainly be interested in X . . . . or Y . . . . and would contact them to see if they were still available.

Cordially yours,

GG . . . . HH . . . .

Chairman

Department of Economics

28 October, 1974

Professor II . . . . JJ . . . .
Department of Geography
University of . . . .

Dear Professor JJ . . . . ,—Thank you for your interest in [our] university as indicated by your letter and vita. We will leave the position open through at least the end of November, at which time our departmental selection committee will begin its screening process. I will be in touch with you again at that time.

I believe that it is in the best interests of fairness (given the current state of the job market) to inform you that . . . universities are now operating under a Department of Health, Education, and Welfare mandate to increase their faculty mixes of minorities and women. Thus, it is becoming increasingly apparent that we will be able to tender an offer to a white male only under the most compelling of circumstances. In other words, I feel that I would be remiss in my obligations if I did not urge you to pursue whatever alternative opportunities you might have with all possible vigor.

Sincerely yours,

KK . . . . LL . . . .

Professor and Chairman

Department of Geography

DRAFT LETTER FROM A STATE COLLEGE IN ILLINOIS

5 February, 1973

Dear . . . . ,— . . . College will have a teaching vacancy in the chemistry department due to the retirement of a faculty member. The new faculty member will be hired at the rank of instructor in a salary range of $8,700-$9,600.

Candidates for the position must have a recent Master's degree in chemistry from an institution recognized by the American Chemical Society. He (or she) should have a strong background in organic chemistry and some course work in biochemistry. A candidate should be especially capable of teaching our introductory courses—General Chemistry 101-102 in inorganic chemistry. Experience as a teaching assistant is highly recommended. Any industrial expertise in the field of chemistry will be looked upon favorably.

Furthermore, . . . College has expressed a strong commitment to Affirmative Action guidelines and a high priority will be given to hiring a person from a minority group, that is, Black or Chicano. For this reason until 15 June, 1975, only those applications from members of minority groups will be actively considered. After 15 June, applications from all qualified persons will be considered, provided the vacancy is not filled by that date. The target date for hiring is 1 July, 1973.

We would appreciate your efforts in our search for qualified candidates, especially candidates from minority groups. Please inform all candidates that a photograph will be required on all letters of inquiry or applications.

If I can provide further information, please feel free to contact me. Thank you.

Sincerely yours,

MM . . . . NN . . . .

Dean

LETTER FROM A LEADING PRIVATE COLLEGE IN CALIFORNIA

Graduate Placement Officer

Department of Economics

University of . . .

Dear Colleague,— . . . College has a vacancy in its economics department as a result of retirement. We desire to appoint a Black or Chicano, preferably female. The appointee would be asked to offer principles and theory courses as well as undergraduate or graduate seminars in his or her areas of specialization.

The department prefers applicants with Ph.D.s in hand, identifiable academic accomplishments, existing reputations as inspiring undergraduate and graduate teachers, aversions to committees and memos, and educations and inclinations to be more than technicians. If you know of persons who may someday meet the above criteria, please ask them to write to me here, sending vita and letters of reference, so that we can arrange to meet at the American Economic Association convention. I shall be at the Roosevelt Hotel. The letters of reference should explicitly comment on present teaching ability and status of the Ph.D. degree.

Salary and rank are open and negotiable. There is no upper limit to salaries at [this college], and there are no written or unwritten percentage quotas on academic rank. Advancement is strictly by merit on the basis of teaching and publication. . . .

Sincerely yours,

OO . . . . PP . . . .

Professor of Economics and Chairman

Department of Economics

LETTERS FROM SOME CALIFORNIA STATE COLLEGES

24 April, 1972

Chairman, Department of Economics

University of . . .

Dear Sir,— . . . State College is currently engaged in an Affirmative Action Program, the goal of which is to recruit, hire, and promote ethnic and women candidates until they comprise the same proportion of our faculty as they do of the general population.

To that end, we would be very interested in receiving names and information about prospective candidates who might be available to teach in the economics department at [this college]. If you could provide us with any details of potential applicants from your graduate students, faculty or professional acquaintances, we would be most appreciative.

Sincerely yours,

QQ . . . . RR . . . .

Assistant Chairone [sic]

Department of Economics

5 April, 1972

Chairman

Department of Economics

University of . . .

Dear Sir,—The department of economics at [this] College is now just entering the job market actively to recruit economists for next academic year. Barring unforeseen circumstances, the department will be hiring one or two new faculty. I am requesting that you bring this letter to the attention of your faculty and graduating students. Enclosed is a reasonably accurate statement of the advantages and disadvantages of teaching in our department.

In general, we are looking for economists who will be strong classroom performers as we are primarily a teaching institution, and who will fulfill our needs in specific subject areas. [This] College is also an affirmative action institution with respect to both American minority groups and women. Our doctoral requirement for faculty will be waived for candidates who qualify under the affirmative action criteria, and who are willing to continue graduate work on a part-time basis. Furthermore, greater latitude in teaching areas would be allowed people hired under the affirmative action program.

We are looking for people in various subject areas. These include: microeconomic theory, government and business-industrial organization, international economics, research methods and mathematical economics, and social and institutional economics.

Thank you for bringing our openings to the attention of your faculty and finishing students.

Sincerely,

XX . . . . YY . . . .

Chairman

Department of Economics

18 April, 1972

Mr. TT . . . . UU . . . .

University of . . .

Dear Mr. UU . . . . ,—I was intrigued by the description you gave of Mr. B . . . . A . . . .and very much appreciate your efforts on his behalf. . . .

Mr. A . . . has not contacted me and I fear that were he to do so we would have no more than pleasant conversation, for we are pledged to the affirmative action policy in our hiring this year.

Again, thank you for your most gracious letter.

VV . . . . WW . . . .

Provost

LETTERS FROM MAJOR STATE UNIVERSITIES
ON THE WEST COAST

Professor TT . . . . BB . . . .

Department of Sociology

University of . . .

Dear Professor BB . . . . ,—The department of sociology here expects to make two or three appointments, most likely at the assistant professor level, in the next two years. I am writing to ask if you know of any outstanding candidates of minority background (Chicanos, Blacks, women) . . . I should mention that we have a substantial number of minority students in our regular Ph.D. program and we are just beginning an NIMH[2] training program in field studies of ethnic and racial communities under the direction of Professors X . . . . and Y . . . . Depending on the research interests of the particular candidate, some connection with the minorities research program is a possibility.

For both minority and non-minority candidates, we are less concerned about fields of interest than we are about general scholarship, creativity, and academic commitment.

Sincerely yours,

SS . . . . RR . . . .

Chairman, Personnel Committee

Department of Sociology

Deans, Directors, Department Chairmen, and all Administrative Officers

Dear Colleague,—The American Indian Culture and Research Center at . . . University is trying to locate and identify American Indians with Master and Doctorate degrees for possible faculty position at . . . University and other institutions of higher learning. Positions are presently available in some academic areas.

If possible please send us their vitae. If vitae are not available, please send us the names, addresses and tribes of each American Indian graduate so we may contact them.

Your assistance will be greatly appreciated.

Sincerely yours,

KK . . . . RR . . . .

Associate Director

American Indian Culture and Research Center

LETTERS FROM TWO PRIVATE UNIVERSITES OF GOOD REPUTATION IN THE MIDDLE WEST

9 December, 1971

Professor GG . . . . HH . . . .

Economics Department

University of . . .

Dear GG . . . . ,—We are looking for female economists and members of minority groups. As you know, ... University, along with a lot of other universities, is under some pressure from the Office of Economic Opportunity to hire women, Chicanos, etc. I would greatly appreciate it if you would let me know whether there are any fourth-year students at [your university] that we should look at. . . .

Sincerely,

MM . . . . LL . . . .

Chairman

Department of Economics

22 December, 1971

Professor YY . . . . ZZ . . . .

Department of Economics

University of . . .

Dear Professor ZZ. . . . . ,—The faculty of arts and sciences . . . University desires to increase the number of faculty members who are either women or members of minority groups.

I would greatly appreciate your drawing to my attention your Ph.D. students who are in those categories.

Sincerely yours,

CC . . . . EE . . . .

Chairman

LETTERS FROM OUTSTANDING MIDDLE
WESTERN STATE UNIVERSITIES

18 October, 1974

Professor CC . . . . JJ . . . .
Department of Economics
University of . . .
Dear Professor JJ . . . .,—Our department is making a strong attempt this year to increase the number of minority and women faculty members in our ranks. Our problem is in identifying and obtaining information on qualified minority and women graduate students in the job market now (for appointments to be effective next fall), seeking positions as assistant professors. We would appreciate your assistance in this matter. Would you please send us the names and vitae of your minority and women graduate students who have passed their preliminary examinations and are thinking about employment next year.

We have openings for several persons in international trade, economic theory, labor, urban and regional, and econometrics. We would appreciate your response as soon as possible as we would like to assemble files and begin interviewing before the December meetings.

Thank you for your cooperation.

Sincerely yours,
HH . . . . TT . . . .
Chairman
Department of Economics

14 February, 1973

Professor JJ . . . . LL . . . .
School of Education Building
University of . . .
Dear Professor LL . . . .,—I am writing to you in your capacity as chairman of the University Civil Liberties Board. I wish to file the following complaint:

On January 31, 1973, the clinical psychology faculty of the psychology department adopted a racial and ethnic quota to govern the admission of graduate students into its training program. The terms of the quota are:

(1) Thirty-three to thirty-five percent of the entering class for Fall 1973 must be of "minority group" origin; (2) "Minority group" is specifically defined as Black, Chicano, Puerto Rican and American Indians; (3) Cubans (unless also black), Asian-Americans and underprivileged whites are specifically excluded from the quota; (4) No minimum standards in terms of grade point average or test scores are to be applied to the "minority group" pool of applicants. (In the past, such standards have been applied to other candidates.) Thus, as written the decision requires the admission of thirty-three to thirty-five percent "minority group" students regardless of the qualifications found within the pool of such minority applicants

It is my belief that this policy is blatantly discriminatory and violates the relevant guidelines of the University. It excludes from equal opportunity certain racial and ethnic groups (including some who are clearly underprivileged) and arbitrarily favors others. It specifies preferential criteria for admission to graduate training solely on the basis of racial and ethnic origin.

I am therefore requesting that the Civil Liberties Board investigates my complaint, and takes appropriate action.

Would you advise me what documentation and information you will need to investigate this complaint? I would appreciate your keeping in touch with me on the progress of your investigation.

Sincerely yours,
CC . . . . BB . . . .
Professor of Psychology

2 March, 1973

Dr. SS . . . . LL . . . .
Chairman, Department of Psychology
University of . . .

Dear SS . . . . ,—I note in the minutes of the executive committee that the department proposes to hire a "black clinician." I would bring to your attention that to do so would be illegal. It violates Section 703 (a) of Title VII of the Civil Rights Act of 1964, which holds it to be unlawful for an employer to "classify his employees in any way which would deprive or tend to deprive any individual of employment opportunities . . . because of such individual's race, color, religion, sex or national origin." In a relevant Supreme Court decision, Griggs v. Duke Power, it was held: "Discriminatory preference for any group, minority or majority, is precisely and only what Congress has proscribed."

I remind you that we are constrained to advertise this position openly and without reference to race, and that we must entertain and consider applications without discriminatory preference. If we fail to do so, I am prepared to file a complaint against the Department with the pertinent University and Federal authorities, and I am further prepared to encourage and support legal action on behalf of candidates who have not been afforded equal opportunity.

Sincerely yours,
CC . . . . BB . . . .
Professor of Psychology

25 January, 1972

Mr. QQ . . . . LL . . . .
Department of Politics

Dear Mr. LL . . . . ,—The department of political science at [this] University has been authorized to make a new three-year appointment in the field of American politics beginning in the fall of 1972. We are looking for a person whose teaching and research interests are in either public policy, judicial process, or minority group politics and who can teach regularly at the introductory level of American politics. The appointment will be at the assistant professor rank if the candidate has completed all of his school's requirements for the Ph.D. Preference will be given to women and minority group candidates in filling this position if candidates of equal quality are identified.

If you would like to be considered for this position, you will need to have your credentials file sent to me by . . . . In addition, the search committee would like some examples of your written work and some syllabi from courses you are teaching for their evaluation.

Since the Department must move very rapidly in this age of budgetary constraint to fill this new position, I must have your reply by February 4. I look forward to receiving your materials so that we can consider you for this position.

Sincerely yours,

BB . . . . RR . . . .

Chairman American Politics Search Committee

Department of Political Science

LETTER FROM A MUNICIPAL COLLEGE IN AN EASTERN STATE

16 August, 1972

Mr. PP . . . . CC . . . .

Dear Mr, CC . . . . ,—The recommendation for your appointment to the department of psychology at . . . College was disapproved by the Board of Trustees on August 15, 1972. The basis for disapproval was primarily that the position presently vacant in that department requires certain qualifications regarding the overall profile of the institution and department as well as educational qualifications of the individual involved.

The disapproval in no way reflects upon your professional preparation or specific background in the area of clinical psychology. The decision was based primarily on the needs of the department in accord with its profile and qualifications. The institution's policy regarding recommendations for faculty appointments does not include the privilege of the chairman of the department presenting a "nearly positive" guarantee for employment. When recommendations are made by the department chairman and concurred by the associate dean and dean, the appointment document is then approved or disapproved by the president; if approved by him, it is then presented to the board of trustees for final approval.

It is with regret that I must inform you of the above decision. However, it is my sincere wish that you will be sucessful in obtaining a position for the academic year ahead.

Sincerely,

KK . . . . KK . . . .

Dean

LETTER FROM A MINOR SOUTHERN COLLEGE

10 January, 1972

Chairman

Department of Political Science

University of . . .

Dear Sir,—We have an opening for an instructor in political science beginning in the fall of 1972. Rank and salary depend on qualifications and experience, but the applicant must have a doctorate. Beyond that, we would prefer a young person between the ages of 30 to 40 years with some teaching or field experience. We are also trying to upgrade our staff with more women and more black people. Courses taught would include International Relations, Inter-American Relations, American National Government, Introduction to Political Science, and Latin America. We would be grateful if you would publicize our need among your doctoral graduates. We would also appreciate your passing on to us any applications you have for positions on your own faculty. There are supposed to be many people looking for positions, but those of us with openings sometimes have a hard time getting together with them.

We appreciate your help.

Sincerely,
Chairman
Division of Social Science

LETTER FROM A STATE COLLEGE IN NEW ENGLAND

10 January, 1972

Mr. RR . . . . LL . . . .

Dear Mr. LL . . . . ,—I have received your letter of January 4 regarding your candidacy here.

It is quite true that we have an opening here and that I have examined your dossier. It is very impressive indeed, and I wish I could invite you to come for an interview. At present, however, the department is interested in the appointment of a woman so we are concentrating on interviews of this kind.

I appreciate very much your interest in the College, and I know that with your excellent qualifications you will find a position of your choice. Naturally, I shall keep you in mind should any changes occur.

Best wishes to you for success.

Sincerely yours,
GG . . . . WW . . . .
Chairman
Department of English

LETTER FROM A LEADING PRIVATE
UNIVERSITY IN NEW ENGLAND

29 November, 1971

Chairman
Department of Political Science
University of . . .

Dear Sir,—My department now expects to add a couple of assistant professors, their appointments to begin September 1972.

We are therefore interested in knowing who the very best of your current crop of Ph.D.s are. If you have already sent us a composite placement brochure, it would be most helpful to have supplementary letters identifying particular individuals and forwarding their vitae.

Also, if you know of well qualified Ph.D.s a year or two "out" who might be moveable to . . . , information about them would be very useful. And . . . is eager to recruit among women and minority groups.

Although we are mainly seeking your ablest candidates regardless of field, it may help you to know that we have conspicuous needs in international relations, West European politics, judicial behavior, public administration and decision theory, urban politics, Afro-American politics, and the politics of education.

Thank you for your help.

Sincerely,
BB . . . . PP . . . .
Chairman
Department of Political Science

AFFIRMATIVE ACTION AT A PRIVATE UNIVERSITY
IN WASHINGTON, D.C.

14 July, 1972

Dear T . . . . ,—When I got back to the office last week I discovered that the Robert X . . .— . . . University case had turned in some interesting directions. We now have documents which clearly confirm what was hitherto X . . .'s unsupported testimony.

Let me summarize the situation: X . . . . , a graduate student here, was asked by BC . . . . CB . . . ., dean of the business school at . . . University, to come for an interview last March. X . . . asserts that he was told that a teaching job was his, pending clearance by Affirmative Action . . . . University agrees that matters got to the point where CB . . . did discuss salary range and affirmative action. Vice-President YY . . . denies that any promise of a job (implied or otherwise?) was made. . . . Acting Dean CB . . . . (5/28/72) says that the equal opportunity officer is overburdened and offers this as an explanation of the delay. Again, it is obvious that the discussion was far more than pro forma.

It seems quite clear from CB . . . .'s letter that he was told by Affirmative Action not to hire X . . . . ; YY . . . ., ZZ . . . and CB . . . all agree that a position exists and that no satisfactory alternative to X has been found. Thus, even though YY . . . may successfully sustain his claim that no legally binding offer of a job was made, there is abundant internal evidence that the decision with respect to X . . . was based not on merit but on race or some other non-admissible criterion. . . .

Sincerely,

W . . . . W . . . .

Mr. Robert X . . .

Dear Mr. X . . . ,—I spoke to Dr. W . . . . this morning and conveyed to him the background of the faculty hiring situation here. The equal opportunity officer of the University had previously been clearing positions in a fairly expeditious fashion, but apparently he became overburdened and he has now requested that the individual teaching units share in the search for minority group faculty. Consequently, I now face delays of the order of months, rather than weeks, in current hiring. I had my secretary call you in order to alert you to this situation.

I have written to Dr. W . . . separately in this regard.

Sincerely,

BC . . . . CB . . . .

Acting Dean

Mr. Robert X . . .

Dear Mr. X . . . . ,—President QHQ . . . . asked me to make a thorough examination of our record of the facts and circumstances underlying the contents of your letter to him. He directed that I respond to you directly upon completion of my inquiries.

Your stated purposes in writing to the University were somewhat imprecise. . . . We are not sure that you contend any remedies due to you from the University and we assume that you do not. Certainly, if it is your contention under the circumstances you allege that a promissory relationship, rooted in contract, existed upon which you relied to your detriment, then we must advise you that upon our investigations we have concluded that no express or implied contract existed in law or fact and your unilateral reliances on preliminary and conditioned exploratory discussions, totally ordinary and customary to the appointment processes in academic institutions, was conjectural on your part. Your reliances based on the record of the circumstances as we have them were your own acts and not reasonably binding upon the University. On advice of counsel, we are prepared to support and defend our position should you choose to take action.

We understand the following summary to recite our record.

Your application for a faculty appointment in our School of Business Administration was unsolicited by us. Dean CB . . . found your credentials impressive and you were invited to visit the campus in late March for an interview. You executed a formal application on March 3, 1972, and you were interviewed by Dean CB . . . . and others here on March 20, 1972. Dean CB . . . . asserts that in his conversations with you on that date that he explained to you University processes for new faculty appointments which included compliances with the University's Equal Employment Opportunity Affirmative Action Program. He also advised you of our salary ranges for new faculty appointees recently awarded the doctoral degree. Dean CB . . . . advises further that at the time of his oral discussions with you he made no firm express or implied offer to you concerning the faculty appointment under consideration.

The University is an equal opportunity employer and all deans and faculties have been directed to comply substantially and fully with our Affirmative Action Program. Dean CB . . . . was in the process of doing so before and subsequent to his interview with you. He so advised you by letter on April 18, 1972, and though he indicated at that time that he personally would recommend your appointment the affirmative action program compliances were not pro-forma and they would be time-consuming. At that point he learned through your intermediary that of your own motion, based on your unilateral reliances on your own assumptions, that you had turned down another position. We have reason to believe that you made no effort to contact Dean CB . . . . on the status of your application prior to April 10, 1972, when we are advised that you rejected an offer elsewhere. Your turn down action on another position was scarcely three weeks from the date of your visit to our campus.

To date the position for which you applied remains open.[3]

We sincerely regret the turn of events which has prompted your recent expressions but we must respectfully submit that they are unjustified under the circumstances.

Very Sincerely yours,

WD . . . . YY . . . .

Vice-President

NOTES

1. The American Economic Association was to meet in New Orleans.

2. The National Institute of Mental Health, a federal body which makes grants to universities for training and research in fields connected with mental health.

3. The associate secretary of the American Association of University Professors (AAUP) wrote to Mr. X on 3 June, 1972, that, according to the report made to her by the president of the branch of the AAUP at the university in question, it was "apparently due to budgetary constraints (that) the School of Business was unable to follow through on the discussions which you had with the acting dean in April. I understand that our chapter president does not believe that there was any suggestion from the university affirmative action office that an appointment

should not be made to you because of a need to recruit minorities." The president of the chapter of the AAUP at this particular university was also at the same time a member of the university committee responsible for the enforcement of "affirmative action" at the university. The president of the local chapter was apparently unaware that the vice-president of the university, with greater authority, asserted that "affirmative action" was involved in this case.

The AAUP for more than half a century interpreted "academic freedom" to be equivalent to the guarantee of tenure against abrogation. It always contended that criteria of politics or religious beliefs or adherence should never be allowed to play any part in determining whether a university or college teacher should be appointed, promoted, or dismissed. But such is the situation in the United States that at least some of the officials of the AAUP now think that racial and sexual criteria should be given prime consideration.

REFERENCES

AB 1725: A Comprehensive Analysis. January, 1989. Board of Governors. California Community Colleges.

Adelson, Joseph. 1978. "Living With Quotas." *Commentary* (May):23-29.

Alleyne, Reginald. 1987. "Everyone Needs Affirmative Action." *Los Angeles Times* (February 15.): V, 5.

Allport, Gordon. 1958. *The Nature of Prejudice.* New York: Addison.

Altheide, David. 1976. *Creating Reality: How T.V. Distorts News Events.* Beverly Hills, California: Sage Publications.

"Ambush at Amherst." 1988. *The New Republic* (June 27): 9-10.

Auerbach, Carl A. 1988. "The Silent Opposition of Professors and Graduate Students to Preferential Affirmative Action Programs: 1969 and 1975." *Minnesota Law Review* 72 (June): 1233-1280.

Beer, William. 1986. "Real-life Costs of Affirmative Action." *The Wall Street Journal*, August 7.

_____. 1988. "Sociology and the Effects of Affirmative Action: A Case of Neglect." *The American Sociologist* 19 (Fall): 218-231.

_____. 1987. "Resolute Ignorance: Social Science and Affirmative Action." *Society* 25 (May/June): 63-69.

Bell, Daniel. 1964. [1955]. *The Radical Right.* Garden Grove, N.Y.: Doubleday Anchor Books.

Berger, Peter. 1967. *Invitation to Sociology.* Garden Grove, New York: Doubleday Anchor.

Biernacki, Patrick. 1986. *Pathways from Heroin Addiction: Recovery Without Treatment.* Philadelphia: Temple University Press.

Bloom, Alan. 1987. *The Closing of the American Mind.* New York: Simon and Schuster.

Bowen, Howard R., and Jack H. Schuster. 1986. *American Professors.* New York: Oxford University Press.

Boyer, Paul, and Stephen Nissenbaum. 1974. *Salem Possessed: The Social Origins of Witchcraft.* Cambridge, Mass.: Harvard University Press.

"Breaking the Code: A New Strand of Black Thought Deals in Difficult Facts." *Newsweek* (October 12, 1985): 84-85.

Brinton, Crane. 1938. *The Anatomy of Revolution.* 1965 ed. New York: Vintage Books.

Broder, David. 1987. *Behind the Front Page.* New York: Simon and Schuster.

Brown, Margaret Wise. 1948. "The Steam Roller." In *Wonderful Story Book*, pp. 54-58. New York: Simon and Schuster.

Bumiller, Kristen. 1988. *The Civil Rights Society.* Baltimore: Johns Hopkins University Press.

Bunzel, H. John. 1980. "Will Colleges' Mission Be Sabotaged?" *Los Angeles Times*, October 22.

_____. 1986. "Affirmative Reactions." *Public Opinion* 9: 45-49.

_____. 1988. "Choosing Freshmen: Who Deserves an Edge?" *The Wall Street Journal*, February 1.

Burstein, Paul. 1982. "Equal Employment Opportunity: What We Believe, What We Know, What Research Can Show." Paper presented at the annual meetings of the American Sociological Association, San Francisco. August 31.

Cafferty, Pastora San Juan, and William C. McCready. 1985. *Hispanics in the United States.* New Brunswick, N.J., and Oxford, England: Transaction Books.

Califano, Joseph A. 1989. "Tough Talk for Democrats." *New York Times Magazine* (January 8): 28-29, 38, 43.

Capaldi, Nicholas. 1985. *Out of Order.* Buffalo, N.Y.: Prometheus.

Carter, Hodding. 1988. "Lily-White GOP Is Bad for Democrats, Too." *The Wall Street Journal* (August 4): 17.

"Caveats Reversed in Workplace Equality." *Washington Times Insight* 3 (April 27, 1987): 9-12.

Coleman, James. 1988. "Response to Sociology of Education Award 8/25/88." *Sociology of Education Newsletter* (Autumn): 6-9.

Cook, Fred J. 1971. *The Nightmare Decade.* New York: Random House.

Coser, Rose Laub. 1975. "Affirmative Action: Letter to a Worried Colleague." *Dissent* 22 (Summer): 366-369.

D'Antonio, William V. 1987. "Observing." *Footnotes* (February): 2

Dorn, Edwin. 1985. "Reynolds' Policies Serve to Perpetuate Injustices of the Past." *Los Angeles Times* (June 20): II, 7.

Douglas, Jack. 1977. "Review of Nathan Glazer's *Affirmative Discrimination.*" *Contemporary Sociology* 6 (September): 539-543.

Doyle, James. 1983. *The Male Experience.* Dubuque, Iowa: Wm. C. Brown.

Dworkin, Ronald. 1977. *Taking Rights Seriously.* Cambridge: Harvard University Press.

Engel, Elliot. 1982. "Of Male Bondage." *Newsweek* (June 21): 13.

Farrell, Warren. 1988. *Why Men Are the Way They Are.* New York: Berkley Books.

"Fire Fighter Hiring Quota Keeps Tension Smoldering." *Washington Times Insight* 3 (April 27, 1987): 13-14.

Freeman, Richard B. 1984. "Affirmative Action: Good, Bad, or Irrelevant?" *New Perspectives* 16: 23-27.

Gallup, George, ed. 1983. *America Wants to Know: The Issues and Answers of the 1980s.* New York: A and W Publishers.

Gann, L. H., and Peter J. Duignan. 1986. *Hispanics in the United States*. Boulder, Colo., and London: Westview Press.

Gans, Herbert J. 1988. *Middle American Individualism*. New York: Basic Books.

Garamendi, John. 1988. "Fiddling as Golden State Crumbles." *Los Angeles Times* (July 24): V, 5.

Glazer, Nathan. 1975. *Affirmative Discrimination*. New York: Basic Books.

_____. 1985. "Affirmative Action as a Remedy for Discrimination." *American Behavioral Scientist* 28: 829-841.

_____. 1988. "The Affirmative Action Stalemate." *The Public Interest* (Winter): 99-114.

Goffman, Erving. 1955. *Presentation of Self in Everyday Life*. Garden Grove, NY: Doubleday Anchor Books.

Goldberg, Herb. 1976. *The Hazards of Being Male*. New York: New American Library.

Gouldner, Alvin W. 1962. "Anti-Minotaur: The Myth of a Value-Free Sociology." *Social Problems* 9 (Winter): 199-213.

_____. 1968. "The Sociologist as Partisan: Sociology and the Welfare State." *The American Sociologist* 3 (May): 103-117.

_____. 1970. *The Coming Crisis of Western Sociology*. New York: Basic Books.

_____. 1976. *The Dialectic of Ideology and Technology*. New York: Seabury Press.

_____. 1979. *The Intellectuals and the New Class*. New York: Seabury Press.

Greenberg, Stanley B. 1985. *Report on Democratic Defection*. New Haven, Conn: The Analysis Group.

_____. 1987. Conversation with the author. June 13.

Gross, Barry. 1978. *Discrimination in Reverse: Is Turnabout Fair Play?* New York: New York University Press.

Gross, Theodore. 1978. "How to Kill a College." *Saturday Review* (February 4): 13-20.

Harrington, Michael. 1984. "Straw Men in Struggle." *The New Republic* (June 11): 37-39.

Harris, Louis. 1987. *Inside America*. New York: Vintage Books.

Hauser, Philip. 1981. "Sociology's Progress Towards Science." *The American Sociologist* 16 (February): 62-64.

Hill, Richard J. 1983a. "Minorities, Women, and Institutional Change." *Sociological Perspectives* 26 (January): 17-27.

_____. 1983b. Conversation with the author, September 29.

Hirschorn, Michael. 1988. "The Doctorate Dilemma." *The New Republic* (June 6): 24-28.

Homans, George C. 1958. "Social Behavior as Exchange." *American Journal of Sociology* 63 (May): 597-606.

_____. 1974. *Social Behavior: Its Elementary Forms*. 2d ed. New York: Harcourt Brace Jovanovich.

Horowitz, Irving Louis. 1987. "Disenthralling Sociology." *Society* 24 (January/February): 48-55.

Huber, Betina. 1985. *Employment Patterns in Sociology: Recent Trends and Future Prospects*. Washington, D.C.: American Sociological Association.

_____. 1987. "The Status of Minorities and Women Within the ASA: Second Biennial Update." Washington, D.C.: American Sociological Association.

"Interviews with Rosalind Rosenberg and Alice Kessler-Harris." 1986. *New Perspectives* 18 (Summer): 21-34.

Jackson, Lester. 1986. "Professor Shortage? Here We Go Again." *The Wall Street Journal* (March 19).

Jacobsen, Cardell. 1983. "Black Support for Affirmative Action." *Phylon* 44: 299-311.

Jencks, Christopher. 1985a. "How Poor Are the Poor?" *New York Review of Books* (May 9(: 41-49.

———. 1985b. "Affirmative Action for Blacks." *The American Behavioral Scientist* 28 (July/August): 731-761.

Johnson, Stephen D. 1980a. "Affirmative Action as a Remedy for Discrimination." *Psychological Reports* 47: 1035-1038.

———. 1982. Letter to the author.

———. 1980b. "Reverse Discrimination and Aggressive Behavior." *Journal of Psychology* 104: 11-19.

———. 1984. Correspondence with the author.

Judis, John B. 1988. "Black Donkey, White Elephant." *The New Republic* (April 18): 25-28.

Kluegel, James. 1985. "'If There Isn't a Problem, You Don't Need a Solution.' The Bases of Contemporary Affirmative Action Attitudes." *The American Behavioral Scientist* 28: 761-784.

Kluegel, James R., and Elliot Smith. 1983. "Affirmative Action Attitudes: Effects of Self-Interest, Racial Affect, and Stratification Beliefs on Whites' Views." *Social Forces* 61: 796-824.

———. 1986. *Beliefs about Inequality*. New York: Aldine de Gruyter.

Kristol, Irving. 1986. "American Universities in Exile." *The Wall Street Journal* (June 17).

Ladd, Everett C., and Seymour Martin Lipset. 1975. *The Divided Academy*. New York: McGraw-Hill.

———. 1980. "Anatomy of a Decade." *Public Opinion* 3 (December/January): 2-9.

Leonard, Jonathan. 1984a. "The Impact of Affirmative Action on Employment." Working paper no. 1310. Washington, D.C.: Bureau of Economic Research.

———. 1984b. "What Promises Are Worth: The Impact of Affirmative Action Goals." Working paper no. 1346. Washington, D.C.: National Bureau of Economic Research.

Levin, Michael. 1985. Letter to the author. March 3.

Lichter, S. Robert, Stanley Rothman, and Linda S. Lichter. 1986. *The Media Elite*. Bethesda, Md.: Adler and Adler.

Lieberson, Stanley. 1988. "Asking Too Much, Expecting Too Little." *Sociological Perspectives* 31 (October): 379-397.

Lipset, Seymour M. 1979. "The New Class and the Professorate." *Society* (January/February): 31-38.

———. 1981. [1960]. *Political Man*. Baltimore: Johns Hopkins University Press.

Lipset, Seymour M., and William Schneider. 1978. "The Bakke Case: How Would It Be Decided at the Bar of Public Opinion?" *Public Opinion* 1: 38-44.

Littwan, Susan. 1986. *The Postponed Generation*. New York: Quill.

Livingston, John. 1978. *Fair Game? Inequality and Affirmative Action*. San Francisco: W. H. Freeman and Co.

Lovelock, Frank. 1985. "Day Labor and Dead Ends." *Newsweek* (September 16).

Lukas, J. Anthony. 1985. *Common Ground: A Turbulent Decade in the Lives of Three American Families*. New York: A. Knopf.

Lynch, Frederick R. 1984. "Totem and Taboo in Sociology: The Politics of Affirmative Action Research." *Sociological Inquiry* 54: 124-141.

———. 1985a. "Affirmative Action, the Media, and the Public: A Look at a Look-Away Issue." *American Behavioral Scientist* 28 (July/August): 807-829.

———. 1987. "On Assessing the Impact of Affirmative Action upon White Males. Some Preliminary Findings." Paper presented at the meetings of the Eastern Sociological Society, Boston, May 1.

McCartney, James L. 1984. "Setting Priorities for Research: New Politics for the Social Sciences." *Sociological Quarterly* 25 (Autumn): 437-455.

McGill, Michael. 1985. *The McGill Report on Male Intimacy*. New York: Holt, Reinhart, and Winston.

Mansfield, Harvey. 1984. "The Underhandedness of Affirmative Action." *National Review* (May 4): 26-32, 61.

Massey, Stephen J. 1981. "Rethinking Affirmative Action." *Social Theory and Social Practice* 7 (Spring): 21-49.

Mathews, Linda. 1987. "When Being Best Is Not Good Enough." *Los Angeles Times Magazine* (July 19): 22-28.

Matza, David, and Gresham, Sykes. 1957. "Techniques of Neutralization: A Theory of Delinquency." *American Sociological Review* 22: 666-670.

May, Lee, and Paul Houston. 1985. "Affirmative Action Finally Wins Grudging Acceptance." *Los Angeles Times* (July 22).

Merton, Robert. 1968. "Manifest and Latent Function." *Social Theory and Social Structure*. 2d ed. Pp. 74-91. New York: The Free Press.

Miller, Stuart. 1983. *Men and Friendship*. Boston: Houghton Mifflin.

Mills, C. Wright. 1956. *The Power Elite*. New York: Oxford University Press.

———. 1959. *The Sociological Imagination*. New York: Grove Press.

Minerva. 1976. "Reports and Documents: The Criteria of Academic Appointment in American Univesities and Colleges." 14, no. 1 (Spring): 97-117.

Moore, Joan, and Harry Pachon. 1985. *Hispanics in the United States*. Englewood Cliffs, NJ: Prentice-Hall.

Mueller, Samuel. 1979. "Underrepresentation of White Males." *Footnotes* (May): 7.

Murray, Charles. 1984a. "Affirmative Racism." *The New Republic* (December 31): 18-23.

———. 1984b. *Losing Ground*. New York: Basic Books.

———. 1988. "The Coming of Custodial Democracy." *Commentary* (September): 19-24.

National Election Study. 1986. Institute for Survey Research. The University of Michigan.

Nelson, Mary. 1970. "Why Women Were Witches." In *Women: A Feminist Perspective*, edited by Jo Freeman. Palo Alto: Mayfield Publishing Co.

Nisbet, Robert. 1969. *Social Change and History*. New York: Oxford University Press.

Noelle-Neumann, Elisabeth. 1974. "The Spiral of Silence: A Theory of Public Opinion." *Journal of Communication* 24 (Spring): 43-51.

_____. 1977. "Turbulence in the Climate of Opinion: Methodological Applications of the Spiral of Silence Theory." *Public Opinion* 41: 143-158.

_____. 1984. *The Spiral of Silence*. Chicago: University of Chicago Press.

Novak, Michael. 1978. "The Terrible Swift Swords of RFK." *The Wall Street Journal* (September 8).

O'Brien, Michael. 1980. *McCarthy and McCarthyism in Wisconsin*. Columbia, Mo., and London: University of Missouri Press.

Orfield, Gary. 1988. "Well Along Toward Separate and Unequal Societies." *Los Angeles Times* (March 22): V, 1.

Parello, Vincent. 1985. *Strangers to These Shores. Race and Ethnic Relations in the United States*. New York: John Wiley.

Pierce, R. Tara. 1986. "'Gypsy' Faculty Stirs Debate at U.S. Colleges." *The Wall Street Journal* (September 25).

Pleck, Joseph. 1981. *The Myth of Masculinity*. Boston: MIT Press.

Podhoretz, Norman. 1979. *Breaking Ranks*. New York: Harper and Row.

Prager, Jeffrey. 1982. "Equal Opportunity and Affirmative Action." *Research in Law, Deviance and Social Control* 4: 191-218.

Richardson, Laurel. 1985. *The New Other Woman*. New York: The Free Press.

_____. 1986. "Another World." *Psychology Today* (February): 22-28.

Rodriguez, Richard. 1982. *Hunger of Memory*. Boston: David Godine.

_____. 1987. "A Scholarship Out of the Barrio, A Ticket to Burn-Out." *Los Angeles Times* (July 26): "Opinion," p. 5.

Rogin, Michael. 1967. *The Intellectuals and McCarthy*. Cambridge, Mass: MIT Press.

Rossum, Ralph. 1980. *Reverse Discrimination: The Constitutional Debate*. Chicago: Marcel Dekker.

_____. 1985. "Plessy, Brown, and the Reverse Discrimination Cases. *American Behavioral Scientist* 28 (July/August): 785-807.

Rubin, Lillian B. 1985. *Just Friends*. New York: Harper and Row.

Russell, Jeffrey. 1972. *Witchcraft in the Middle Ages*. Ithaca, N.Y.: Cornell University Press.

Schrecker, Ellen W. 1986. *No Ivory Tower: McCarthyism and the Universities*. New York: Oxford University Press.

Schneider, William. 1988a. "An Insider's View of the Election." *The Atlantic* (July): 29-58.

_____. 1988b. "Anti-Government Mood Fuels Politics of Race." *Los Angeles Times* (October 28): II, 7.

Schwieder, Robert M., and Gary A. Cretser. 1986. "We Will Survive But Will the Discipline?" Paper presented at the annual meetings of the Pacific Sociological Association, Denver, Co., April.

Smelser, Neil J. 1962. *Theory of Collective Behavior*. New York: Free Press.

Smith, James P., and Michael P. Ward. 1984. *Sexual Inequality in the Work Force*. Santa Monica, CA: Rand Corporation.

Smith, James P., and Finis R. Welch. 1986. *Closing the Gap: Forty Years of Economic Progress for Blacks*. Santa Monica, Calif.: Rand Corporation.

Sobran, Joseph. 1987. "The Use and Abuse of Race: Howard Beach." *National Review* (March 27): 28-38.

Sowell, Thomas. 1981. *Ethnic America*. New York: Basic Books.

_____. 1984. *Civil Rights: Rhetoric or Reality*. New York: William Morrow.

Stahl, Bill. 1987. "The Problem of People Becoming the Problem." *Los Angeles Times* (August 2, 1987): V, 1.

Tamarkin, Bob. 1978. "Is Equal Opportunity Turning into a Witch Hunt?" *Forbes* (May 29): 29-31.

Thomlinson, Ralph, and Larry Hong. 1987. "The Resurgence of Sociology at Cal State Los Angeles." *Footnotes* (October): 2.

Turner, Ralph, and Lewis M. Killian. 1987. *Collective Behavior*. 3rd ed. Englewood Cliffs. NJ: Prentice-Hall.

Tyrrell, R. Emmett. 1987. "A Conservative Crack-up?" *The Wall Street Journal* (March 27).

United States Commission on Civil Rights. 1987. "The Economic Progress of Black Men in America." Washington, D.C.

Vago, Steven. 1988. *Law and Society* 2d ed. Englewood Cliffs, NJ: Prentice-Hall.

van den Berghe, Pierre. 1971. "The Benign Quota: Panacea of Pandora's Box?" *The American Sociologist* 6 (June): 40-43.

_____. 1972. "Neo-Racism in America." *Transition*. 41: 15-18.

_____. 1984. Letter to the author.

_____. 1988. Letter to the author.

Vander Zanden, James. 1980. *American Minority Relations*. 4th ed. New York: Alfred A. Knopf.

Verba, Sidney, and Gary R. Orren. 1985. *Equality in America: The View from the Top*. Cambridge, Mass.: Harvard University Press.

Weber, Max. 1946. "Science as a Vocation." In *From Max Weber*, edited by Hans Gerth and C. Wright Mills, New York: Oxford University Press.

Weiner, Steve. 1986. "Sears' Costly Win in a Hiring Suit." *The Wall Street Journal* (March 18).

Wessel, David. 1986. "The Last Angry Man: Some Companies Begin Confronting Men's Resentment of Successful Women." *The Wall Street Journal* (March 24): 18D.

White, Theodore. 1982. *America in Search of Itself*. New York: Random House.

_____. 1984. "New Powers, New Politics." *The New York Times Magazine*. (February 5).

Whitehurst, Daniel K. 1983. "California's Taxes Are Too Low." *Los Angeles Times* (April 27): II, 5.

Will, George F. 1985. "Battling the Racial Spoils System." *Newsweek* June 10: 96.

Williams, Walter E. 1982. *The State Against Blacks*. New York: McGraw-Hill.

Wong, Linda. 1987. "UC Admissions Changes Raise Specter of Bias." *Los Angeles Herald-Examiner* (March 27).

Zajonic, Robert. 1968. "Cognitive Organization and Processes." *International Encyclopedia of the Social Sciences*. Vol. 15: 615-622.

INDEX

About the Author

FREDERICK R. LYNCH is Senior Research Associate at the Salvatori Center, Claremont McKenna College. He is the author of numerous articles on affirmative action and other social issues in scholarly journals and popular publications.